Rock Hunter's Guide

Igneous dikes cutting stratified rocks with West Spanish Peak in the background, Huerfano county, Colo. (U.S. Geological Survey, R. C. Hills)

Rock Hunter's Guide

How to Find
and
Identify Collectible Rocks

Russell P. MacFall

Thomas Y. Crowell, Publishers
New York / Established 1834

Also by the author
Gem Hunter's Guide
Minerals and Gems

Grateful acknowledgment is made for permission to reproduce the following drawings: page 5, top, Hearst Books; page 5, bottom, Field Museum of Natural History; page 101, Illinois State Geological Survey.

FIRST EDITION

Library of Congress Cataloging in Publication Data

MacFall, Russell P
Rock hunter's guide.

Bibliography: p.
1. Rocks—Collectors and collecting. I. Title.
QE433.6.M33 552'.075 78-22457
ISBN 0-690-01812-6

80 81 82 83 10 9 8 7 6 5 4 3 2 1

contents

Acknowledgments vii

1. The rewarding realm of rocks 1
2. Getting acquainted with rocks 13
3. The fine-grained rocks 43
4. The rock hunter in the field 73
5. Our many-splendored continent 92
6. The collector and the craftsman 125
7. Locations for the rock collector 140

Glossary 220

Official state stones 227

Metric equivalents for rockhounds 228

Sources of information 229

For further reading 239

acknowledgments

Obviously, a work of this kind must depend upon the accumulated wisdom of the untold hundreds of geologists and other investigators who have studied the geology and petrographic resources of North America. Relatively little, however, has been written about rocks as a hobby interest, so that even a survey of available outcrops available to the collector has had to be made through a wide variety of secondary and somewhat unrelated sources. Moreover, anyone who presumes to write about geological forces in this era of novel and controversial concepts and theories must accept that he is treading on unstable ground. For this reason, I wish to thank Professor J. Reid Macdonald for his careful reading of the manuscript of this book. His emendations were stimulating and have given the author some feeling of confidence that the book will serve a useful purpose. I am also indebted to my editor, Hugh Rawson, for his contributions of advice and criticism and his patience with an occasionally dilatory author. To the many others whose discoveries may be mirrored here, the author wishes to acknowledge his indebtedness and gratitude.

Eroded spires of loosely consolidated sedimentary rocks in the Badlands National Monument, South Dakota. (South Dakota Dept. of Highways)

1.
the rewarding realm of rocks

Speak to the earth and it shall teach thee.
Book of Job

Familiar as it is, the earth will repay closer acquaintance. Land, sea, and sky constitute a laboratory for exercising every field of interest from astronomy to zoology, and for gaining a deeper appreciation and understanding of the earth's bounty. The rocky firmament on which we live, for example, not only affords delightful landscapes but also provides the materials for our houses and skyscrapers, the fuels that keep us warm and power our automobiles, the water we drink, and the soil that grows our food. How to be a friend to the earth? How to use its gifts wisely? The answers to many such social, economic, and political problems must be found in the sciences of the rocky crust of the earth.

But closer acquaintance with the earth can also be a pleasant recreation; it can be fun and a hobby, such as the hobby of collecting rocks. Enjoyment of rocks seems almost a human instinct. Nearly every person has at some time picked up an attractive pebble and taken it home. Those who keep on picking up rocks become collectors. They may be called beachcombers, treasure hunters, or even packrats, but they have found a lifetime interest.

Collecting is rooted in curiosity, eagerness to understand, and the desire to own. The collector can also enjoy the companionship of kindred spirits, whether they are brought together by rocks, pots of African violets, postage stamps, or an evening looking at the stars.

Interest in rocks knows no bounds of class, society, or eminence. Perhaps as many women as men are numbered among collectors, often following the example of their children. The Morgans and other wealthy families have enriched museums with their treasures; other fortunate individuals have had rocks or fossils they discovered named after them.

Even some presidents have shared this interest. Abraham Lincoln appears to have been a rockhound. Writing in his magazine *Earth Science Digest,* the late Ben Hur Wilson recalled that he had seen in the museum at Iowa Wesleyan College, Mt. Pleasant, Iowa, a cigar box marked "collection of rocks made by A. Lincoln," with Lincoln's signature on the lid. Presumably, Wilson wrote, the box reached the college through James Harlan, who was Secretary of the Interior during Lincoln's second term in office. Harlan later became president of the college, and his daughter became the wife of Lincoln's son, Robert Todd Lincoln.

Thomas Jefferson collected fossil bones, wrote about them, spread them out in the unfinished White House, and even had the fossil of a ground sloth, *Melalonyx jeffersoni,* named after him. He was active in encouraging the study of rocks by the American Philosophical Society and in supporting Peale's Museum in Philadelphia, where the first complete fossil skeleton of a mastodon from North America was set up. And in this century a mining engineer and geologist, Herbert Hoover, occupied the White House, and he and his wife, Lou Henry Hoover, translated Georgius Agricola's book, *De re metallica,* a landmark volume in geology and mining.

Geology—Science of the Earth

The science of the physical fabric of the earth is geology, a term that comes from two Greek words meaning "earth" and "doctrine." Geology embraces the broad panorama of continents and oceans, plains and mountains, raging rivers and placid lakes. It is concerned with the atom as well as the universe, and it looks back 4.5 billion years into time.

Such a science could not be an abstract, intellectual exercise, limited to classrooms and laboratories, nor is it. For centuries scientists have fought for the freedom to discover and proclaim the truth. Today geology is in the midst of one of the most exciting revolutions in its long history.

Ancient peoples speculated about the nature of the earth; such a practical Roman as Pliny the Elder studied the phenomena of an erupting volcano so intently that he lost his life. But medieval theology made martyrs of those who doubted that Noah's flood had created the landscape and that the earth's age could be estimated by biblical chronology.

In the eighteenth century, however, geology began to break these chains. In 1788, James Hutton, a Scotsman, advanced the revolutionary theory that eruptive rocks from beneath the surface of the earth, as well as sedimentary rocks laid down in water, had created the earth's crust. He also voiced a fundamental principle that in the history of the earth there is "no sign of a beginning and no prospect of an end."

Just as Hutton's insights were becoming generally accepted, along came Charles Darwin with his theories of the origin of species by natural selection, and a new theological battle was joined.

Without the immense vista of time revealed by the pioneers of geology, the theory of natural selection posited by Darwin would not have been tenable. Natural selection adequate to create all the different species requires time, and lots of it. Biology and geology, along with astronomy, held the attention of thinking minds through the nineteenth century. But the sciences move at varying paces. Physics and chemistry took center stage in the decades after World War I with major discoveries about the structure of the atom and the nature of matter. Geology and biology were reborn in the 1960s and 1970s, the latter through the discovery of the double-helix structure of the DNA molecule and controversial research in genetics.

Geology's metamorphosis in this century began with the publication in 1915 by a German, Alfred Wegener, of *The Origin of Oceans and Continents,* in which Wegener advanced the startling theory that the continents had drifted into their present positions. The theory was dismissed as science fiction by most geologists, but finally it brought geology to the battlefield again and to a revolution in the 1960s in our knowledge of the earth's history. This was aided by instruments developed during World War II that for the first time made possible exploration of the floors of the oceans.

Plate Tectonics—What It Means

From research stimulated by the controversy over Wegener's dream emerged the comprehensive theory of plate tectonics. This theory has won acceptance because it explains and gathers together phenomena previously difficult to harmonize. It opens new windows for geological science.

According to plate tectonics theory, the continents have been drifting over the earth's surface for millions, perhaps billions, of years. They ride piggyback on six rigid major and several small plates that make up the crust of the earth. The crust, of course, is comprised of both the continents and the ocean basins. It is comparatively thin and rests on mantle, a region of intensely hot, semi-plastic rock materials.

The boundaries of the crustal plates are marked by a vast system of two midocean ridges. One, rising from the depths of the Atlantic, extends down past the tip of Africa and thence into the Indian Ocean, where it joins the other. The Pacific ridge passes between Australia and Antarctica and into the Pacific. From here it runs north, skirting the west coasts of the two Americas.

From the ridges, 600 miles wide, flows white-hot lava, which fills the gap between the older lava flows on both sides of the ridges. These have been moved aside by currents within the underlying mantle. For example, the plates that bear North and South America on their backs move westward about 2 centimeters (nearly an inch) a year. This has been going on for 75 million years. As the Atlantic plate is shoved against the Pacific plate, it overrides the latter at the contact point off the coast of South America, narrowing the Pacific Ocean, and in the north shoves the Pacific plate northwestward.

Iceland, which lies directly on the mid-Atlantic ridge, lives with the fire of about twenty active volcanoes, one of which in 1783 poured a flood of lava on the island after a series of violent earthquakes. In 1963 a new volcano popped up out of the sea off

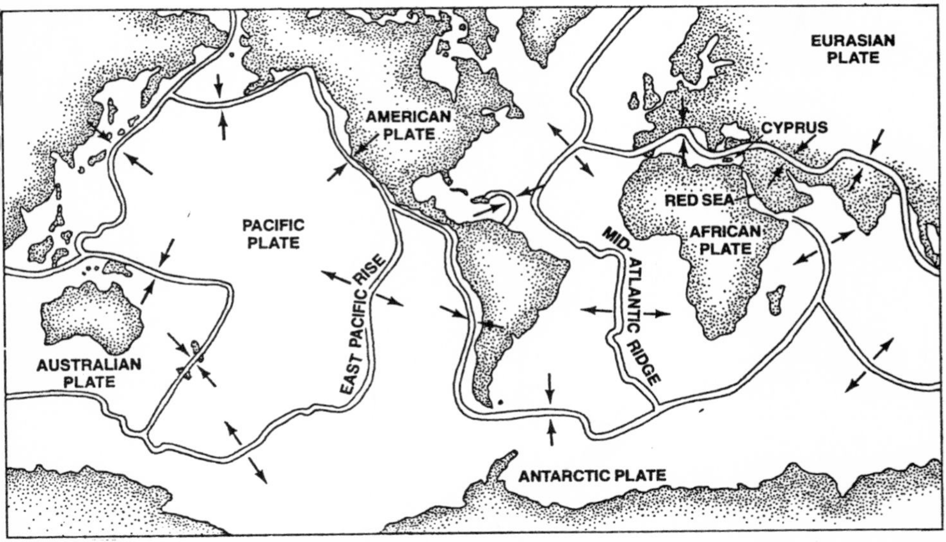

EURASIAN PLATE
AMERICAN PLATE
CYPRUS
RED SEA
PACIFIC PLATE
AFRICAN PLATE
MID-ATLANTIC RIDGE
EAST PACIFIC RISE
AUSTRALIAN PLATE
ANTARCTIC PLATE

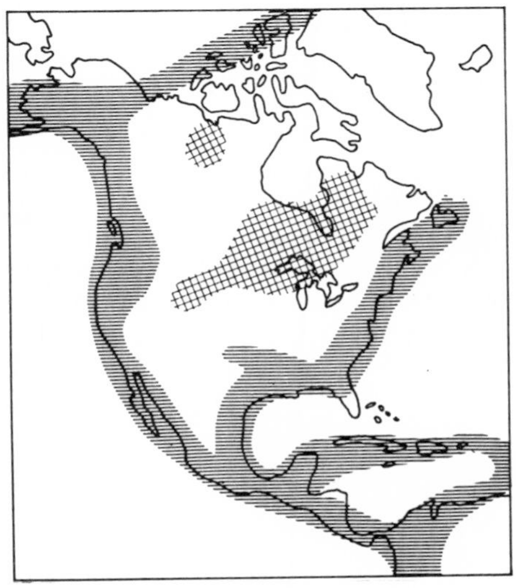

OLDER THAN 2 1/2 BILLION YEARS
1 BILLION TO 2 1/2 BILLION YEARS OLD
YOUNGER THAN 1 BILLION YEARS OLD

Tectonic plates in the earth's crust. Arrows show how some plates are moving apart, while others are converging.

The sequence of the North American continent's growth can be determined from the ages of the various rock belts within it.

the Icelandic coast and after a spectacular eruption created an island, Surtsey, with its cone.

The Pacific plate, which is one-third the surface of the earth, sinks at its contacts with the American and Asian plates into deep trenches where its edges are melted. Along these contacts exist the so-called Ring of Fire, made up of active volcanoes, and the earthquake zone around the Pacific Ocean that extends to Iran, Turkey, and Italy. Along the contacts, mountains rise, such as the Andes, the Cascades, and the Japanese peaks. Peru, California, Alaska, Japan, and China have suffered heavily from earthquakes in the last few decades, and so has Asia Minor.

The evidence of rock cores drilled from ocean bottoms supports the theory of continental drift, but some elements are not yet clearly understood. Why does the lava force itself to the surface in the midocean ridges? One theory likens the action to that of liquid in a pot on a stove. As it is heated, the liquid on the bottom grows lighter and rises to the top. There it cools as it is moved to the side, and sinks again. This is called convection, from the same root as the word *convex.*

Parting of the Continents

Some types of rocks become magnetized as they are formed, and retain this fossil magnetism. This quality enables geologists, by means of delicate tests, to identify the presumed position of the rocks when they were formed and the pathways of the drifting continents as they spread apart following the breakup of the primitive supercontinent, known as Pangaea. South America parted from Africa, a theory that explains the complementary shapes of their facing coasts. Comparison of the similarity of rock types and fossils further confirms this hypothesis.

North America was forced west from Laurasia (the Europe-Asia mass). Consequently, rocks in Newfoundland and Scotland match neatly, and some of the southeastern United States can be related to North African origins. Antarctica drifted south, Australia parted from it, and India swept north into collision with the Laurasian continent, raising the Himalayas where its edge slid under the larger body. In a similar way, pressure from Africa is believed to have raised Europe's Alps.

Two hundred million years ago, the magnetic studies of the rocks reveal, the present site of New York was on the Equator, and India lay close to Antarctica, which had just broken away from Africa. Ten million years hence, Los Angeles will have moved northwest with the Pacific plate along the line of the San Andreas Fault and will be abreast of San Francisco. Forty million years later, Los Angeles will have been devoured in the Aleutian trench. Perhaps later, the American plate will have maneuvered to collision with the Asian continent, with a new supercontinent as the possible result.

Energy and Environmental Problems

Profoundly stirring as the new geology is, its major importance to collector and citizen alike lies in the hope that it will help relieve some of the world's critical mineral shortages and solve some environmental problems. Among these are depletion of metal ore deposits, dwindling resources of oil and uranium for energy production, pollution of water supplies despite a growing demand, and the loss of cropland to deserts.

Perhaps it is not too farfetched a comparison to say that the person who has developed an interest in rocks and geology has a similarly wider view of such matters as energy sources. The United States, for example, has an enormous oil resource that is virtually untapped—the oil shales of western Colorado and Wyoming. Why spend billions to go to the Arctic Circle for oil when it is close at hand? But even a slight knowledge of geology makes clear the problems of exploiting these oil shales. The rock must be heated to distill off the hydrocarbon content; the spent shale must be disposed of without destroying the natural beauty of a mountain region; and an abundant supply of water must be made available in an arid land. Competitive costs and politics also obscure the prospect. In Alberta, Canada, however, oil is being economically recovered from vast beds of tar sands by similar but less complicated methods.

Prudent use of water resources also often calls for some insight that the serious collector has acquired through study and practical experience. Florida is an obvious example. Like much of the Midwest and South, Florida draws its supply of fresh water from the rocks. Anyone interested in physical geology knows that the Florida peninsula is a limestone shelf extending from the mainland. Through the pores of this tilted ledge, water slowly trickles south. But when developers flood the state with thirsty people, the demand for water outruns the supply, the wells dry up, and salt water from the surrounding ocean begins to contaminate them.

Energy does grow on trees, but it takes nature some millions of years to turn logs into coal, and organic matter into oil and natural gas. By revealing now-obscure relationships of areas parted by continental drift, the study of plate tectonics should help to guide prospectors for coal and oil to former continental shelves and other previously ignored regions. Antarctica, for example, has coal deposits formed before it drifted into latitudes of lifeless cold. The new geology's insights into the relationships of the crust and mantle of the earth may also be helpful in the utilization of geothermal power, which is derived from steam rising from within the earth.

Copper, lead, and tin resources cannot hope to keep up with the demand, estimated to be growing at 10 percent a year. But if continental fragments that have drifted apart from known ore deposits can be traced under the new theory, metal ore reserves can be increased. Another avenue in the same direction leads out from a collateral theory of "hot spots," which are presumed to be protrusions of a bit of the earth's mantle into its crust. Cyprus, where metal has been mined for ages and which gave its name to copper, appears to be such a spot. Nearby in the Red Sea, mineral-rich solutions are creating what may be another Cyprus. The origin of ore deposits remains a live subject in the current ferment of geological thinking and may be the best hope for an answer to critical shortages in the next century. Allied with it, of course, is the utilization of the metallic nodules that litter certain parts of the ocean bottoms. How to mine them and distribute the metals fairly to the have and have-not nations are problems that will stand in the way.

Water supply or the lack of it on the 29 percent of the earth's surface that is not ocean determines where crops grow, people live, and factories produce goods. Some regions, such as the American Midwest, are well watered year after year, but the Russian steppes have their good years and bad. Washington State wheat-growers husband the water of two years in the soil to grow a crop the third year. There is evidence that virtually every region has had a variety of climates as the continents drifted and glacial epochs came and went. Today one-fifth of the world's land surface is desert; a 4,000-mile strip of sterile sand runs across Africa and is growing wider year by year. Egypt is 96 percent desert; its people are fed from the irrigated remnant.

Nature makes deserts, but they are spread by overgrazing of grass cover, destruction of forests for fuel and timber, and bad crop practices. The new geology may be able to make clear the rate and processes of climatic change and show that any present solution to the growth of deserts must be found in wiser use of the land within the limits set by nature.

Insights from Outer Space

Insights of the new geology, some of which may have practical application to human problems, were strengthened in the last two decades by the most dramatic incident of the century. Astronauts walked on the moon and brought back rocks from its craters and highlands. What they saw there, interpreted by study of the moon rocks they collected, has resulted in a better understanding of the earth's early years. This has come about because the moon's surface appears to have changed little in the last 3 billion years, while the earth's youthful face has been eroded away and replaced by younger rocks. Like the earth, the moon appears to have been born as a hot body. As its surface cooled, the crust was battered by meteorites, and lava from volcanoes filled the scars. Since its lively beginning, the moon has become geologically inactive except for an occasional moonquake. The earth, too, must once have been a lifeless ball of lava plains and craters before its atmosphere and moisture began their never-ending work of weathering and rebuilding.

Out of space exploration has developed another useful tool for science—photography of the earth's surface from artificial satellites. Mapping with special techniques has been of great service to geology because it reveals many hidden details of the structure and mineral resources of the rocks, details beyond the capabilities of conventional prospecting.

Enjoyment of the Earth

As the Italian playwright Carlo Goldoni once said: "The earth is a beautiful place but of little use to him who cannot read." Interest and knowledge are the twin keys to enjoyment, especially enjoyment of the outdoors. A forest abounds in delights for the person who has become familiar with the many species of trees, but to the uninformed it is nothing more than a spot of green or, at most, a cool refuge from the hot sun. In the same way, to the rock collector on vacation the desert will tell its story, the rolling prairie will make plain the marks of the passing of a great glacier, and the meandering stream will testify to the gentle grade of its valley. Acquaintance with geological formations and rock types will be the collector's clues to finding desirable specimens.

The Sierras, the Grand Canyon, the Great Lakes, and Niagara Falls speak for themselves, even to the casual tourist. They are spectacular. Most of the earth is less dramatic, but to anyone who can read in nature's book, even the placid cornfields of Iowa and Illinois, for example, reveal an eventful past.

These two states, geologists have determined, were the playground of the mighty Mississippi River and of several continental glaciers that remodeled this region in the last million years. The Mississippi in the distant past flowed diagonally across Iowa west of Mason City and Iowa City, but glacial ice shoved it east and forced it to cut a channel through the rocks above Dubuque—a channel much like its present one. But glacial ice later forced it even farther east into Illinois along a line from Clinton to Hennepin to Peoria and down to St. Louis. Another glacier came from the east, pushed the river west again, and blocked tributaries, forming a great lake over the rich land near Iowa City. Only about 75,000 years ago did the river become our familiar Father of Waters, and that is only yesterday on the geological time scale.

Perhaps such a homely example testifies to the truth of the statement that John A. Dorr, Jr., and Donald F. Eschmann make in *Geology of Michigan:* "Once a person learns how to observe earth features and to ask questions of nature, he may wander at will anywhere in the world and he will seldom be without the thrill of discovery."

In sum, the rock collector has a hobby as wide as the earth and the sky above us. Within this hobby the collector can find relaxation, a stimulating reason for being alone or in chosen company in the outdoors, and satisfaction for the instinct to own and show examples of nature's handiwork. As a citizen the collector has put himself or herself in a position to understand many of the problems of society.

Collecting within the earth sciences has many facets, such as gems, minerals, fossils, rocks, photographs of formations and ghost towns, and artifacts from old mines. Gems have glamour, like gold, and hunting for them has all the allure, like gambling, of striking it rich. Few, though, have the luck of the couple who took their baby along on a trip to the Arkansas state park where diamonds are found in disintegrated volcanic rock. While the parents scratched in the soil, the baby lay on a blanket in the shade of a tree. The watchful mother saw the baby pick up something and put it in its mouth. When she cupped her hands under the baby's chin and commanded, "Spit it out," a small diamond crystal fell into her hands.

Desirable minerals, especially crystals, have beauty in their own right and also can lead the collector into all the intricacies of mineralogy. But specimens are no longer easy to find, since many old mines have been worked out or have become inaccessible. Fossils lead into a world of their own, the historic past, but again depletion of sites and growing governmental restrictions have limited one's opportunity to collect.

Rocks—Beauty in Abundance

Rocks themselves will always be abundant and yet rich in beauty and interest. Besides being assured of finding desirable specimens, the collector has a wide choice of places to enjoy the fresh air, for communion with the earth, and for the wholesome exercise of swinging a geologist's hammer. The field experience gained with rocks will be invaluable later in more specialized branches of the hobby.

Nowhere in the world has collecting been made so convenient and so generally rewarding as in the United States and its neighbor, Canada. Libraries and museums abound in such resources as books, maps, and exhibits; adult education courses are popular, and more than 1,000 clubs with more than 80,000 members offer their facilities, leadership, and congenial associations to anyone interested in earth science hobbies. In the United States these clubs are organized into six regional federations that hold annual conventions and shows in addition to those put on by individual clubs. Dealers in specimens, equipment, and books bring their wares to the shows, and facilities are provided for individuals to swap specimens. A dozen magazines from the most elementary to the most professional levels serve the collector audience with news of collecting sites, discoveries, techniques, and research. Modern roads and motels, automobiles, buses, and recreational vehicles make access easy to mountain, plain, and desert alike. State geological and tourist agencies encourage collectors with advice and maps.

Showcases of the mineral kingdom exist everywhere on the North American continent: New England with its granite mountains, New York City with its traprocks, Florida with its coral, Alabama with marble, Indiana with limestone, Minnesota with pipestone, South Dakota's rose quartz, Colorado and Utah with many-hued sandstone, California with serpentine, Arizona with copper-stained rocks, and Washington with petrified wood. Nature has scattered rocks lavishly throughout the land.

Most land in the eastern United States is privately owned and open to collectors only by permission, but the western states and western Canada generally invite reasonable use of their vast tracts of publicly owned land.

The chapters following this introduction to the hobby of rock collecting will classify and describe systematically the major species of rocks in sufficient detail to make them recognizable. This descriptive material will be augmented with illustrations. Later chapters will contain information about preparing for a collecting trip, equipment, conduct in the field, map use, and safety, as well as an outline of the geological history of North America and the rewarding opportunities it offers for collecting.

2. getting acquainted with rocks

Let rocks their silence break.
Samuel F. Smith

History's memory, long as it is, does not run back far enough to record that moment when a remote ancestor first picked up a rock and recognized that in his hand he held a tool with which he could pound wild seeds into meal or drive away a hostile animal. That example was imitated and improved on; for archaeologists discover stone artifacts—arrowheads, scrapers, knives, hoes, axes, and ritual ornaments—around prehistoric campsites. Many are so skillfully crafted for daily use that they deserve to be called man's first art forms.

Stoneworking Through the Centuries

Stone was flaked or ground with high skill into sharp knives and points; some cultures even discovered that heating flint improved its chipping qualities. Central Ohio's colorful flint was bartered over much of North America. Farther west, Indians fashioned quartz, agate, and petrified wood into jewellike points, and they and the Maya of Central America worked wonders with glassy black obsidian. Tough diorite stones were grooved and lashed to rude handles for use as clubs and axes. Thousands of such hammers were found where ancient tribesmen of a mysterious race broke copper from pits in Upper Michigan's Keweenaw peninsula and Isle Royale.

Central American jade ornaments and monumental sculptures in granite attest to the sophistication of the artisans of these civilizations.

Egypt's pharaohs built temples and pyramids that are reckoned among the wonders of all time. The exhibition in the United States of objects from the tomb of King Tutankhamun drew millions to marvel at the splendor with which he was buried 3,000 years ago. The jewels of carnelian, lapis lazuli, and other gem materials that adorned his body are even more remarkable when it is remembered that they were fashioned without the use of hard abrasives or steel tools. Contemporaneously, Chinese lapidaries were patiently sawing tough jade boulders into slabs with sand and creating beautiful jade bowls and carvings.

Tutankhamun's mummy wore more than 140 pieces of jewelry, but not for adornment alone. Stones in those days were believed to have magical properties that would protect the king on his journey through the underworld. Alabaster vases carved with incredible craftsmanship were placed in the tomb to hold the unguents and perfumes he would need for that journey. These were decorated with petitions to the gods to show the dead king their favor.

Through history since those ancient days runs the record of the faith placed by humanity in the magical and medicinal powers of stones. In the Gem Room of the Field Museum of Natural History in Chicago rests a case of amulets used by many peoples in many ages—the worry stones and lucky pieces of credulous times. Jade gets its name, for example, from the Spanish *piedra de ijada,* meaning "stone of the loin," deriving from the belief that a person wearing a piece of jade would be spared diseases of the kidneys. So common were such prescriptions that the habit of wearing jewelry as ornament may have come about from the example of ancestors who wore it for a more vital reason.

Belief in amulets dies hard; in fact, it remains alive today. A former resident of Michigan's Upper Peninsula recalled recently a boulder that rested on the porch of a house where an Indian family lived in the town of L'Anse. This "thunderbird egg," so the family believed, had kept lightning from striking their house, although their neighbors had not been so fortunate. Some folk still have faith that if they count their warts and then bury an equal number of pebbles, the warts will go away. No doubt that remedy is as effective in its way as a copper bracelet is against arthritis.

The usefulness of stone to the human race through the ages is evident in large as well as small examples. The ancient Greeks built the Parthenon of marble carved by their greatest sculptors. Rome's monuments of stone still testify to the power and glory of its classical civilization. Over the centuries, Europe became a continent of substantial stone dwellings. Many, like the rows of cottages in England's Midlands, are still in use. Even today, stone remains the material of choice for national capitals and heroic monuments. The limestone monoliths of Washington, D.C., express both the usefulness of stone and the power of government.

The stone-paved roads where Roman legions marched have not lost their usefulness. Likewise, stone remains the basic material of our roads and streets; cars and trucks roll on highways built of concrete made with crushed stone and gravel. Measured in dollars, such construction uses constitute the most important mineral industry in the United States.

Minerals and Rocks

Like air and water, rocks and pebbles are so much a part of our daily life that it is easy to take them for granted and ignore their nature and their origin. Geologists, the men and women who interpret the mineral kingdom to us, recognize two major divisions in their domain: minerals and rocks. A mineral is a naturally occurring inorganic substance with a definite chemical composition. If they have had room to grow freely, most minerals will express their orderly internal structure by the characteristic external shapes that are called crystals.

Minerals are individuals; rocks are crowds of minerals, aggregates of crystals or crystalline particles. Quartz, for example, is a mineral, a compound of an atom of a metal, silicon, with two atoms of oxygen, the life-supporting gas in the air we breathe. Quartz is not formed by animal or vegetable life, so it is inorganic; it has a fixed chemical composition, and it expresses its internal order by a characteristic crystal form that usually resembles a sharpened hexagonal pencil. Quartz, or silica, as it is often called, using a group name for the many varieties of quartz, fully qualifies as a mineral. It should, for it is the most abundant mineral on earth.

Granite, on the other hand, is a rock, made up of minerals, including quartz, as well as such other common ones as feldspar and mica. The crystals of these several minerals are crowded together in granite so closely that they do not stand out as individuals.

For convenience, some materials such as coal and coral that owe their origin to organic rather than inorganic sources are classified as rocks. They have become essentially inorganic by geological processes and they occur in massive deposits like other rocks. Likewise, for convenience certain minerals such as limestone and its cousin dolomite are usually thought of as rocks. The former is calcium carbonate, the latter is calcium magnesium carbonate, so technically they answer all the requirements for minerals.

Origin of the Earth

According to what is known as the "big bang" theory, fragments of a previous universe coalesced into a mass that exploded, sending its particles out in all directions to form the galaxies that astronomers see through their telescopes. This explains the fact that the universe is still expanding as the fragments continue their flight.

Our own galaxy, visible from earth as the Milky Way, is believed to have formed in this way. Within it, the solar system of which earth is a part apparently developed when a cloud of gas and dust began to rotate and finally took shape as a flat disc with the sun in the center.

Composition of the Earth

The earth must have taken shape as a seething hot mass, but over this a rocky crust developed. Hot escaping gases accompanying volcanic eruptions created an atmosphere; the crust thickened, and the earth's interior took form. Measurement of the passage of earthquake shock waves through the earth has provided information about the probable structure of our planet. The crust of surface rocks and soil ranges in thickness from 20 to 30 miles (35 to 50 kilometers) on the continents to as little as 3 miles (5 kilometers) in deep ocean basins.

Beneath the crust lies the mantle, composed of several diverse layers of dark rock about 1,800 miles (3,000 kilometers) thick and so hot that the rock is a plastic mass. Deep mines, such as the gold reef workings in South Africa, give impressive evidence of the internal heat of the earth. Temperatures there rise so rapidly that water becomes scalding hot 1.5 miles (2.5 kilometers) down in the mines. Some calculations indicate that temperatures increase 30 degrees Fahrenheit (17 degrees Celsius) per mile. In the famous silver mines of the Comstock lode at Virginia City, Nevada, one of the ever-present perils was that a blast might open up a pocket of boiling water and scald the miners.

Readings from earthquake shocks place at the center of the earth a solid core surrounded by an outer liquid core made up of elemental iron, cobalt, nickel, and perhaps some sulfur. The dual cores are about 2,160 miles (3,250 kilometers) thick. Their nature is suggested by pebbles of josephinite, a natural iron-nickel alloy found in Josephine County, Oregon. Some geologists have speculated that these pebbles are perhaps samples of the outer core brought to the surface by profound earth movements.

A heavy core for the earth would reconcile global arithmetic. Land surface rocks have a specific gravity of about 2.7, less than three times the weight of an equivalent volume of water. But the average specific gravity of the earth is known to be 5.5. A heavy iron-nickel core would bring up the average to the proper figure. On cosmic scales, the earth weighs in at 6×10^{21} tons, which is the figure 6 followed by 21 zeros.

Age of the Earth

The age of the earth remained a subject of speculative and theological controversy for centuries until it was estimated in this century from the evidence of isotopes of radioactive elements in rocks. Such isotopes form and change slowly over long periods of time. By these reliable cosmic clocks the earth is roughly 4.5 billion years old. Meteorites bring the news that the solar system is just about as old.

The earth's primeval crust disintegrated eons ago, leaving no trace of its nature. The continents have drifted, as Chapter 1 has described; they have been repeatedly drowned beneath the seas; mountains have risen and been worn away; volcanoes have

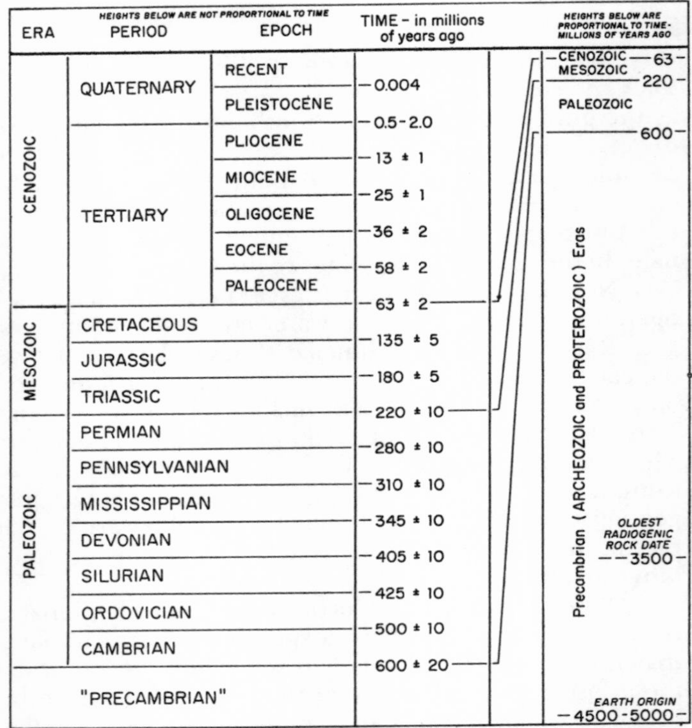

ERA	PERIOD	EPOCH	TIME – in millions of years ago
	HEIGHTS BELOW ARE NOT PROPORTIONAL TO TIME		
CENOZOIC	QUATERNARY	RECENT	0.004
		PLEISTOCENE	0.5 - 2.0
	TERTIARY	PLIOCENE	13 ± 1
		MIOCENE	25 ± 1
		OLIGOCENE	36 ± 2
		EOCENE	58 ± 2
		PALEOCENE	63 ± 2
MESOZOIC	CRETACEOUS		135 ± 5
	JURASSIC		180 ± 5
	TRIASSIC		220 ± 10
PALEOZOIC	PERMIAN		280 ± 10
	PENNSYLVANIAN		310 ± 10
	MISSISSIPPIAN		345 ± 10
	DEVONIAN		405 ± 10
	SILURIAN		425 ± 10
	ORDOVICIAN		500 ± 10
	CAMBRIAN		600 ± 20
	"PRECAMBRIAN"		

Geologic time scale

poured their fiery torrents on land and sea. Endless change, an inorganic birth, maturity, and extinction, is nature's way with rocks as it is with living things.

The first 3 billion years of the earth's development is prehistory written dimly in the rocks. Not until about 600 million years ago did life begin to leave an abundant fossil record that could be deciphered. On this fossil record the chronology of life and change on the earth is based.

Forces That Formed the Rocks

Geology concerns itself not only with the age of rocks but also with the circumstances of their origin. Rocks can be classified in this way into three major groups. Those forced up from pools of melted material, called magma, that lie deep beneath the crust are described as igneous rocks from the Latin word for fire.

Igneous rocks include those that reach the surface and solidify there and those that harden beneath the surface. The former, such as lava, are known as extrusive rocks; the latter, such as granite, as intrusive rocks.

The continental crust is made up largely of igneous rocks, such as the intrusive granites of the Sierra Nevada that have been exposed by erosion of the older rocks under which the granite hardened, and the vast extrusive lava plateau on which Oregon, Washington, Idaho, and parts of several other states rest. Appropriately, that corner of the continent has not lost its volcanic disposition. Geologists detect signs that Mount Baker and Mount Saint Helens may again erupt. The crust under the oceans is composed of basalt, an extrusive rock.

While intrusive rocks take their places slowly and imperceptibly, no manifestation of the earth's elemental forces is more awe-inspiring or destructive than a major volcanic eruption, such as the one that took place in 1883 in the strait between Java and Sumatra. From the island of Krakatoa poured pumice that blanketed the whole region many feet deep, choked the strait with huge floating blocks of pumice, destroyed villages, and took thousands of lives; then Krakatoa added the climactic touch of exploding and hurling 4 cubic miles of rock into the air. This gigantic blast sent a tsunami, or tidal wave, roaring into the devastated region. Heard three thousand miles away was the bang of the volcano's final moment.

A second group of rocks owe their origin to the ceaseless work of wind and rain. These destructive agents are never weary. Weathering breaks up the rock in place; mass wasting such as landslides hurls the rock downward by gravity; and erosion by wind, water, and ice in motion completes the process. These natural agents combine to sort the eroded rock debris and deposit it into beds where it is compacted or cemented into new rocks, such as sandstone. Shale and limestone are the other major sedimentary rocks, along with pebbly conglomerate. Unlike the others, limestone also owes its existence to the work of another natural agency—precipitation of calcium carbonate (lime) by chemical action in sea water as well as to an ooze formed of the shells of tiny organisms.

Earth forces create new rocks from old in another way, known as metamorphism, from the Greek words meaning change of form. As pressures within the crust cause mountains to rise and fold and valleys to sink, magma gets a chance to break through wherever the surface is faulted. The tremendous forces at play change existing rock both physically and chemically into new kinds of rock.

Snow's change into ice offers a homely illustration of metamorphism. As it piles up throughout a cold winter, snow presses on the bottom layers. Without melting, they slowly change to ice; the delicate flakes have taken a new form. Likewise, metamorphism's agents—pressure, heat, active fluids and gases —make solid rock plastic, so that it folds and bends without breaking. In the process the granular crystals of one kind of rock may change to the flaky crystals of a new rock.

Metamorphism operates on both a grand scale and a limited one. Regional metamorphism transforms more widely but usually not so intensely as contact metamorphism. It may be felt throughout a major mountain range, changing its granite to gneiss. But where an intruding magma can bring all its powers to bear in a limited way, such contact metamorphism melts some of the older rock, crushes some, and creates a whole array of new minerals.

Contact metamorphism's effects may be felt for hundreds of feet within the preexisting rock. As is true in so many of the chemical processes in nature, water plays a major role in the transformation. Water acts as solvent and reagent in chemical change; it may penetrate the existing rock farther than the heat of the magma itself, and the amount of water present may even determine how fluid and active the magma itself is. Minerals in metamorphic rock are often flattened, like mica, or the grains are stretched in the direction of flow.

Rock Identification and Classification

A collector acquainted with the general characteristics of igneous, sedimentary, and metamorphic formations has taken a long step toward identifying specific rocks as well as formations that are most likely to be of interest to him. Rocks, like people, can be found as well as known by the company they keep. Field identification of a rock can be so confusing at times that the clues afforded by those associated with it are welcome.

The nature of their origin is only one of the properties by

which rocks are known. The size, composition, and interrelationships of the minerals that compose a rock obviously determine its identity. That identity can be established by the amateur only if he or she has some acquaintance with the language of chemistry. The chemical elements that are the building blocks of all things number more than 100, but fortunately for the rock collector, all except about 1.5 percent of the earth's land, sea, and air is composed of just eight of these elements. These and the symbols by which they are named in chemical and mineral formulas are: oxygen (O), silicon (Si), aluminum (Al), iron (Fe), calcium (Ca), sodium (Na), potassium (K), and magnesium (Mg). The first two make up nearly 75 percent of the crust, which is often referred to as the lithosphere, from the Greek word for stone. Familiar metals—gold, silver, copper, lead, and zinc—common as they may appear, are comparatively rare, and so are such useful ones as sulfur and carbon.

Not only do a few elements make up the bulk of the rocks, but out of the nearly 2,500 mineral species only a comparatively small number are common enough to concern the average collector.

Nature of origin and mineral composition constitute the basic distinctions by which rocks are classified, but for the collector they must also be described in such terms that field recognition becomes possible. Census takers list individuals by sex, race, age, and occupation as they go about compiling a picture of the nation's population. This information becomes the basis of business and political judgments, but it is of no value to a person trying to identify a stranger in a crowd. Recognition in such a situation requires particulars, not generalizations—such details as whether the individual is thin or fat, has blue or brown eyes, has blond or brown hair or no hair at all, his or her posture, height, and habits of dress. Possessed of such details, a person could go up to a stranger with some confidence and say, "You must be Joe Smith."

So it is with rocks. The key to identification can be simply stated: Let the rock itself respond to questions put to it by an informed mind, just as a skillful television or newspaper interviewer encourages a celebrity to talk.

Pick up a rock—a pebble, a jagged fragment, a water-worn slab. What does it mutely tell you? What is most apparent to a critical glance? Usually texture and color. Face-to-face with a rock, the collector can for the moment forget chemistry and circumstances of origin, and concentrate on its texture, visible minerals or lack of them, and, to a lesser degree, on color, weight, hardness, and signs of fracture or cleavage.

Texture is usually the most significant clue noticeable in field examination of a rock. If the crystals or particles are 1/5 inch (5 millimeters) or larger, the texture is coarse; if 1/25 inch to 1/5 inch (1 to 5 millimeters), it is medium; and below 1/25 inch (1 millimeter) it is fine-grained. Anything below the level of vision is described as microcrystalline.

The collector will also ask whether the grains are interlocked and all about the same size—equigranular, as in granite; lumpy and very coarse, as in pegmatite; glassy or frothy, as with some volcanic rocks; sandy, as in sandstone; earthy, as in shale; fibrous, as in some types of gypsum; or so fine that they are invisible to the unaided eye. Many metamorphic rocks can be recognized by distinct layering, like a pile of leaves, a condition known as foliation. The igneous porphyries display large crystals in a fine-grained mass; pebbles and rock fragments find their home in conglomerate. Flow structure—cavities or crystals elongated or aligned in the direction the once-plastic magma flowed —can be a significant textural detail.

Other questions remain to be answered. How hard is the rock? A century and a half ago, Friedrich Mohs devised the scale for measuring the hardness of minerals that bears his name. In it talc (1) is the softest mineral. A fingernail will scratch it easily, but will barely do the same for gypsum (2). Calcite (3) is easily scratched by a copper coin, and fluorite (4) by a knife blade. Apatite (5) also yields to a knife blade, and glass will scratch it. Orthoclase feldspar (6) resists a knife blade, and quartz (7) is harder than a steel file. At its upper end, the Mohs scale places topaz (8), corundum, which is ruby and sapphire in the gem world (9), and diamond (10). The Mohs scale, though designed for minerals, is also commonly used to indicate the hardness of rocks.

Color in the rock world means essentially the proportion of light and dark minerals in the specimen. The former may be white, pink, pale gray, or some shade of brown or red; the dark ones are mostly dark brown, green, or black. Hardness and color

GRANITE: Cumberland, R.I. Typical texture of coarse, easily visible, closely compacted granules of gray quartz, white, gray or pink, even red, orthoclase feldspar, and white albite feldspar, all of about the same size, speckled with crystals of black hornblende and dark biotite mica.

GRANITE: Hurricane Island, Me. Very coarse, porphyritic crystal granules of gray quartz and light-colored feldspars with crystals of hornblende and biotite.

GRANITE: Llano Co., Tex. An unusual and decorative porphyry of bluish quartz and pink feldspar in a fine-grained brown ground mass. It occurs as dikes in granite and is locally known as llanite.

PEGMATITE: Pala area, San Diego Co., Calif. Black tourmaline in a mottled rock of giant-size feldspar and quartz granules.

should always be determined from a fresh surface where the rock has been chipped or split. Weathering easily puts a false face on it.

Luster is the appearance of a surface when light strikes it. It can be described as metallic, glassy, pearly, or dull. Like color, luster helps to identify some major rock constituents, such as grayish, glassy quartz and pale, pearly feldspars in granite.

Wood can be split along the grain; so can some minerals along a plane of weak cohesion in the crystal structure. This is cleavage. Mica has perfect cleavage into sheets thin enough for windows; calcite and feldspar cleave into characteristic forms, and quartz does not cleave at all. It fractures instead to a shape described as conchoidal, like the curved surface of a shell. Some other minerals fracture in a fashion described as hackly or fibrous.

Rocks differ markedly in weight. Pumice is feather-light; some of the iron-rich jaspers and basalts are noticeably heavy. Weight is measured as specific gravity, which is the comparison of the weight of a substance with that of an equal volume of water. Quartz, for example, is nearly three times as heavy as water; its specific gravity (sg) is 2.65; that of lead is 7.5. Specific gravity can often be reckoned in the field by hefting a rock.

Identification of rocks is based in this book on classification according to texture, starting with the coarse-grained rocks, then the others in their order of grain size, down to those in which grain is imperceptible. As each rock type is taken up, details of its origin, associates, and the chemistry of its constituent minerals will be treated in such detail as will be useful in recognizing it.

Petrologists—specialists in the study of rocks—use some highly technical terms based on microscopic and chemical examination. For the amateur, however, the more general and traditional classifications are adequate, and by organizing this study around the master key—texture—the collector can identify most rocks by name sufficiently accurately for his or her purposes.

Granite

The earth's continental crust—the part with which the collector will be concerned—is made up largely of granite, granite-

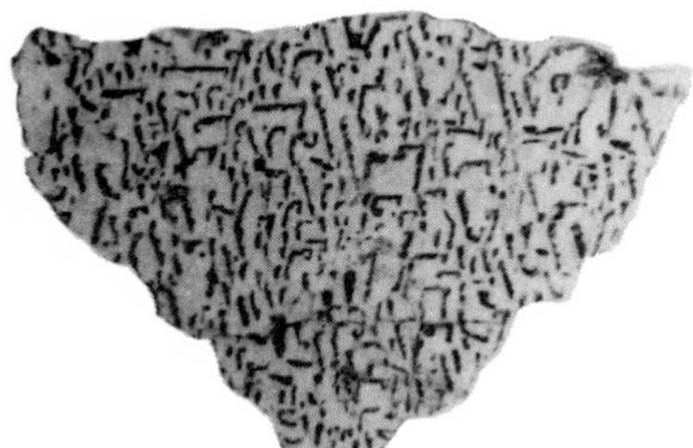

GRAPHIC GRANITE: Ontario, Canada. A form of pegmatite consisting of coarse feldspar crystals intergrown with gray quartz in a pattern that resembles cuneiform writing.

APLITE: Boulder Co., Colo. Quartz and orthoclase feldspar crystals in a sugary-textured rock associated with pegmatites.

GRANODIORITE: St. Cloud, Minn. Moderately coarse and grayer than granite, with white plagioclase feldspars replacing much of the orthoclase. Much so-called granite is granodiorite.

DIORITE: Salem, Mass. Mostly light to dark gray plagioclase feldspars with little or no quartz and a heavy proportion of dark minerals such as hornblende, augite, and biotite.

like rocks and igneous lavas iced with a thin coating of sedimentary rocks. Granite is relatively coarse and easily recognized; it affords a good starting point for a systematic exploration of the rock world.

The granitic rocks have their origin in reservoirs of molten material, magma, that form in the lower crust and the upper part of the mantle. This magma is forced upward toward the surface by internal pressures and earth movements. Magma is versatile. What kind of rock it will make depends on whether it reaches the surface, how fast it moves, and its water content, physical state, and chemical composition. If the melt is rich in silicon and oxygen and it cools slowly below the surface, typical granite may form. If magnesium and iron are present in sufficient quantity to combine with and use up the free silicon, dark-colored minerals will predominate in the rock. Iron and magnesium minerals are the most aggressive, the first to form from magma, and the feldspars and finally quartz take what silicon is left. The texture, such as the size of the crystals, is determined by the temperature of the melt, its viscosity, and the length of time that circumstances allow for it to crystallize.

The origin of granite has provoked a lively discussion among geologists. Some attribute it to the melting of sedimentary rocks forced down deep within the crust by their own weight, such as the eroded material from a mountain range that piled up in a valley. But whether granite is metamorphic or igneous is of more academic than collecting interest.

As the invading magma moves up in a weak spot in the crust, absorbing older rocks on its way, it may spread beneath the surface rocks and harden slowly there. Fragments of the older rocks, called xenoliths from the Greek words for stranger and rock, may be picked up in the mass. If the magma fills a vertical or sharply angled fold or crack, a dike will be the result. If the zone of penetration is horizontal, it will harden as a subsurface sheet of rock called a sill. The Palisades of the Hudson River are such a sill.

In a major thrust, the magma may hump up the rocks into what is called a laccolith, from the Greek word for cistern, or create a bowl-shaped lopolith, like the formation from which nickel is mined at Sudbury in Canada. The Henry Mountains in

SYENITE: Cuttingsville, Vt. A fairly uncommon coarse igneous rock, mostly light-colored orthoclase and microcline feldspars with prominent laths of black hornblende.

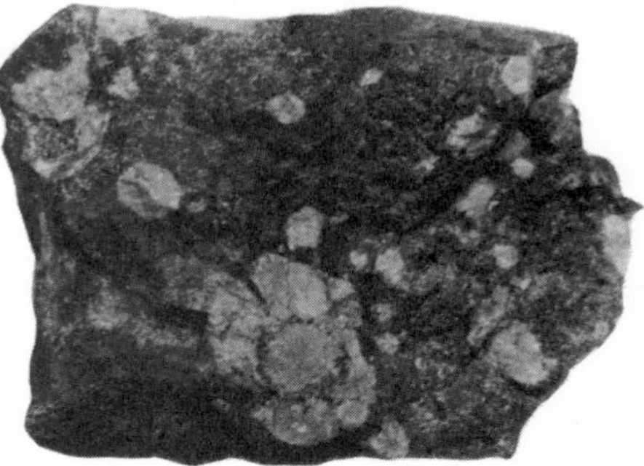

SYENITE: Magnet Cove, Ark. A syenite containing porphyritic structures of pseudoleucite, a replacement of leucite by nepheline.

NEPHELINE SYENITE: Gooderham, Ontario, Canada. Resembling a coarse granite, but one in which nepheline takes the place of quartz and the orthoclase is darkened by augite and other iron-magnesian minerals.

MONZONITE: San Juan Co., Colo. In color and texture monzonite lies midway between syenite and diorite. It is gray and composed of feldspars, mica and augite and a bit of quartz.

Utah are textbook examples of laccoliths. A gigantic intrusion, such as the several that formed the mighty mass of the Sierra Nevada, is called a batholith, from the Greek word for depth stone. A small batholith, like Stone Mountain in Georgia, is a stock. Erosion gradually removes the older surface rock and exposes the magmatic intruder.

If the magma pours to the surface through a volcano or a rift, it will cool much more quickly than magma which is permitted by its cover of older rocks to crystallize at leisure. The lava will contain only small crystals or none at all. Different as they are in appearance, the intrusive (buried) rocks and the extrusive (ejected) rocks may be much alike in chemical composition, just as fudge can become grainy or be smooth depending on the length of time it is exposed to heat. Extrusive and intrusive rocks will be discussed in detail later, and so will the rocks that form in magmas too poor in silicon to find a place in the granitic series.

Granite breaks apart with a coarse, rough surface, the grains of quartz evident by their characteristic shell-like fracture and glassy, grayish appearance, and the feldspar by pearly cleavage faces. The orthoclase feldspar predominates. It is opaque white, pink, or even reddish; the less plentiful albite feldspar is an inconspicuous white. Granite's quartz and feldspar crystals usually are about the same size, closely interlocked, and sprinkled with tiny rods of black hornblende and lustrous flakes of biotite mica.

The components of granite's tweedy mix include several of the commonest rock-forming minerals. Quartz, whose chemical formula is SiO_2, is harder than most other rock-forming minerals, is chemically inert, and has no cleavage that would facilitate mechanical breakdown. For these reasons it survives as sand when granite is weathered away. Pebbles of such varieties of silica as quartz, agate, chalcedony, flint, and jasper make up a high proportion of the pebbles in streams and on beaches.

The feldspars are many and various in appearance, but they fall into two classes. Orthoclase and microcline comprise one, the plagioclase feldspars the other. Orthoclase is a mineral composed of potassium, aluminum, silicon, and oxygen. Its chemical formula, $KAlSi_3O_8$, indicates that orthoclase is a compound of one atom of potassium (K), to one of aluminum (Al), three of silicon (Si), and eight of oxygen (O). Orthoclase is an important mineral of such rocks as granite, syenite, pegmatite, and gneiss.

GABBRO: Wichita Mountains, Okla. The granite rocks are all intrusive. Gabbro is the darkest of the coarse extrusives, made up of plagioclase feldspars, largely labradorite, with augite, magnetite, and olivine.

GABBRO: Davie Co., N.C. A pegmatitic variety of gabbro with some eyelike phenocrysts of dark minerals.

ANORTHOSITE: Essex Co., N.Y. Frequently found with gabbro, anorthosite is lighter in color, brown to gray, often displays bluish labradorite crystals and elongated crystals of its dark constituents. Like gabbro, it may show some layering, as in this specimen.

PERIDOTITE: Syracuse, N.Y. A dark green to black rock composed mostly of olivine and magnetite and other dark minerals. Like this specimen, it may be porphyritic. It is associated with gabbro.

Microcline has the same chemical formula as orthoclase. In its green version, amazonstone, it is often cut as a gem. So is perthite, a feldspar curiously constructed of a stack of thin plates that reflect light with a shimmering luster.

Albite, one of the group of plagioclase feldspars, is like orthoclase except that sodium (Na) takes the place of potassium in its chemical formula, $NaAlSi_3O_8$. Albite, as its name implies, is white or light in color, and resembles orthoclase in hardness and luster. The other plagioclase feldspars will be discussed later with the rocks in which they appear.

Dark flakes of mica sprinkle the surface of granite like tiny mirrors. The common micas are muscovite, a hydrous potassium aluminum silicate, and biotite, a hydrous potassium magnesium iron aluminum silicate. Hydrous indicates that the compound contains an oxygen-hydrogen (OH) group. Muscovite occurs as colorless, light brown, or reddish scales in many common rocks; biotite, which is dark brown to black, is the common mica of granite.

Granite often appears to be weathering in a curious fashion, but the thin shells thrown off by such masses as Half Dome in Yosemite National Park are a gradual unloading of the pressures stored up in the rock from its creation in the batholith. Likewise, granite shrinks into hexagonal pillars like huge posts or develops a complex joint system. Frost and plant roots exploit these weaknesses to disintegrate the rock.

The most storied piece of granite in the United States is Plymouth Rock in Massachusetts, where, according to popular belief, the Pilgrims first set foot on this continent. Man has done more than weather to disfigure this storied boulder. It has been moved four times; it has broken apart each time, and fragments were peddled to tourists. In 1920, what remained of Plymouth Rock was cemented together and laid to rest under a roof of granite supported by Grecian columns.

Pegmatite, Aplite, and Porphyry

Unlike granite, pegmatite may not be in demand for tombstones or facings of office buildings, but for collectors it is perhaps the most exciting member of the granite family. As a silica-rich magma cools and begins to crystallize, still-liquid material may find its way into crevices in the cooling mass. It hardens

DIABASE: Somerville, Mass. A rock of plagioclase feldspars speckled with augite. It is usually found as dikes and sills associated with volcanic basalts.

DIABASE: Cape Ann, Mass. The dark background brings into prominence the lathlike feldspar crystals in this diabase porphyry.

PORPHYRY: Well-defined augite crystals in a fine-grained matrix of predominantly plagioclase feldspars.

DIABASE: Suffern, N.Y. Hexagonal column characteristic of basaltic rocks, exemplified by the Palisades of the Hudson River.

there very slowly; shells of coarse quartz and feldspar form a central core around which the remaining watery fluids accumulate. These fluids pick up elements that have not found a home in the chemical community. Mica grows slowly into huge sheets; such highly valued lithium minerals as spodumene and lepidolite appear in the growing pegmatite, along with the beryls and other useful beryllium minerals, as well as tourmaline and topaz. Some spodumene crystals found in the Etta mine in South Dakota and in Southern California were giants of many tons' weight. Not only have pegmatites yielded many minerals of industrial importance, but they have also been a major source of gems and mineral specimens.

A rock made up of very coarse intergrown crystals of quartz and feldspar is easily identified as pegmatite. One curious form, however, is graphic granite, so called because the gray quartz traces patterns in the light-hued feldspar that have a fancied likeness to cuneiform script.

Another unconventional granitic rock resembles sugar. This is aplite, composed almost entirely of quartz and colorless feldspar grains. Aplite occurs in small dikes associated with pegmatites.

The term *porphyry* frequently appears in descriptions of igneous rocks. Porphyry owes its origin to a not uncommon set of circumstances. As magma rises into the crust, it may loiter along the way long enough for some mineral crystals to form and float, like berry seeds in jam, in the melt. If the cooling melt subsequently hardens too rapidly for other large crystals to develop, the result will be a porphyry—a fine-grained ground mass dotted with well-formed, distinct, contrasting crystals called phenocrysts. Like stars in the sky at night, they stand out against the background. Porphyry is not a rock in itself; it is a word that describes a particular texture of a rock, such as a granite porphyry or a basalt porphyry. In granite porphyry, the large crystals are usually white, gray, or pink orthoclase feldspar in a ground mass of quartz and dark minerals.

Granite's Many Associates

Granite's closest relative, granodiorite, is grayer than granite because it contains less quartz and the warm-colored feld-

KIMBERLITE: Murfreesboro, Ark. A greenish or bluish porphyry of peridotite, containing calcite, much mica, xenoliths of other rocks. It is the host rock of diamond pipes.

GNEISS: Uxbridge, Mass. A metamorphic equivalent of igneous granite in composition and texture except that its dark and light constituents are separated into layers.

GNEISS: St. Lawrence Co., N.Y. Layering is evident here, as well as the segregation of feldspar and quartz into eyelike (German augen) forms that give it the name of augen gneiss.

TOURMALINE SCHIST: Shelby Co., N.C. A dense mass of black tourmaline needles aligned in one direction from the effects of metamorphic force.

spars. In their place, granodiorite substitutes as much as 30 percent of dark minerals. Much of what is commonly called granite, such as in the Rockies, is granodiorite.

As the name indicates, granodiorite lies midway in composition between granite and diorite. Dark pink or gray, diorite contains little quartz, a large proportion of the dark iron and magnesium minerals, and is often porphyritic. But like granite and granodiorite, it is coarsely crystalline, and is found in the margins of the two related rock masses. Veins of quartz often thread through these rocks. From these veins has come much of the world's gold.

Syenite, a light-colored, coarse-grained rock less common than other granitic rocks, is made up mostly of orthoclase and albite feldspars. Its rarest form, nepheline syenite, is usually gray. Nepheline is a granular sodium potassium aluminum silicate ($NaKAlSiO_4$) that to the eye looks like a gray or pink quartz in the feldspar mass. It is softer than quartz and has an easy cleavage and a greasy luster. Nepheline syenite contains no quartz, but it may be figured with crystals of blue sodalite, which help identify it.

Midway between syenite and diorite lies monzonite, made up of pale yellow feldspars with muscovite mica, black augite, and traces of quartz.

Granodiorite and diorite, as the descriptions indicate, are at the head of a series of coarse-grained igneous rocks that have originated in a magma less rich in silica than one that would normally harden as granite. This series darkens as orthoclase and quartz gradually disappear and the plagioclase feldspars, the pyroxenes and amphiboles, take their place.

These names describe minerals so important in the study of rocks that acquaintance with them is as necessary to the serious collector as the multiplication table is to the mastery of arithmetic. The plagioclase feldspars comprise a series from albite, the sodium aluminum silicate ($NaAlSi_3O_8$), to anorthite, the calcium aluminum silicate ($CaAlSi_3O_8$). The other members of the series incorporate less sodium and more calcium in their formulas as they approach anorthite in composition. These intermediate plagioclase feldspars, in order, are oligoclase, andesine, labradorite, and bytownite. They become increasingly major constitu-

TALC TREMOLITE SCHIST: St. Lawrence Co., N.Y. Pale tremolite needles against a background of talc. Tremolite alters to talc.

ACTINOLITE SCHIST: Chester, Vt. Green needles of actinolite, an amphibole, form the bulk of this metamorphic rock. Actinolite is an iron-rich tremolite. The two are the minerals of nephrite jade.

CHIASTOLITE SCHIST: Lancaster, Pa. Twinned crosslike brown crystals of chiastolite in a dense schistose mass.

MUSCOVITE SCHIST: Manhatten Island, N.Y. Bright cream-colored mica flakes make up a large part of this rock. It has a platy texture.

ents as the darker rocks grade into black gabbro, basalt, and peridotite. Striations caused by twinning can often be observed on the surface of plagioclase feldspars.

The amphiboles are complex silicates of potassium, sodium, calcium, magnesium, iron, and aluminum. Hornblende, the black laths common to granite, is an amphibole. Other rock-formers among the amphiboles are actinolite, usually greenish and sometimes fibrous like asbestos, and tremolite, which is white or gray. Actinolite is commonly found in schist and gneiss, and tremolite in schist and marble, as products of metamorphism. The amphiboles are slightly harder than the feldspars, and softer than quartz.

The pyroxenes resemble the amphiboles chemically but differ from them in crystal form. Augite, a pyroxene, can be expected in such dark rocks as gabbro. It is dark green to black and has a glassy luster. Diopside, another common pyroxene, may be white or gray but is more often light green with an oily luster. Marble is frequently host to it.

For rock identification purposes, the collector needs to be able to distinguish only between orthoclase and plagioclase feldspars. In the laboratory, fine distinctions can be drawn. Some plagioclase feldspars, however, have notable individuality, such as labradorite, which can display a peacock range of colors on a polished surface, or in another variety can be faceted into a golden-colored gem.

Gabbro and Its Associates

As the dark minerals become predominant, the coarse-textured intrusive rocks grade into gabbro, which is dark gray to black. Gabbro is almost entirely composed of plagioclase feldspars and the pyroxene augite, together with blackish magnetite and greenish olivine. Magnetite is an iron oxide; olivine is a silicate of iron and magnesium. The finest crystals of olivine, found at Saint John's Island in the Red Sea, are cut as gem stones under the name of peridot. Smaller but clear granules from Arizona and New Mexico are also used in jewelry. Olivine is nearly as hard as quartz.

Gabbro has the curious habit, rare among igneous rocks, of sorting some of these constituents into layerlike segregations. It often contains small cavities lined with crystals of calcite or some

MICA SCHIST: Hoosac Tunnel, Mass. Coarse flakes in easily parted layers, one of the commonest schists. Like the others it is named for its most prominent mineral.

AMPHIBOLITE: Mitchell Co., N.C. A dense, fairly coarse, tough metamorphic rock made up largely of hornblende needles and plagioclase feldspars with little schistose foliation. It is dark green to black and the needles are usually pointed in one direction. If it has more quartz the rock is called hornblende schist.

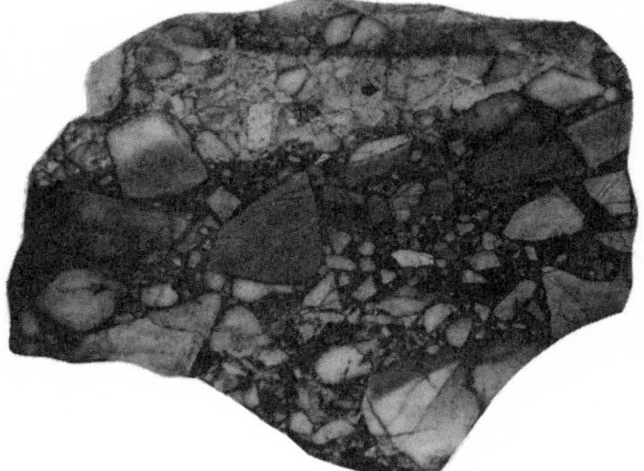

BRECCIA: Ontario, Canada. Angular fragments of rock in a cementing matrix. Conglomerate is similar but is made up of rounded pebbles.

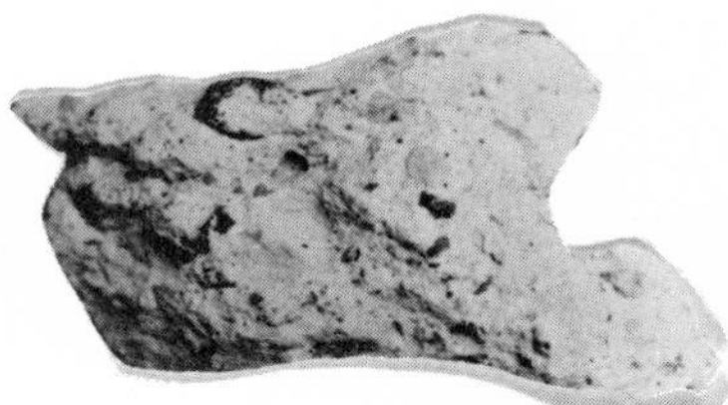

AGGLOMERATE: near Scotty's Castle, Death Valley, Nev. Much like a breccia, a mass of unsorted volcanic material, lava fragments in ash.

of the zeolites. The zeolites are a family of silicates containing water in their structure that they lose when exposed to heat or even to dry air. They are usually white in color and transparent or translucent. An extensive batholith of gabbro underlies the whole Lake Superior region from Duluth, Minnesota, into Ontario.

An uncommon coarse igneous rock is found associated with gabbro. This rock, anorthosite, is almost entirely composed of labradorite, one of the plagioclase feldspars. Usually brown or gray, it may display light bluish crystals and show a layered texture. Beds of it exist in the Adirondacks, Quebec, and Minnesota.

Two other dark, coarse-textured rocks are frequently encountered on a collecting trip. These are peridotite, composed of olivine, augite, and the iron-magnesian minerals, and diabase, mottled with long feldspar crystals in a mass of grains of black augite, and often porphyritic. The Palisades of the Hudson River are a classic example of a diabase sill, and the greenstone of the Upper Michigan copper country is derived from the same rock.

Basalt, diabase, and other dark, heavy igneous rocks are often described as trap, a word taken from the Swedish and German words for step.

Peridotite in a variety known as kimberlite is the host rock of the diamonds found in South Africa and Arkansas. Kimberlite is a breccia, a broken mass of a number of types of rocks in dark green or bluish peridotite. The name comes from the city of Kimberley in South Africa, where diamond "pipes," which are the necks of volcanic vents, were first discovered. Dunite, a rock related to peridotite and almost entirely composed of olivine, is host to the rich nickel deposits at Sudbury, Ontario.

Their iron and magnesium content makes the gabbros and other dark intrusive rocks heavier than the granites. The continents are built of granite and other light-colored rocks, which have an average specific gravity of 2.65, but the oceans rest in basins of gabbro and similar rocks with a specific gravity of 3.0 or more. The continents float; the ocean basins sink.

Gneiss and the Schistose Rocks

Granite and most of the igneous rocks almost never segregate their crystal constituents into layers. This difference helps to

PUMICE: Millard Co., Utah. A light-colored, frothy form of lava ejected in a volcanic eruption. It is so light it floats in water.

TUFF: Frying Pan Basin, Mont. A fine-grained volcanic rock that looks like sandstone and may smell earthy when wet. It is often layered through deposition by a series of eruptions.

VOLCANIC BOMB: Calif. A blob of lava ejected while molten that hardened into this shape as it fell to earth. The color is dark brown to black and the texture is crusty.

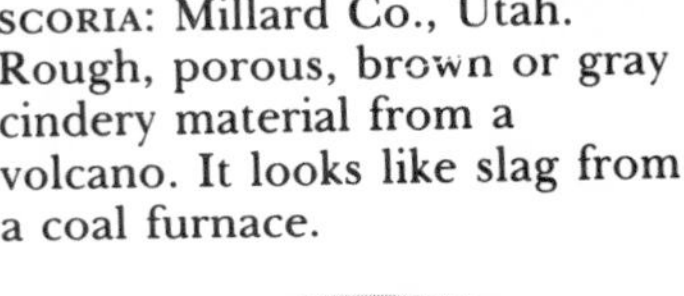

SCORIA: Millard Co., Utah. Rough, porous, brown or gray cindery material from a volcano. It looks like slag from a coal furnace.

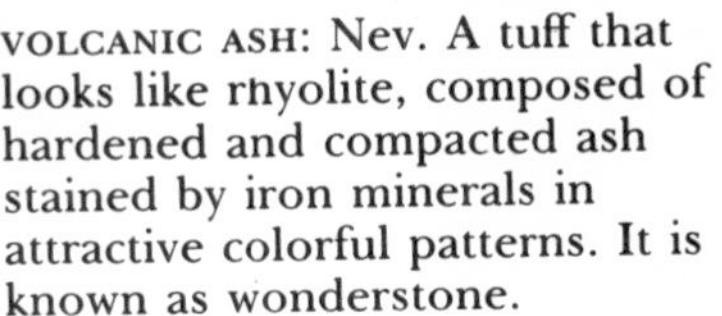

VOLCANIC ASH: Nev. A tuff that looks like rhyolite, composed of hardened and compacted ash stained by iron minerals in attractive colorful patterns. It is known as wonderstone.

distinguish them from the coarse-textured but layered rocks with which they are most likely to be confused, such as the metamorphic gneisses and schists. Gneiss (pronounced *nice*) closely resembles granite in texture, grain size, and color, but in gneiss the light gray or pink quartz and feldspar alternate as layers with dark bands of mica, hornblende, and some related minerals. Such segregation or banding of constituent minerals is the most obvious difference in appearance between gneiss and granite. Augen gneiss, from the German word for eye, is a curious form marked with large, rounded groupings of feldspar, quartz, and dark minerals in a fine-grained matrix. Mylonite is the general name given to such metamorphic alterations of coarse igneous rock.

The association of granite and gneiss has long excited the attention of geologists. Presumably, most gneiss has been derived from granite wherever regional metamorphism has occurred. Heat and pressure of major earth movements could transform granite into gneiss without actually melting it. The problem is complex, as is illustrated by the rock called migmatite, which is made up of gneiss or schist streaked with granite.

Schists, the most common metamorphic rock, vary widely in appearance, but most of them are coarse-grained and light in color. Unlike gneiss, in which light and dark layers tend to alternate, most schists are uniformly layered with glistening flakes of mica or chlorite and rodlike crystals of hornblende or other dark minerals, all oriented in one direction. Along these layers schists split readily, leaving an irregular surface.

Among the major types, named for the predominant mineral, are chlorite schist, green and flaky; glaucophane schist, bluish or even purplish and fairly compact; albite schist, dotted with white grains of albite feldspar; coarse, flaky, dark staurolite schist, distinctive for its crosslike crystals of staurolite; garnet schist, reddish from crystals of garnet in mica; and kyanite schist, with bladed crystals of the bluish mineral kyanite. Muscovite and biotite mica schists represent the family most distinctively with their gleaming flakes of pale muscovite mica and brown to black biotite mica mingled with grains of quartz and feldspar.

Amphibolite, often called hornblende schist, is found with other schists and marble. Hard, heavy, more massive than most schists, even to the point of resembling slate, it yet shows a schistose texture of layers of black hornblende needles and lighter-colored feldspar, actinolite, and chlorite. Garnet schists are also less flaky than other schists but, like amphibolite, may appear streaked.

Several unfamiliar minerals have been mentioned in connection with schists. Chlorite, a common rock-former, is a hydrous magnesium iron aluminum silicate, softer than feldspar, with a cleavage like that of mica and a pearly luster. It lends its distinctive green color, shading into darker hues, to many rocks.

Glaucophane, an amphibole like hornblende, ranges in color from azure blue to black. Staurolite forms the curious fairy crosses and is usually reddish brown and associated with garnet and kyanite. The latter is easily recognized by its light blue, bladed crystals. Both it and staurolite are silicates common to metamorphic rocks.

Schists are derived from alteration of shales, several igneous rocks, and other metamorphic rocks, such as slate. Their coarse texture makes schists easy victims of the erosive forces of nature. Like granite, therefore, they become major sources of sand and soil.

The Rock Called Conglomerate

Just as conservation-minded families reclaim waste paper and glass and tin containers, so nature refashions the products of weathering. Some of the waste goes into a rock called conglomerate. Pebbles, stony fragments, and sand collect in outwash plains of mountain streams and other places and become cemented into rock with silica, lime, or iron oxides. From its appearance such recycled rock is called puddingstone, a pudding mainly of pebbles of such siliceous rocks as quartz, flint, chert, jasper, and other tough materials.

Some conglomerates are firmly cemented, such as the Lake Superior district examples mottled with red and black pebbles derived from ancient Canadian formations. By contrast, the high cliffs that line the shores of the Mediterranean Sea in the Italian Riviera are so feebly bound that every storm at sea cuts them back and strews its spoil of fresh gravel on the beaches.

If the conglomerate is composed of angular rock fragments, it is called breccia, from the Italian word for broken. Breccia usually forms from the piles of broken rock that accumulate at the base of cliffs, while pebble conglomerates represent material collected by streams or worked over by waves and currents on the shores of seas and lakes.

Conglomerates are common enough and varied enough to entice the collector to bring together a group that will exhibit the range of color and texture of these rocks. They have also been popular for fashioning into bookends and other ornaments.

Conglomerate and agglomerate are two words with essentially a single meaning, but geology reserves the latter for lumps of volcanic rock called lapilli, cinders and other ejecta cemented together by volcanic ash and pumice. Pumice is a white, powdery, glassy froth. If the agglomerate is fairly fine-grained, the compacted mass is tuff, a rock that resembles sandstone, feels sandpapery, and when wet smells earthy, like shale. Both it and pumice are light-colored and can be expected wherever volcanoes have been active, such as in the Sierra Nevada, the Cascades, and Yellowstone National Park. A bed of tuff filling former lakes near Florissant, Colorado, is famous for its excellent preservation of delicate fossils of insects and leaves.

Through the circumstances of their formation, most conglomerate materials have been roughly sorted. But in the complex interplay of forces within a continental glacier, a wall of ice a mile thick grinding and planing the land, then retreating and spilling its spoil indiscriminately, sorting is almost accidental. The loose mass of glacial till may include giant boulders as well as broken rock, pebbles, clay, soil, and sand piled up in moraines along the edges of the ice as well as at its terminus.

But meltwater pouring from the glacier, like any stream, may try to sort the debris into hills of sorted gravel called kames. The area northwest of Milwaukee, Wisconsin, known as Kettle Moraine State Forest, displays textbook examples of such glacial activity.

When in glaciated country, which includes much of North America, the collector who finds a rock, especially a rounded one, that is unlike those common to the area in which he or she is searching has reason to suspect that it has come there through glacial action. In such a region, the collector may also come across rock strata gouged or deeply scratched by rocks that were fixed like teeth in the moving glacial ice.

3. the fine-grained rocks

Though the mills of the Gods grind slowly,
Yet they grind exceedingly small.
Longfellow

If the coarse-grained rocks do not always speak distinctly to the collector, they at least speak loudly. The fine-grained ones are often less voluble; they may even mumble. But if they are not always as communicative about texture and the like, many of them are no less interesting than their rougher cousins.

Granite, as the preceding chapter explained, is composed of granular, close-packed, coarse crystals of quartz, feldspar, and a sprinkling of mica and dark minerals. Its fine-grained analogue, composed of the same minerals, is rhyolite. Rhyolite formed from a siliceous magma that reached the surface of the earth and cooled there, perhaps from a volcanic eruption. Rapid cooling of the lava cut short the formative period; crystals had little time to grow. If the same magma had cooled slowly in a snug pocket underground, it would have formed granite.

A magma of proper composition to form rhyolite would have a viscous texture that would not flow far and would harden as relatively small masses close to the volcano or vent from which it emerged. Rhyolite is light-colored—white, gray, reddish, or brown—and may exhibit phenocrysts of quartz or feldspar in the fine-grained mass. Often it is a tuff or breccia of volcanic fragments. Rhyolite may also betray its volcanic origin by mottling and flow patterns.

As Chapter 2 explained, syenite is one of the coarse-grained granitic rocks. Its fine-grained equivalent, trachyte, also has little quartz and is essentially feldspar and some dark-colored minerals. Gray, pink, or greenish, it has a porphyritic texture. Phonolite resembles trachyte but is darker and has the curious habit of splitting into slabs that respond like chimes when they are suspended by cords and tapped with a mallet. South Dakota's Black Hills and Devil's Tower afford representative specimens.

Latite comes close to coarse-grained monzonite and granodiorite in composition among the fine-grained rocks. Like them, it has a larger proportion of dark minerals than rhyolite and may show porphyritic structure of feldspar crystals in a glassy groundmass.

Andesite, commonest of the fine-grained volcanic rocks except for basalt, and dacite often occur together in lava flows and dikes, such as are found around Mount Rainier. They are usually gray, reddish, or gray-green. Most andesites are porphyritic with flow lines and bubblelike cavities. Latite, trachyte, dacite, and andesite look so much alike that often only a laboratory test can tell them apart.

Obsidian is chemically identical to granite and rhyolite; it is the extreme member of the fine-grained granitic rocks. Obsidian is a glass, transparent in slivers, but black or reddish in the piece. Some specimens display beautiful snowy spheres of cristobalite, a form of silica. Inevitably this is known as snowflake obsidian and is in demand as a lapidary material. Obsidian is easily recognizable by its glassy luster and shell-like pattern on a fracture surface. Indians obtained it from cliffs in what is now Yellowstone National Park and the Glass Buttes in Oregon and traded it across the continent for chipping into ornaments and weapon points. Collectors dig in the perlite beds in Arizona for obsidian nodules called Apache tears. A brown, waxy form of the same rock is known as pitchstone, and pumice forms vast beds of an obsidian froth in volcanic regions.

Basalt's Mighty Empire

Gabbro's fine-textured equivalent is basalt, variously colored dull green, brick-red, or black by a heavy content of iron minerals, augite, and olivine, as well as plagioclase feldspars. Basalt, the most abundant volcanic rock, as it flows hardens into several characteristic forms. Smooth, ropy masses are called pahoehoe, and rough, fragmental lava is aa—both words from the Hawaiian language. Hawaii, of course, has had long experience with volcanoes, since the islands are the tops of volcanoes, and two of the world's most active ones are on the island of Hawaii. Basalt erupting under the sea forms masses known as pillow lava.

A huge basalt plateau occupies much of the northwestern United States. Northwestern India's basalt flow, known as the Deccan Trap, covers some 250,000 square miles of that subcontinent. In Oregon, collectors dig to get chalcedony and opal nodules that fill gas pockets in the basalt. These are prized for their landscape and flowerlike patterns. The shores of Lake Superior and the Upper Peninsula of Michigan expose extensive flows of basalt. The hardened rock, as is true generally of basalt, contains small pockets called amygdules from their almond shape. Calcite, zeolites, chlorite, opal, and agate formed in these cavities as mineral-laden water seeped through the rock. Likewise, copper was deposited in the amygdules and provided the rich ore mined for more than a century. This mineral-rich basalt is composed of labradorite, one of the plagioclase feldspars, diopside, augite, and iron oxides. It weathers dark green, brown, or red.

In general, the presence of rounded, bubble-shaped cavities, such as those found in basalt, is indicative of volcanic origin. The cavities are formed by gases trapped in the hardening mass. Intrusive rocks often contain cavities, but they are more irregular in shape.

Basalt shrinks as it cools; this release of heat may cause it to part into hexagonal columns, so even and regular in shape that they appear man-made. The Devils Postpile near Mammoth, California, and the Giant's Causeway in Ireland are notable examples.

Sandstone, Quartzite, and Shale

One of the most easily recognized of the fine-grained rocks is sandstone. Its gritty, even texture resembles that of no other natural material. Sandstone strata are laid down where wind and water have sorted rock debris, dissolved or powdered some, rounded the durable grains, and spread the latter as beds and dunes. In the process much of the rock became soil or clay, but the quartz grains remained to be cemented into stone by silica, iron oxides, or calcium salts. Though water is usually thought of as the prime mover of sand and other rock debris, wind transports nearly as much sand as water and does it faster and over a wider area.

Beds of sandstone normally are level, but they may preserve crossbedding, ripple, and raindrop marks—even dinosaur tracks—from ancient beaches and dunes. Crossbedding arises where wind or stream action creates ripples or pockets in the bottom or in a layer of sand. These later fill with sand placed at an oblique angle to the preexisting bed. Sandstone created under such conditions may exhibit striking contrasts of pattern and color. That from the area around St. George, Utah, for example, is sawed into slabs and framed as landscape pictures.

Iron oxides color sandstone intensely, ranging from the brown of the fashionable mansions of the last century to buff or red. Some is colored green by glauconite, a mineral related to the micas. Most sandstone, however, is gray, tan, or even colorless. Its many-hued cliffs lure tourists to the national parks and scenic wonders of the Colorado Plateau. Snow-white St. Peter sandstone—pure quartz—in Illinois and the Oriskany sandstone of West Virginia become the windshields of the nation's cars and glass containers for food and drink.

Sandstone's major economic importance lies, however, in its role as a reservoir for petroleum and natural gas. Geologists map sedimentary rock strata in the hope of discovering a sandstone whose pores are filled with oil and gas trapped in a pocket by impermeable strata.

Impure sandstone containing a high proportion of mica and feldspar is called arkose, a gray, buff, or reddish, unevenly textured rock. Arkose grades into graywacke, a dark stone of angular, poorly sorted grains and fragments in a fine-grained matrix, often colored green by chlorite. A deposit of graywacke may show evidence of sorting into beds of pebbles and smaller fragments cemented by clay.

RHYOLITE: Castle Rock, Colo. Rhyolite is the extrusive fine-grained equivalent of intrusive igneous granite—quartz, orthoclase and albite—and is light gray, pink or brown in color. It may be vesicular.

RHYOLITE: Chaffee Co., Colo. Streaks show flow structure in the fine-grained rock.

TRACHYTE: Bannockburn Township, Ontario, Canada. The ground mass is fine-grained and fairly light in color with some dark minerals and usually is porphyritic with crystals of sanadine feldspar, as in this specimen.

PHONOLITE: Cripple Creek, Colo. Usually darker in color than trachyte, phonolite often can be split into plates so dense that they can be used for chimes, hence the name.

Sand Claims Attention

Some years ago a magazine article under the title "Sand—Why Take It for Granted?" called attention to the collector interest that can lie in the stuff of which sandstone is formed. A large proportion of the world's surface is covered with sand. Monotonous in the mass, sand under the magnifying glass reveals an astonishing variety of shape and mineral substance, as well as color.

Sand is defined as grains no larger or smaller generally than 1/18 inch (1.5 millimeters), about the diameter of a pencil lead. It is mostly quartz, but more than twenty-five other minerals may be associated with the quartz, such as feldspar, hematite and magnetite, garnet, hornblende, mica, tourmaline, zircon, and ilmenite.

Under the glass, sand can tell the informed collector much about its origin and history. Glassy particles may owe their being to volcanic action; angular particles are young, unworn sand, usually from disintegration of granite or other coarse-grained rock. Water and cold weaken the cohesion of the crystals and they fall as sand.

Rounded sand has been worked over by streams and wind. The latter forms and moves dunes with silent but mighty power, and mountain streams tumble sand until the particles are tiny gemstones. When the particles become too small, they float rather than tumble, and end up as siltstone.

Sand collecting has an enthusiastic following that takes its devotees to the beaches and deserts and has built up an active swapping interest across the nation.

Sandstone exposed to heat and pressure from a major igneous intrusion may become fused into one of the toughest and most durable of all rocks, quartzite. Its appearance is little changed, but the grains become a coherent mass; a fractured surface will run through the grains rather than around them; it will be smooth and glassy, not gritty as it was before the metamorphosis. Quartzite and marble are not unlike in appearance, but the former is much harder. A knife blade will scratch marble but have no effect on quartzite. One commercial form of quartzite is novaculite, the fine-grained material from Arkansas used as a whetstone.

LATITE: near Victor, Colo. Fine-grained and dark like trachyte and often porphyritic. It is one of a group of these rocks that can be told apart only by analysis of the feldspar content.

ANDESITE: Mount Shasta, Calif. Like trachyte, gray, brown, green or black, composed mostly of plagioclase feldspar with phenocrysts of the dark minerals. Andesite is second only to basalt in abundance among fine-grained extrusive rocks.

ANDESITE: Ouray, Colo. A breccia of fragments of andesite in an andesitic, fine-grained ground mass.

DACITE: northwest of Helena, Mont. Much like andesite in appearance, predominantly plagioclase feldspar.

Like sandstone, shale is not difficult to recognize. It is compacted mud, often mixed with organic carbon from leaf mold, and colored red or black by carbon or iron minerals. Shale is usually soft enough to be scratched by a fingernail; it splits readily into thin sheets and flakes that weather quickly back to mud again.

Clay, one of the principal constituents of shale, is a major product of the decomposition of rocks, just as shale itself forms more than half the bulk of the sedimentary rocks. Besides quartz sand and mud, these products consist of iron oxides and soluble sodium and potassium salts that wash away to sea. Chemical decay of feldspar provides material for calcite and the calcium rocks and the silicate minerals, such as kaolin ($Al_2O_3 \cdot 2SiO_2$), that are collectively called clay.

Marl is a clay rich in calcite particles and occasionally shell fragments, such as would be deposited in a marine basin or lake. It is earthy, loosely compacted, and often colored green by glauconite.

Anyone who has driven along a highway that cuts through limestone hills may have noticed that the strata are often interleaved with layers of shaly rocks. The alternation of beds reflects the changing shorelines and the character of available sediments the seas had to work with. Limestone is deposited in deep water, and shale in the receding sea, often in pools and swamps. Virginia's Great Dismal Swamp is a modern example of conditions that prevailed in remote ages.

The Midwest of the United States is surfaced with limestone and shale over deeply buried ancient crystalline rocks. As has been mentioned, one major shale deposit lies in Colorado and Wyoming, an oil shale rich in organic matter that will be a major source of petroleum once economic and political conditions make utilization feasible.

Metamorphic forces change shale into slate, which retains the layered nature of its parent but becomes much harder and develops its own slaty cleavage without reference to the shale bedding. It also becomes much more assertive in color. Black, red, green, and purple rooftops everywhere display slate's attractiveness and exploit its durability. Mining and splitting of slate is a major industry in the eastern United States, where mountain-building forces created large deposits. Slate splits so easily be-

DACITE: Ward, Boulder Co., Colo. Feldspar porphyry with biotite, augite, and hornblende.

OBSIDIAN: Millard Co., Utah. Glassy black obsidian notable for the phenocrysts that give it the common name of snowflake obsidian. Obsidian has a bright luster, breaks with a shell-like (conchoidal) fracture and may be brown, red, or gray, often with a silvery or golden sheen.

PERLITE: Chaffee Co., Colo. Perlite is a gray or creamy mass of fractured shells of obsidian. In this specimen the shells enclose obsidian nodules, often called Apache Tears.

BASALT: Boulder Co., Colo. Basalt is the fine-grained extrusive equivalent of intrusive gabbro. Like the latter, it is dark—gray, green, or black—composed of plagioclase feldspars and silicate minerals, heavy, and the commonest of the volcanic rocks. In this specimen the rows of feldpar crystals mark the direction of lava flow.

cause metamorphosis changed the grains of shale into tiny, flat plates aligned along a common plane of weak cohesion. The edges of a piece of slate will usually show traces of this platy structure, and its face may be spotted in a variety of colors.

Slate has two fine-grained relatives, hornfels and phyllite. Whether the shale becomes one or the other depends on the intensity of metamorphism it has undergone. Under increasing force, shale is converted into slate, then hornfels, then phyllite, and finally schist. The crystal structure becomes coarser as the process proceeds.

Hornfels is usually gray, dense like baked clay, and, although it does not split like slate, it may show some trace of the layers from which it was formed. Like slate, it may be spotted, and it may contain crystals of chiastolite. Phyllite is readily recognized by the satiny sheen of its surface. It is light gray or green and parts easily into thin slabs that have a blistery, wavy surface and glisten with microscopic flakes of mica. Both hornfels and phyllite are common in the Appalachian slate regions.

Limestone and Its Manifestations

Limestone, light in color and fine-grained, is one of the rocks most familiar and most useful to man. It is calcium carbonate ($CaCO_3$), with a hardness of 3 on the Mohs scale, hence easily scratched with a knife blade. Crystalline calcium carbonate is calcite, studied and collected for its scores of crystal forms and its beauty, such as the transparent Iceland spar. Aragonite, much less common, is also calcium carbonate, but it belongs to a different crystal system from calcite. Flos ferri, a lacy, branching aragonite formed in caves, and hexagonal twinned crystals of the mineral are collector's treasures.

Limestone originated on the floors of oceans, formed there partly by chemical precipitation of calcium carbonate and partly by an accumulation of the skeletons and shells of organisms that had extracted lime from sea water as part of their life processes.

Much like limestone is dolomite, carbonate of calcium and magnesium [$CaMg(CO_3)_2$]. Dolomite is slightly harder and more even-grained than limestone and has a slightly colder bluish cast. Touched with a drop of acid, limestone fizzes with the release of carbon dioxide gas; dolomite reacts similarly only when pow-

BASALT: Keweenaw Co., Mich. When the flowing lava hardened, trapped gas caused pockets in the rock, called amygdules from their almondlike shape. As in this specimen, these later filled with calcite, zeolite, chlorite, or copper crystals.

BASALT: Island of Hawaii, Hawaii. Brownish mass of lava from Mauna Loa, the world's largest volcano, It is twisted like shiny taffy.

SANDSTONE: Wyoming. Ripples in the once sand surface appear at the top, and alternate layers of quartz grains and darker minerals in the cross section. The mass was formed and deposited in water, then hardened into sugary rock.

SANDSTONE: Buffalo Gap, S.Dak. Bands of varicolored sands warped by earth movements before they hardened into rock.

dered and when the acid is warm. Dolomite is believed to have formed where seawater rich in magnesium salts circulated through the limy ooze, a process known as dolomitization. Ankerite, a brown iron calcium carbonate, is often found with dolomite.

Where limestone has been laid down intermittently, the strata may be interbedded with shale and stained with mud, iron minerals, sand, glauconite, and organic remains. For building stone, only high-grade, compact, clean deposits are worth working; others may be suited by location or nature for use as crushed stone, cement, or agricultural lime. Limestone can be quarried, shaped, and carved easily, as it is soft when in place. It hardens when exposed to the air. It is also durable, abundant, and remains white if the atmosphere is reasonably clean.

From Indiana quarries comes a limestone favored for public building for its consistent texture and quality. This oolitic limestone formed in seas some 300 million years ago where minute grains and bits of shell, when gently agitated, coated themselves with the limestone substance from the mineralized waters. The egg-shaped particles, called oolites, settled to the bottom, became packed together, and over millions of years turned into stone.

These ancient seas also left behind fossil graveyards of the life that once teemed in them. In shale and limestone, paleontologists and amateurs hunt for superbly preserved fossils of sponges, algae, corals, trilobites, crinoids, molluscs, and other organisms. These colonies flourished along the shallow waters of the sea and died; their bodies were replaced by stone, were heaped up by the waves, and became enclosed in a bed of limestone. Such an assemblage is known as a bioherm, a mound of fossils cemented together, usually with a facing of fragments where an ancient reef was pounded by storms. Such a reef, the Great Barrier Reef, exists today off the Australian coast. Bioherms, where the rock is stained with oil and tar from organic remains, are a favored source of crushed stone because the oily fragments adhere well to asphalt paving materials. In quieter environments, fossils were laid down in the limestone strata and can be exposed by splitting the rock.

Fossils are prime clues to help the collector know that he or she is working in sedimentary rock, and they are also indicative

SANDSTONE: Garfield Co., Utah. Specimen clearly shows the gritty texture of this reddish sandstone and the even sorting of the grains by wind or water before the rock formed. (Photo Field Museum of Natural History)

ARKOSE: Mount Tom, Mass. A coarse aggregate of poorly sorted quartz grains with much feldspar and mica and some rock fragments. Arkose is a product of the disintegration of granite.

ARKOSE: Boulder Co., Colo. A typical arkose resembling a finely fragmental granite. Such rock is commonly pinkish or gray. In granite the granules are more intimately united.

GRAYWACKE: Grafton, N.Y. A gritty, poorly sorted rock of quartz, feldspar, grains and rock chips in a clay or similar fine-grained matrix. It is commonly gray to dark gray or green and fairly tough.

of the age of the formation. They are rarely as well preserved in dolomite as in limestone or shale, and its coarse texture makes sandstone a poor resting place for fossils.

Some limestones are composed largely of one type or species of fossil, such as the one from which Petoskey stone corals are collected in Michigan, the coquina stone of Florida, or the crinoidal limestone around Crawfordsville, Indiana, and LeGrand, Iowa.

Most caves owe their being to the patient work of water on limestone. Carbon dioxide from the air becomes dissolved in rainwater, forming a weak carbonic acid, like that of a carbonated soft drink. The weak acid trickles into a crevice in the stone, and over millions of years it etches out giant caverns such as the appropriately named Mammoth Cave in Kentucky and the Carlsbad Caverns in New Mexico. Inside the cavern the slow dripping of the carbonate-laden moisture causes stalactites and exotic cave formations to grow. In a similar way, lime deposits build up in iron water pipes and teakettles in hard-water country.

Mineralized waters of springs, such as those in Yellowstone National Park, deposit a spongy, light-colored, limy material known as tufa. A denser form is the travertine used for tabletops and wall paneling. Translucent onyx, a favorite material for vases, carvings, and ornaments, owes its attractive banding to the variation of mineral content in the spring waters that deposited it. Like marble, onyx is a crystalline member of the limestone family. It is often called alabaster, but that name properly belongs to a fine-grained, translucent gypsum.

Some sea dwellers, such as minute diatoms and radiolaria, have shells of silica that also became part of the limy ocean ooze. Silica is feebly soluble in water. Moisture in limestone strata picks up the silica and deposits it in voids as chert, an impure, compact form of chalcedony. These hard nodules weather out and collect at the base of limestone cliffs and in stream gravels. From them the Indians fashioned arrow points and other aboriginal weapons and tools. Like other members of the quartz family, chert has a conchoidal fracture that made it an ideal raw material for the Indian's purposes. The shell-like fracture pattern as well as its homogeneity and hardness—it is harder than a knife blade—are sufficient to identify chert, which is much the same material as flint. Both rocks, worn smooth to a waxy luster, are common in gravels.

QUARTZITE: Baraboo, Wis. Fused grains of quartz sandstone, usually white to brown or pink or, as in this specimen, purple. Quartzite is notably hard and strongly coherent.

MARBLE: Pittsford, Vt. A gray specimen with well-defined marbling in white. Most marbles are light colored; the glint of calcite crystal faces can be seen in coarse-grained marble. This distinguishes it from many limestones that look like marble. It is much softer than quartzite, another often similar rock.

MARBLE: Tate, Ga. Light pink, uniformly crystalline material from famous Georgia quarries.

SHALE: Garfield Co., Colo. Shale is hardened, compacted silt and clay, soft, usually dark in color and layered with an easy cleavage, as is evident in this specimen of oil shale from the extensive Colorado deposits.

Chalk, a porous, snowlike variety of limestone, is composed mainly of the skeletons of coccophores, foraminifera, and other tiny sea dwellers. Kansas chalk deposits are a famous collecting ground for fossils, and the white cliffs of Dover, England, are chalk from which come black nodules of flint, used in medieval times as a building stone for walls, as well as for musket flints.

Nodules, Geodes, and Concretions

Limestone is commonly the home of hollow, rounded bodies called geodes. These are usually lined with crystals of quartz, calcite, iron minerals such as hematite and limonite, barite, and a few less common minerals. Such curious formations are fairly easy to find in streams and around quarries in the Mississippi valley. Rattlestones, as the name suggests, are hollow, geodelike bodies containing loose particles.

Nodule, geode, and concretion are words used to describe several different types of bodies found in a rock mass, usually a sedimentary one. Each has its proper place in the vocabulary of the rock collector. A nodule is a foreign body in a rock mass that is different in nature from the nodule itself. The manganese bodies found in sediments in the bottom of Green Bay in Lake Michigan and in the Pacific Ocean are nodules. A geode occupies a cavity in a rock mass, is usually rounded and hollow, and is separated from the mass by a wall of chalcedony. A concretion is a concentration of some elements in the mass, cemented together by silica, iron salts, or calcite. It usually exhibits a concentric structure. The name comes from the Latin *concrescere,* to grow together.

South Dakota's sand calcites, Oklahoma's barite roses, and the gray mudstone concretions that look like Oriental statues and are often mistaken for fossils are common examples. Rough, rounded septaria, concretions divided inside by radiating spears of white calcite, are eagerly collected in the Mississippi valley, New York, Pennsylvania, and Ohio. Sawed in two and properly shaped and polished they make handsome bookends.

Mysterious markings of ridged, toothy vertical lines often appear in limestone and marble, especially where strata meet in the rock. These curious patterns, called styolites, may represent foreign particles segregated by pressure as the rock hardened.

SHALE: Keweenaw Co., Mich. So-called ripple rock, a shale formed of decomposed basalt silt and preserving the marks of waves on an ancient beach. The rock is deep red.

OOLITE: State College, Pa. Oolites are tiny spherical bodies, in this specimen in a matrix of silica. They form around a nucleus, a small particle, usually in water or a gel.

OOLITIC LIMESTONE: Bloomington, Ind. Fine grained, light colored, evenly textured and formed of oolites cemented by limy materials. This is a favorite building stone quarried in the United States and Great Britain.

COQUINA LIMESTONE: St. Augustine, Fla. A loosely cemented cream-colored mass of limy shells of the coquina, used as a building stone in Florida.

Where intruding magma comes in contact with limestone, intense metamorphism may take place, creating a rock known as skarn. Skarn is fairly coarse-grained, dark, and host to collectible crystal specimens of such silicates as olivine, serpentine, and garnet, as well as some of the metallic sulfides.

Serpentine is a little harder than limestone, has a waxy luster and fibrous fracture, and may feel slightly greasy. Composed of hydrous iron and magnesium silicates, it forms by alteration of such rocks as peridotite. Chrysotile asbestos is a commercially valuable fibrous form of serpentine and so is the dark green verd antique used for ornamental purposes. Serpentine is usually some shade of green or yellow; the translucent serpentine of a clear green shade found on the Maryland–Pennsylvania line is cut as a semiprecious gem stone.

Soapstone is often found with serpentine. It is soft, white, or gray-green from inclusions of chlorite, and is essentially massive talc, a magnesium silicate. Chinese-sculptured groups of soapstone are eagerly collected, and amateurs find it a desirable rock to carve. Soapstone's inertness to chemicals makes it an admirable material for laboratory sinks. Steatite is a form of soapstone that displays a silvery sheen. All these talcose rocks are associated with schists and gneiss. Greenstone, common in the Michigan copper country, is related to these rocks by its content of chlorite and epidote and its derivation from basic igneous rocks.

A much tougher associate is nephrite jade, a felted mass of fibers of the minerals tremolite and actinolite. Although generally thought of as a green gem stone, nephrite ranges in color from a tallowlike white through shades of green and brown to an intense black. It ranks slightly less hard than quartz on the Mohs scale.

The large family of minerals known as garnets are not uncommon silicates in metamorphic rocks. They range in color through almost every color except blue, but are usually green, brown, or red. Most of the half-dozen species are easily recognized by their ball-like crystals, but garnet occasionally occurs in large masses such as are mined for abrasive purposes at Gore Mountain, New York.

Limestone and dolomite metamorphose into marble, which is a crystalline calcite, the mineral form of calcium carbonate.

LIMESTONE: southern Wisconsin. A fine-grained limestone in which casts of fossil shells of brachiopods and mollusks are imbedded. From shales and limestones come much of the evidence we have of ancient life.

DOLOMITE: Little Falls, N.Y. Gray, dense dolomite containing a vug in which a crystal of quartz has formed. Dolomite is usually coarser, grayer, and harder than its fellow carbonate, limestone.

SLATE: Bangor, Pa. Gray slate from the principal quarry area in the United States. The layered structure which makes it useful for roofing is evident in the specimen.

SLATE: Pa. Dark slate containing fern fossils outlined in white calcite.

Some material sold as marble is, in fact, a fine-grained limestone, but true marble makes its texture evident on a freshly broken surface by the glint of the faces of tiny calcite crystals. Marble is about as hard as limestone, but its compact crystalline nature makes it quite durable.

Marble quarried for building purposes usually is white, gray, or pink, often veined or mottled in a fashion from which the language gets the word *marbling* to describe fat and lean in beef. Verd antique, usually classed as a marble, is serpentine, and the dark marble with a bluish flash of colors is composed of one or more of the plagioclase feldspars, such as labradorite. Every large city has several stone-cutting shops where scraps of marble can be had. Quarries also build up enormous piles of marble that is not salable but would supply excellent specimens for a collection of this beautiful stone.

Coal and Iron-Rich Rocks

The continental seas that repeatedly overran the lowlands of North America created deposits of sedimentary rocks of all kinds. Where they drained into the seas, rivers flowing from the hills left swamps and pools of fresh water at their mouths. Into the mud of the bogs washed trees and limbs from the tropical forests of that age; other organic matter as well as the bodies of fishes and animals accumulated there, and all this fiber and flesh was preserved from decay in a sterile, airless tomb. Slowly the mass, pressed down by the weight of clay above it, ripened into lignite, a brown coal, and finally into coal itself. Vast beds of lignite exist in the Dakotas and other western states, but because it is subject to spontaneous combustion, lignite has found only limited use as a fuel. Subbituminous and bituminous coal beds in Wyoming, Utah, and Colorado supply a major part of the nation's fuel.

Peat beds—spongy, damp mats of vegetable matter—long used as fuel in Scotland, Ireland, and elsewhere in Europe, are modern equivalents of the ancient environments in which lignite and coal formed. Scotch whisky derives its prized smoky flavor from grain dried over peat fires. Under average conditions, about a foot of peat will form in ten years. The waters of the bogs in which it is found inhibit decay so well that human bodies hun-

PHYLLITE: Lancaster Co., Pa. A pale gray, red, or green rock with a satiny sheen from the tiny flakes of mica and other minerals of which it is composed. This specimen contains crystals of the iron sulphide pyrite.

TUFA: Mumford, N.Y. Typical porous texture and light color of this sedimentary rock deposited by hot springs. Travertine is a more compact tufa, often banded, used for tabletops and ornaments.

CHERT: Joplin, Mo. A nodule of this earthy, minutely crystalline form of silica. Chert is light in color, hard, and fractures with a shell-like (conchoidal) surface, as in this specimen. Flint is a term often used for darker specimens. Nodules are irregular foreign bodies in rock masses, such as this formed by deposition of silica from solutions in limestone cavities.

NODULE: Oreg. A so-called thunder egg formed by deposition of agate and opal in a gas cavity in the lava that covers much of northwestern United States. The lava is reddish; the nodule may show a variety of colors and patterns.

dreds of years old have been found well preserved in them.

Coal itself had been for nearly two centuries the major fossil fuel until petroleum and natural gas crowded it into second place. Bituminous coal, also known as soft coal, is black, friable, and breaks to a bright surface. Anthracite, which is a product of metamorphism and mined almost entirely in the eastern United States, is almost pure carbon, with a hard, jetlike luster. Not unlike it in texture is cannel coal, which is also fine-grained and so rich in volatile oils that it can be ignited with a match.

Jet, nearly as hard as calcite and compact, became fashionable in Victorian times for use in jewelry. Brooches and necklaces were carved from this form of coal washed by ocean waves from the cliffs at Whitby in Yorkshire, England. Jet is also found in the mines near Las Vegas, N.M.

Balls of fossil vegetable matter indurated by clay and iron sulfides, and potato-shaped, reddish concretions called clay ironstones are often unearthed in the operation of strip coal mines. Giant shovels remove soil and rocks so that coal seams near the surface can be mined. The coal balls, when sliced into paper-thin sections, disclose under the microscope many details of the nature and structure of fossil vegetation. The concretions, broken open by a hammer blow, may contain carbonized impressions of leaves, stems, insects, worms, shrimp, or other evidences of ancient life. Collectors have hunted them in the streams and hills south of Chicago for more than a century, and they are also plentiful in eastern coal fields. The cement that holds together the clay ironstone is composed of an iron carbonate, siderite, and the iron-aluminum silicate, chamosite.

Minnesota's iron ore mines fed the blast furnaces of the United States with rich soft ore for scores of years. Vast beds were formed in the Hibbing area by bacteria that concentrated the metal in their bodies from ocean waters. Similar ores are mined near Birmingham, Alabama, and in Colorado. Now that the soft ore has become depleted, Minnesota relies on an iron-rich rock called taconite. Taconite is dark red, tough, and hard. It is crushed, and the iron particles are extracted by magnets, then mixed with clay into pellets for the furnaces. Some of the Minnesota mines yielded beautifully patterned iron rocks, known by such names as Mary Ellen jasper and binghamite.

Ishpeming, Michigan, is known to collectors for jaspilite, a

CONCRETION: Norman, Okla. A barite concretion known informally as a barite rose from its petallike shape. Concretions are made up of particles of mineral material cemented around a nucleus, usually by percolating waters.

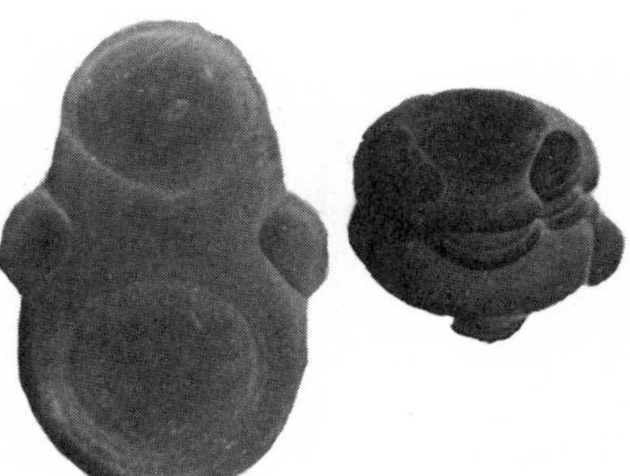

CONCRETIONS: Calif. Concretions of mudstone or shale, such as these two grotesque figures, are often mistaken for fossils.

CONCRETION: Rattlesnake Butte, S.Dak. Sand grains cemented by calcium carbonate solutions into the crystal shape of their mineral, calcite.

GEODE: Uruguay. Many fine crystals occur in geodes, such as these amethysts. Geodes are roughly spherical, usually found in limestone cavities with a shell of chalcedony and a lining of crystals.

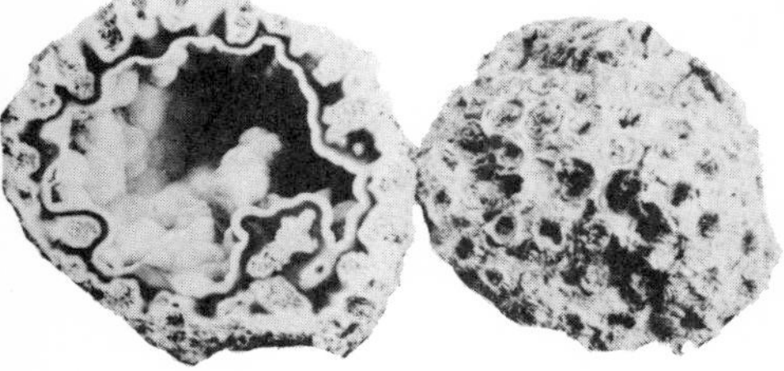

GEODE: Hillsborough Bay, Tampa, Fla. Geode lined with chalcedony and opal of a variety of colors, formed where coral colonies decayed and left cavities in the limy mud of the bay.

rock made up of alternate layers of blackish hematite and red jasper. Steel-gray hematite, an iron oxide (Fe_2O_3), is the principal ore of the mines around Ishpeming, which lies at the eastern end of an iron-mining region that extends west to Ironwood, Michigan, and south to Menominee and Crystal Falls, Wisconsin. The Clinton ores of the Appalachians are another rich source of iron-related rock, principally hematite compacted with clay.

Salt, Gypsum, and Phosphate Rock

The continental seas that rose and fell, advanced and retreated from the land left behind not only sedimentary rocks but also deposits of salt and gypsum, such as the ones that underlie Detroit, Michigan, and Syracuse, New York, as well as a number of other places in the United States. Encroaching saline waters filled basins in the land. These did not drain as the seas withdrew. Instead, the salty waters evaporated, leaving a deposit of gypsum and salt. Repetition of this ebb and flow laid down thick beds that were preserved by burial under clay and rock.

The substances in the seawater crystallized in the order of their solubility, the least soluble first, then the others. Gypsum, hydrous calcium sulfate, first to precipitate from the solution, is quite soft (1.5–2.0 on the Mohs scale), and in its crystalline form, selenite, has a slightly pearly luster and a marked cleavage like mica. Crystals can be bent with the fingers without breaking. One of gypsum's most attractive forms is fibrous satin spar. Anhydrite, which is calcium sulfate without the water molecule, is found interbedded with gypsum and salt. It is granular, pearly, slightly harder than gypsum, and, like gypsum, transparent in cleavages and colorless or pale blue.

A major deposit is worked near Grand Rapids, Michigan, close to the Detroit salt mines. Under proper conditions, gypsum can form dunes like sand, such as the White Sands National Monument in New Mexico, one of the continent's natural wonders. Gypsum is an important industrial material for the manufacture of plaster and, in its striped, gaily colored form of alabaster, for vases and carvings.

Salt is the second material to crystallize from the saline waters, followed by chlorides of potassium, magnesium, and other elements. Salt is so much a part of daily life that its chemical

ASBESTOS: Lowell, Vt. Silky strands of chrysotile asbestos, one form of serpentine. The solid mass itself is green.

SKARN: Willsboro, N.Y. Skarn is quite variable in texture and color because it is formed through recrystallization of rocks involved in contact metamorphism. This specimen shows crystals of garnet and white wollastonite resulting from the reaction of granite magma with limestone.

PEAT: Minn. Peat is bedded, brown, fibrous plant debris undergoing the first stage of natural decomposition that results in coal.

JET: Whitby, England. A piece of jet picked up on the shore and a brooch carved many years ago of this organic rock. Jet is hard, dense, and has a tougher consistency than other coals.

ANTHRACITE: Pa. A metamorphic rock that is nearly pure carbon, the most completely developed form of coal. It is glistening black and fairly hard.

name, sodium chloride (NaCl), is common property. Under a magnifying glass it can be seen that salt, even as it comes from a salt shaker, crystallizes as tiny cubes. It may be white, pink, or blue, and is known by its mineral name, halite. Not only is its crystal shape characteristic, but it is easy to identify by the tongue alone. As the major source of two important industrial elements, salt is mined like coal, whole rooms being excavated in the thick beds.

Although it has few charms for the collector, phosphate rock supplies vital agricultural and industrial chemicals. Found as brown or yellowish nodules in clay or sandstone, the rock is associated with the bones of marine animals in the extensive deposits worked in central Florida. Phosphate rocks are also mined in Tennessee and several western states where ocean basins once existed.

Meteorites—Messengers from the Sky

Paradoxical though it may be, perhaps the most eagerly sought rocks on earth have come from the sky. These rocks—meteorites—are believed to fall from a belt of celestial debris, the asteroids, located in the solar system between Mars and Jupiter. Millions of these visitors fall every day; most of them burn to dust from friction in their descent through the earth's atmosphere. Some die gloriously in a great burst of light and a fiery trail. Because water covers so much of the surface of the earth, many meteorites are lost; many others that fall on land weather away before they are discovered.

Despite all the hazards and perils, some meteorites reach the earth, and a few are found each year through chance and the search for them inspired by scientists eager to study the evidence meteorites bring of the nature of the solar system and of the universe.

Meteorites fall into three major classes: irons, stony irons, and stony meteorites. The irons are masses of a nickel-iron alloy. Irons are easy to identify; they are three times as heavy as other rocks, attract a magnet, may appear rusty, and show pits on the surface that look like thumbprints in dough. Stony irons resemble gray concrete in which a network of sharp bits of metal appears. Stony meteorites are compact masses of the concretelike rock with some silvery specks of metal. Stony meteorites are the

GYPSUM: North Holston, Va. Gypsum, hydrous calcium sulphate, is light in color, soft and usually layered, as in this specimen. It forms in beds, along with beds of salt, by evaporation of sea water.

METEORITE: Tonopah, Nev. The Quinn canyon nickel-iron meteorite, an excellent example of the effect of air friction that shaped the conelike nose as the mass fell to earth. (Field Museum of Natural History)

METEORITE: La Porte, Ind. Characteristic crystal figures of iron-nickel alloys known as Widmanstätten figures found in many metallic meteorites. (Field Museum of Natural History)

METEORITE: Long Island, Kan. Stony meteorite weighing 1,184 pounds, with some of the fragments from the fall. It, too, shows a well-developed nose cone. It is in the Field Museum of Natural History collection, Chicago.

most common but are also the most difficult to recognize and the ones most readily destroyed by weathering.

All meteorites are alike in a few respects. They are compact, not cindery; they have a brown or black crust when freshly fallen; and they are irregular in shape. The first test of a suspected meteorite is to grind off a corner and look for traces of metal inside. Many meteorites, especially the irons, have been discovered on farms where they had been turned up by a plow and often used as a doorstop.

Gold is where you find it; so it is with meteorites. Some environments are more favorable places to hunt than others where vegetation would conceal the celestial stranger. On deserts, weathering is less severe than elsewhere; hunters are few, and ground cover is sparse. Even better conditions were encountered by an expedition for meteorites to the Antarctic in 1977. The snowy ice caps were examined from a helicopter. Dark rocks were few, but eleven of them were meteorites. One of 900 pounds had broken into thirty-three pieces. All in all, the expedition made a major addition to the world's known 1,900 different falls.

As this and the preceding chapter have demonstrated, the familiarity with rocks that the collector needs in the field and at home in working with the collection cannot be mastered in a few easy lessons. It must come from some study, some experience, and the enthusiasm that makes learning a pleasure. Nature has lavishly endowed the American continent; a diversity of handsome rocks can be found from New England to California and from the Arctic Circle to Central America. The next chapter will describe preparations for a collecting trip, the equipment and clothing needed, and some of the techniques and precautions for safety and success in the field.

CROSS-EXAMINING YOUR ROCK

I. Is rock made up of crystals of roughly the same size and readily visible without magnification? If so, see A below. If not, see III below.
   A. Are crystals coarse and interlocked, not layered? If so, see 1 below. If not, see B below.

1. Mainly light-colored quartz and feldspar. If so, see a, b, or c below. If not, see 2 below.
   a. Grains about 1/5 inch (5 millimeters), **granite.** Varying in size to much larger, **pegmatite.**
   b. Grayer than granite, about a third dark minerals, **granodiorite.**
   c. Light color, minor quartz, **syenite.**
2. Mainly feldspar and dark iron-magnesium minerals. If so, see below.
   a. Dark gray, hornblende, augite, little quartz, **diorite.**
   b. Blackish, plagioclase feldspars and augite, may be layered, **gabbro.**
   c. Dark green to black, much olivine, **peridotite.**
   d. Dark feldspars and augite, mottled with white, medium texture, **diabase.**
3. Soft, light color, calcite crystals visible, **marble.**

B. Does the rock show pronounced layering or banding? If so, see below.
   1. Platy minerals, marked irregular layering, often much mica, **schist** (many types).
   2. Green to black mat of hornblende needles in parallel orientation, **amphibolite.**
   3. Alternating layers of light and dark segregated minerals, otherwise like granite, **gneiss.**

C. Igneous rock showing fine-textured groundmass with large crystals scattered through it, **porphyry** (described by rock type).

II. Is rock made up of firmly cemented particles, pebbles, or rock fragments? If so, see below.
   1. Rounded pebbles, **conglomerate.**
   2. Angular fragments, **breccia.**
   3. Light-colored grains, mostly quartz, **sandstone.**
   4. Mixture of quartz and feldspar grains and mica, **arkose, graywacke.**
   5. Unsorted volcanic fragments and pumice, **agglomerate.**
   6. Glassy minute volcanic fragments in volcanic ash, **tuff.**

III. Is rock composed of materials visible only under magnification? If so, see A or B below.

A. Is rock uniform in texture, microcrystalline, not layered? See below.
   1. Light-colored, quartz and feldspar, may be banded in color, **rhyolite.**
   2. Fused grains predominantly of quartz, **quartzite.**
   3. Green to gray, breaks readily into slabs, **phonolite.**
   4. Gray, pink, yellow, mostly feldspar, porphyritic, **trachyte.**
   5. Purple, brown, black, flow structure, **andesite.**
   6. Dense, dull black, crystal-filled gas cavities, **basalt.**
   7. Green to gray, fairly soft, greasy, **serpentine.**
   8. Green, cream, quite soft, **talc, soapstone.**

B. Is rock layered? If so, see below, if not, see IV.
   1. Soft, dull gray, reddish or black, splits easily, fossiliferous, **shale.**
   2. Hard, red, purple, gray, black, splits easily, **slate.**
   3. Hard, tough, shows traces of layering on edge, **hornfels.**
   4. Light gray, silky sheen on split surface, **phyllite.**
   5. Light color, fairly soft, usually stratified, fossiliferous, **limestone.**
   6. Light color, bluish cast, much like limestone, **dolomite.**
   7. Colorless, often transparent, with salt deposits, **gypsum.**
   8. Salty taste, colorless or tinted, often stratified, **salt.**
   9. Layering not evident, brown to black, soft, brittle, **peat, lignite, coal.**

IV. Is texture glassy, porous or nodular? If so, see below.
   1. Glassy, hard, black or red, may show white inclusions, **obsidian.**
   2. Light, porous, soft, **chalk.**
   3. Hard nodules, siliceous rock, conchoidal fracture, waxy luster, **flint, chert.**
   4. Frothy white, glassy, minute particles, **pumice.**
   5. Hard, usually brown or red, often iron-rich, **jasper.**

4. the rock hunter in the field

Nature and books belong
To the eyes that see them.
Emerson

The sports fisherman planning his vacation prepares for it by learning how the trout are biting in Ontario or the Rockies, where to buy a license, and how many fish he may catch, then gets his tackle and his gear in shape for the trip. A deer hunter likewise investigates the situation in the Carolinas, Wyoming, or Maine, for example, before he makes up his itinerary.

Rock hunters too, must give some attention to where to go for good hunting, favorable weather, and a happy outing. The great decision has then been made, and preparations for the trip can be started. A few hours of planning may make the difference between a glorious holiday and a disappointing one.

How much time is available for the trip? Is it to be a strenuous excursion with a few seasoned fellow collectors or a vacation outing for the family? The former presumably will have some precise predetermined destination—a quarry, a mine dump, or a tempting rock exposure. For a family vacation trip, try to discover what accessible collecting sites are located along the route, and approach them in the spirit of an outing.

Too tight a schedule can defeat even the most carefully planned trip. Collecting conditions in an unfamiliar area may not turn out to be what they seemed. Access to a quarry may be unexpectedly difficult because of poor roads or bad weather. The quarry may refuse to admit collectors or may be open only on weekends; it may object to admitting children. Experienced collectors try to have an alternative site in mind when they run into such situations.

Local conditions can be investigated in several ways. One is to call or write the geology department of a nearby college or museum, the Chamber of Commerce of the nearest town, or someone in a local mineral or fossil club. Names of club officials appear in the annual April issue of the *Lapidary Journal* (see "Sources of Information"). Most public libraries have collections of telephone books that list construction companies and other likely sources of information about mines and quarries. State geological surveys (see "Sources of Information") may reply to inquiries about producing quarries and mines. A local contact may even be able to arrange for a collecting permit.

Prepare by Reading

State and federal publications can be mined for suggestions about forgotten or little-known sites. Although these books and pamphlets soon go out of print, they will usually appear in university or large museum libraries, or they can be obtained through the interlibrary loan system. This enables a library to borrow books for its patrons from other libraries, even from the Library of Congress.

A literally textbook example illustrates the reward of study and preparation for a trip. Mrs. Win Robertson of Surrey, British Columbia, is reported to have borrowed a geology textbook. In intervals in her tasks as a housewife, she read that jade could be found where granite was in contact with serpentine, and she located such a contact on a geological map of the area near Smithers. She and her sixteen-year-old son and two helpers rented a helicopter and searched the rugged northwest of British Columbia. Working up a stream, they found jade boulders, and at the top of a waterfall, huge masses of jade and "an area that ran up the mountain about a mile and a quarter of a mile wide." Later, they took out 38 tons of jade by helicopter, for which they were paid $250,000, according to a Vancouver newspaper. And that appears to be only the start of Mrs. Robertson's adventure.

Scratch test for hardness. Quartz crystal (Mohs hardness 7) scratches glass (hardness 6).

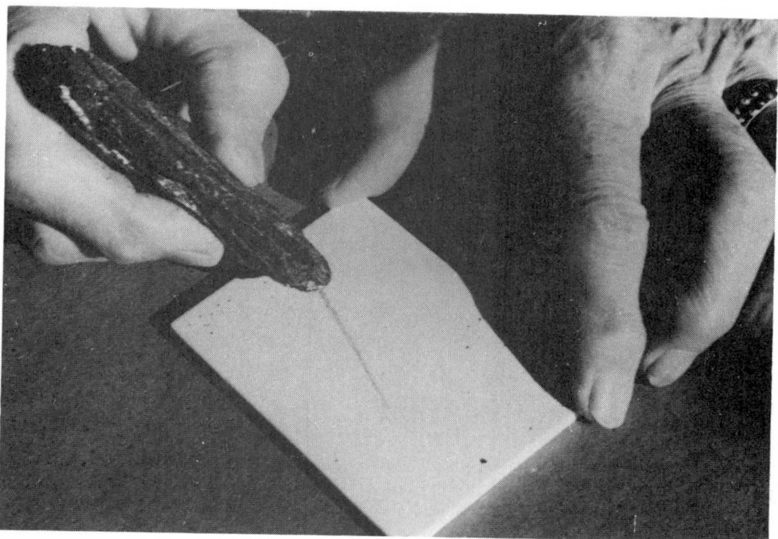

Streak test for color of specimen. Hematite leaves red streak on an unglazed porcelain streak plate.

The moral: "No one had ever gone into the area looking for jade," she said. "But I figured there was jade there because of the geology of the area. It had to be there somewhere; it was just a matter of finding it."

Weather must be one of the most serious considerations in planning the trip. The United States, Canada, and Mexico offer a choice of almost every climate, from the jungles of southern Mexico through the Sonoran deserts of northern Mexico and the American Southwest, through the plateau region and mountains of Utah, Colorado, and California, to their gentler counterparts in the eastern United States. Alaska and Hawaii extend the range with their contrasting climates, and Canada offers its own unique variations. Arizona is more comfortable in the winter than in the blazing sun of summer; Wyoming's snows fall in September and melt late in the spring. In summer, early morning offers the best temperatures for collecting. The afternoon can be devoted to looking over the trophies of the morning's hunt.

State tourist bureaus and geological surveys will supply information about sites and conditions, but only by personal effort can the collector become familiar with the appearance of what he or she will be seeking. Most museums display systematic specimens of rocks and have sets of representative rock types that the collector can consult and handle. Labels on the specimens will often give definite location information. Some of the locations may have been lost through urban expansion, or a once-prolific quarry may have become degraded into a refuse pit.

Clothing and Equipment

Clothing for an adventure outdoors should be comfortably loose, durable, and, above all, it should cover the entire body. Only in this way will the skin be protected from sunburn, insect bites, and scratches and bruises caused by abrasive contact with rocks. Jeans or other types of stout cotton slacks, thick socks and army-last shoes, and a shirt fill the bill admirably for both men and women. For proper collecting style, these should be supplemented with durable work gloves, a hat or cap that shades the eyes, and a windbreaker of some sort, such as a ski jacket. Shoes should be broken in by some weeks of wear, and most persons find two pairs of socks—thin next to the skin and thick next to the shoe—ensure foot comfort. Socks get wet from wading streams and walking in sudden showers; carry an extra pair. Sunglasses may be desirable, especially at high altitudes.

Deserts are warm during the day, abruptly chilly as soon as the sun sets. There, as well as generally in the outdoors, comfort comes from dressing in layers. A sweater can go over a shirt in the cool of the evening; a raincoat can double for warmth as well as protection from the rain when that is needed.

The collector's basic tool is the geologist's pick, which has a square hammer face on one end and a sharp pick on the other. With it, rocks can be broken out, strata can be pried apart, and specimens can be trimmed. For heavier work, a crack hammer—a short-handled sledge—will be useful. So will a flat-bladed chisel for splitting, and another with a four-sided point. Some locations will call for a full-sized sledge, a long-handled pick or mattock, a shovel with a pointed nose, and small and large crowbars. With them, overburden can be stripped away and massive ledges of stone can be broken apart. A rake is needed where the collecting will be done in talus or gravel. The collector's pockets should contain a pocketknife and a magnifying lens, and safety glasses or welder's goggles should be worn when attacking rock with a sledge. More than one collector has lost the sight of an eye or suffered serious loss of blood from an artery cut by a flying chip. A hard hat, goggles or safety glasses, and metal-tipped safety shoes are prescribed by federal regulations for anyone entering a quarry. Such protective equipment is useful anywhere that natural hazards may be encountered in the field.

Knapsacks for carrying specimens, gunnysacks or boxes, and wrapping paper for storing them in the car or shipping them should not be forgotten. Rocks worth bringing home should be numbered with a felt-tipped pen. The number can be written directly on the specimen or on a short strip of adhesive tape placed on it. The number will refer to a like-numbered entry in a notebook or on a file card recording the place where the rock was found, the stratum or deposit from which it came, any associated rocks, and the date. Specimens are more convenient to handle if they are wrapped, and they are also better protected from contact with others.

Most collecting trips presumably will not involve camping out. But there are a number of books on this aspect of the enjoy-

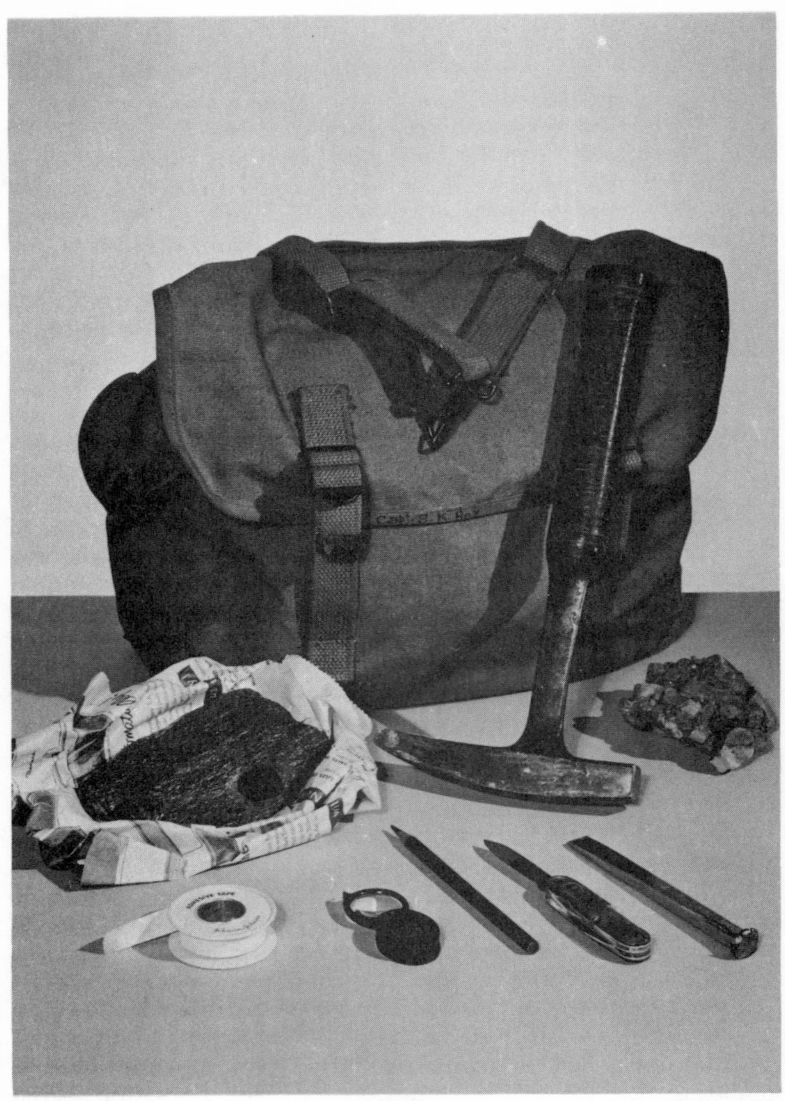

Items to take on a collecting trip: collecting bag, rock pick, tape to mark specimens, magnifying glass, pencil, knife and chisel, as well as wrapping materials. (Field Museum of Natural History)

ment of nature. Manufacturers have developed some tough new vehicles for invading nature's last remaining fastnesses. Information about them is freely available. For all except a few exceptional trips, the family car in A-1 shape, with a driver whose physical condition corresponds, will suffice. The spare tire should be tested and dependable; its companions should be a tow rope, bumper jack, extra fan, air-conditioner belts, and perhaps cans of fuel and drinking water if the itinerary leads off well-traveled roads.

Some advice about driving: observe speed limits; remember that night driving is far more dangerous than day driving; be especially alert on narrow, backcountry roads; keep the car well ventilated; stop occasionally for refreshments and to change drivers; don't drive when tired or sleepy; and don't drive too far in a day or overload the car. The one thing sure to spoil a vacation is an accident.

The rock collector enjoys at least one major advantage over those who hunt primarily for gem materials, fossils, and mineral specimens. Often the locations the latter collectors have to seek and exploit are difficult to find, small, and soon exhausted. But rock sources are usually large, virtually inexhaustible, dependable, and not far from major highways. Nor is there any reason why the rock collector cannot bring home agate, amethyst crystals, pyrite specimens, and fossil shells and corals, to name only a few, that may be encountered while mining the mother rock in which they formed.

The Importance of Maps

For many excursions, road maps such as are obtainable at filling stations will suffice, supplemented by the annually published highways atlases. But there are exceptional circumstances, such as the search for a forgotten old quarry or mine deep in thickets at the end of a rutted dirt road. Here exploring instincts come into play, a delightful game in itself, and more specialized maps with longer memories are needed.

The United States Geological Survey has created a series of large topographic maps on sheets 2 feet across and 2 1/2 feet long, which answer that need in minute detail. Each covers a relatively small area of a state on one of several scales, such as

1 inch to 62,000 inches, about 1 mile. The scale is given on the map, which is identified for ordering by the name of a town or prominent natural feature included in it.

Man-made features appear in black, major roads in red, water in blue, and forests are green. In addition, contours—the hills and valleys—are delineated by means of brown contour lines. These give a third dimension of height and depth to the flat map surface. Each contour line traces a single elevation of the surface, such as 500 feet above mean sea level, as that level appears in objects on the map. The contour line for a lake, for example, would follow its shoreline because water finds a constant level. Contour lines curve up a valley, showing the rising level that would cause a stream to flow down it. The lines are spaced a uniform distance apart, such as 20 feet. Where the surface rises rapidly, as on a hill, they will be close together; on a plain they are far apart. Familiarity with such maps makes it easy to visualize the mapped area, as well as to note obstacles and trace roads or paths that lead to a mine or quarry marked on the map.

More specialized are the U.S.G.S. geologic maps based on topographic maps but with additional information overprinted in color and texture. These indicate the nature and structure of the surface rocks of the area delineated on the map. Easily identified, distinctive rock units are called formations and are given names, such as the St. Peter sandstone. Formations are colored on the map to correspond with symbols placed on the right-hand margin of the sheet. On the lower margin is a cross section of how the area of the map would appear if it were sliced vertically like a layer cake. Such detailed data are obviously of great value to the rock collector because they pinpoint exposures of the material sought. Unfortunately, geological maps are not yet available for all parts of the United States.

Further information about rock formations is given on geologic maps by inconspicuous lines that mark their dip and strike. Strike is the compass direction that a more or less vertical stratum or dike makes along its top edge. It may strike north, for example, or a certain number of degrees off one of the major directions. Dip is the vertical angle in degrees that the strike plane of the rock makes with a horizontal ground surface. Think of a staircase running up the wall of a room or hall. Measurement across a step with a compass would give its strike. The angle that the staircase makes with the floor would be its dip. Or balance a book on its long edge on a table. The compass direction across its back is its strike; then tilt the book and measure the angle in degrees it makes with the table to get its dip. The symbol on geologic maps is ⟋ ; the longer line is the strike, and the shorter is the dip; they are both related to the orientation of the map, which is to the north. The figure gives the angle of dip.

Maps of areas east of the Mississippi River are obtainable from the Distribution Branch, Geological Survey, 1200 South Eads Street, Arlington, Virginia 22202. Those for areas west of the Mississippi River are for sale at the Distribution Center, Geological Survey, Federal Center, Denver, Colorado 80225. Either office will supply the pamphlet *Topographic Maps,* a list of available maps, index sheets for each state's maps, and a list of dealers in various cities who stock some maps.

A series of regional maps issued by the American Association of Petroleum Geologists, P.O. Box 975, Tulsa, Oklahoma 74101, is an excellent source of information about formations, caves, national parks, and other matters of geological interest.

Maps of national forests are for sale from the Forest Service, U.S. Department of Agriculture, Washington, D.C. 20250. The following Bureau of Land Management offices supply maps and information about public lands under their control:

Alaska—555 Cordova Street, Anchorage 99501
Arizona—2400 Valley Bank Center, Phoenix 85073
California—Federal Building, Sacramento 95825
Colorado—Colorado State Bank Building, Denver 80202
Idaho—Federal Building, Boise 83724
Montana, North and South Dakota—Granite Tower Building, 222 North 32d Street, Billings, Montana 59101
Nevada—Federal Building, Reno 89502
New Mexico and Oklahoma—Federal Building, Santa Fe, New Mexico 87501
Oregon and Washington—729 Northeast Oregon Street, Portland, Oregon 97208
Utah—University Club Building, 136 East South Temple Street, Salt Lake City 84111
Wyoming, Kansas, Nebraska—Federal Building, Cheyenne, Wyoming 82001

States east of the Mississippi River—7981 Eastern Avenue, Silver Spring, Maryland 20910

Canadian maps are supplied by the Geological Survey of Canada, Ottawa, Ontario, and the geological surveys of the various provinces. Both the U.S. Geological Survey and that of Canada publish catalogs of their professional papers and bulletins. These can usually be seen in public or university libraries. Price lists of geological publications are obtainable from the Superintendent of Documents, Government Printing Office, Washington, D.C. 20402.

State Geological Survey offices are listed in the the section "Sources of Information," along with major museums and universities. They also issue reports, monographs, and maps, often of primary usefulness to the collector because they are specialized and detailed. Even publications on gem and mineral locations may contain some information that will lead the collector to interesting rock formations, such as pegmatites and geode sources.

The ABCs of Safety

A collecting trip should be taken in the spirit of an adventure, but it will be a fun adventure only if common sense is not left behind. Prudence is always a virtue when facing unaccustomed circumstances and the possible hazards they may present. An ABC of safety on the collecting trip and in the field includes:

1. Leave word where you are going and when you will be back. If you have a mishap or get lost, you still have the comfort of knowing that help will come. Stay with your vehicle; it is easier to find than you are, and it is shelter. Woodsmen say that if you are lost in forested country, find a stream and follow it down. Usually there will be an inhabited place along the way.
2. At the collecting site, start the day by looking the site over for obvious hazards, such as shattered overhanging rock, excavations, crumbling pathways, or loose, sliding rock.
3. Don't collect above or below anyone. A dislodged rock

can do serious mischief. Be careful when breaking rock; a flying chip can cut an artery or blind an eye.

4. Don't make too long a day of the collecting excursion. Accidents happen at the end of a fatiguing day. Collect only as much as you can carry comfortably. Walk slowly, look around occasionally, take a few deep breaths, and enjoy the landscape. To avoid falls, learn to feel for a secure footing and walk so that your body is never off balance.
5. Stay out of old mines unless you have an experienced guide with you. Deadly gases, touchy explosives, and hidden shafts make them unsafe. Mines are baffling places to collect in, anyway, unless you are familiar with the conditions under which you have to work. If you find what looks like a long .22 cartridge around a mine, don't touch it. It is a blasting cap, far more dangerous than a rattlesnake, and just as touchy.
6. Every year, several collectors dig their own graves when the walls of an excavation they are making fall in on them. Pits in sandy soil are particularly treacherous.
7. Sunburn is more likely to make the trip unpleasant than some more spectacular catastrophe. Keep the skin covered, especially at high altitudes. Insect repellent will discourage most flying pests; sulfur pills are recommended to repel chiggers, and the collecting kit should include bandages and ointment for cuts and abraded skin. Ticks lurk in brushy areas, where they can hop aboard the body of a passerby. Inspection each evening for tick bites is recommended in infested country. The insect crawls beneath the skin to feed and can be induced to back out by gentle squeezing or the touch of a warm object. The bite area may become infected if the tick is crushed or broken in the skin.
8. Scorpions may be encountered in some desert areas, such as the American Southwest. They are small, straw-colored, spiderlike creatures with a painful, even dangerous sting. Campers are advised against sleeping on the ground lest a scorpion, which enjoys warmth, too, crawl into the sleeping bag. Bedrolls, shoes, and clothing should be shaken out before use, and gloves

should be worn whenever the collector is turning over rock slabs by hand or moving brush or wood piles. Wild animals may be delightful to watch, but playing or handling them, alive or dead, has its risks. They may bite or be diseased.

9. The black widow spider is brown or black, and the female, the poisonous one, has a red or yellow hourglass marking on the underside. It lurks in long grass, brush piles, under stones, in barns, and especially in outhouses. The bite is painful, dangerous to children. Keep the victim of a bite quiet and get a doctor. Wear gloves when working where spiders may lurk.

10. The best advice about snakebite is to avoid being bitten. Snakes are not aggressive; they fight back only if cornered. So walk slowly and noisily, and don't put foot or hand into any place where you cannot see clearly, such as under fallen logs or on ledges where a snake may be sunning itself. Loose slacks and stout shoes that protect the ankles and loose-legged slacks will break the force of a snake's attack.

    Rattlesnakes are the most common poisonous species. As a safeguard, some physicians prescribe carrying an antivenin kit in rattlesnake-infested country. Others say that the best treatment is to keep the victim quiet and get him or her to a doctor as quickly as possible. In general, if a bitten area swells or discolors rapidly, the poison is acting locally and probably is not dangerous. If the bite does not swell, the poison may be circulating and could reach vital organs. An astonishingly small number of persons are fatally bitten by snakes each year; far more die of allergic reactions to bee or hornet stings.

11. Some rocks contain or are coated with unpalatable substances; it is advisable to wash hands after handling them. Drink only water that is known to be unpolluted; a sparkling mountain stream may not be as pure as it appears. Sandwich fillings, salads, cream cakes, and other picnic-type foods left unrefrigerated in the warm trunk of a car may harbor toxins that can cause serious illness.

Places to Collect

If the collector has not previously made a scouting trip to the site, it is well to begin the day by looking it over to note any hazards and then systematically plan how to work and where to work. One rock formation may promise a geode bed in porous limestone, or rose quartz in a pegmatite dike may lie at the end of a trail of mica and quartz chips. Often better specimens can be won from pieces fallen at the base of a cliff than would reward an arduous attack on those in place. Collect freely, discard thoughtfully, selecting only the best specimens, and take only as much as you need and can carry comfortably. Greedy collecting is unfair to other collectors and burdens you with material that will have lost its charm when you get home. A house or garage will hold only so much.

In breaking rock, several collectors can often work together with better success than if each worked alone. Each may know some trick that makes the job easier. Rock parts most readily along a stratum, as in limestone, or a micaceous layer in schist. In attacking a rocky wall, search for a projecting piece, strike it repeatedly on one side, then the other, to loosen it along a layer, then break it out. Before leaving the site, each person should make sure that no tools or garments have been left behind. It is surprisingly easy to forget a jacket that has been casually laid aside in the heat of the day.

Collecting should not be done from the surface of an outcrop, but from the fresh rock below the weathered crust. If weathering, however, has revealed some features of the texture not obvious on the fresh surface, leave some weathered surface on the specimen for study.

This rocky earth abounds in places to collect. Anywhere that nature or man has exposed its firm foundation is worth at least a casual visit. Some of the most memorable discoveries in the eastern United States were made during excavation of the underlying traprock for foundations for New York's skyscrapers. In Richmond, Virginia, a laborer digging a garage foundation uncovered a wealth of crystals of the blue iron phosphate vivianite. Trenching for a pipeline, sewer, or tunnel always affords an opportunity. Dredging in Hillsborough Bay, off Tampa, Florida,

Acid test to differentiate between limestone and dolomite. Step 1: Effervescence when hydrochloric acid is dropped on limestone. (University of Missouri)

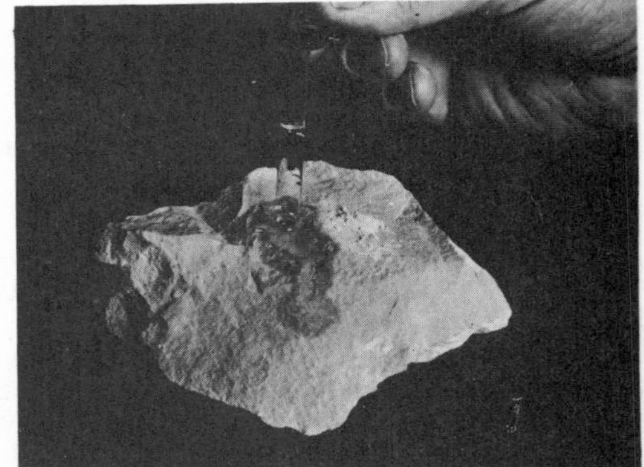

Step 2: Dolomite does not react when same acid is applied. (University of Missouri)

Step 3: But powdered dolomite (upper right) does respond, especially to warm acid. (University of Missouri)

bared magnificent fossil coral, and strip mining for phosphates near Bartow, Florida, has exposed a rich source of fossil mammal bones. Construction of a large dam displaces millions of tons of rock; so does roadbuilding or an excavation such as was required to construct underground reservoirs for Chicago's floodwaters.

Quarries, Road Cuts, and Beaches

Quarries, both active and abandoned, can be bonanzas for the collector. Slate quarries in the Appalachians produce huge piles of discarded material, and so do granite and marble quarries in Vermont, Alabama, Colorado, and Tennessee. Old quarries often become dumps for a nearby town's refuse. As the debris settles and becomes overgrown, it may provide a platform from which long-inaccessible strata in the quarry can be reached.

Glaciers dragged and then abandoned rocks throughout much of the northern United States. In clearing their fields, farmers usually pile glacial rocks and boulders in a corner or build dry walls of them. If permission to look over the rock piles is obtained, a sample of rocks of half a continent may lie before you.

Road cuts through a hill can be productive if the collector contrives to stop off the pavement or on a side road. Many freeways are paralleled by frontage roads that make this possible. Maintenance crews frown on collectors who allow rocks and debris from their digging to litter the roadway. Several states publish roadside geology guides designed for the motorist, and some state highway departments regularly make public their construction programs.

Modern mining methods have reduced the amount of waste rock brought to the dump from shaft mines, and open pit mines crush all the material trucked to the mill. Old dumps, however, exist by the thousands, some near active mines.

Coal mines usually have little to offer the collector except coal balls and concretions, which have been previously described. Washing plants in Indiana, Illinois, Kentucky, and Kansas discard coal balls by the thousands because the sulfur and clay content reduces their value as fuel.

Some coal, salt, and gypsum mines arrange tours for visitors. *Mining and Mineral Operations in the United States,* a publication of the U.S. Bureau of Mines, lists mines that receive visitors, and gives other useful information. It can be ordered from the Superintendent of Documents, Government Printing Office, Washington, D.C. 20402.

Beaches are great places to swim, sunbathe, fish, skip flat stones across the water, and collect. Several years ago, a Chicago woman won a blue ribbon at a collectors' convention for her polished granite pebbles picked up on Lake Michigan beaches. They cost her nothing except the labor of polishing them; the collections she was competing with represented investments of thousands of dollars. Some beachcombers have made a hobby of collecting the fossil corals known as Petoskey stones. In Oregon and Washington, agates, petrified wood fragments, and other treasured stones wash down onto the beaches from the hills and are soon picked up by rockhounds. Handsome masses of conglomerate are tossed up on shore by Lake Superior, along with collectible driftwood.

Gravel pits work the sand and pebbles accumulated by an ancient river or lake beach. Dozens of open pits and dredges exploit such industrially valuable material along the Mississippi River. They are marked on topographic maps and listed in telephone directories under "Sand and Gravel." Equally attractive to the rock collector are the vast heaps of cobbles and pebbles from gold dredges and hydraulic mining operations in California and Alaska. Just outside the hamlet of Dutch Flat, California, tower such piles left by the fortune hunters of a century ago.

Restrictions on Collecting

Wide and open as the rock hunter's world may appear to be with all these choices, it should never be forgotten that there is no unlimited right to collect, even on public lands. Vandalism and abuse of the privilege of access to public land have brought about restrictions and even prohibition of collecting there. Most public land is in Alaska, Arizona, California, Colorado, Idaho, Montana, Nevada, New Mexico, Oregon, Utah, and Washington, a total of one-fifth of the land area of the United States. But collecting is forbidden in national parks, national monuments, areas such as dams under the control of the Army Corps of Engineers, and occasionally in national forests when there is a fire risk or other hazard. Collecting on Indian reservations can be done only with the permission of tribal authorities.

The Bureau of Land Management limits entry to areas where vehicles cause environmental damage or where prehistoric rock carvings must be protected from vandals. Subchapter C of Circular 2147 of the Bureau sets out rules for mineral material disposals, including collecting on public lands. Collectors should also remember that mining claims must be respected as private property.

Some land in the eastern United States is public domain, but most is privately owned. Entry without the owner's permission to camp, collect, or even cross is trespassing. Land need not be fenced or otherwise identified as being privately owned. A trespassing collector may be faced by an angry owner armed with a loaded shotgun, or even worse. Furthermore, such conduct by rock hunters gives the whole hobby a bad image and makes owners unwilling to cooperate.

One problem lies in the fact that by giving permission for entry, the owner becomes responsible for an injury or other mishap suffered by the collector through hazards the owner has permitted to exist on the property. This is an acute problem for a quarry and mine owner, whose insurance company may refuse to accept such a risk. Some quarry owners will refuse permission but allow the collector to enter, and so the collector is then a trespasser. Some states, such as Texas, have passed owner-release laws that relieve an owner of responsibility for a guest. This has been done primarily for the sake of sportsmen but would seem to apply to collectors, too. Some owners ask that the collector sign a waiver of responsibility and set some terms, such as refusal to admit children. If the owner charges a fee for access to the property, he or she becomes responsible for the safety of guests. Many rewarding localities for agates and geodes are now operated on a fee basis.

A typical waiver of responsibility is that required by the owners of the Pugh quarry, at Custar, Ohio. The collector signing it agrees to hold harmless and release the company and its employees of any claims for damages resulting from injury to the collector or any loss in the quarry. Besides the signed release, the quarry regulations require that a minor must be accompanied by an adult, and put machinery, buildings, and some parts of the quarry off limits.

Most states restrict or prohibit collecting in state parks and other areas set aside for special purposes. A survey of state regulations that would affect the rock collector discloses that only a few, in particular California, Nevada, Oregon, Utah, and Wyoming, are concerned enough to have special collecting regulations.

A federal rule applies to collecting of petrified wood on public lands. The individual may take 25 pounds a day, plus one piece, and no more than 250 pounds a year. Explosives and power equipment may not be used, and the material taken must be for personal use, not for sale.

A Code of Ethics for the Collector

To summarize all this, a code of ethics would include:

1. Be careful to get permission to enter private property, even an open range. Reach an agreement with the property owner about where you may go, what you may do, and how long you plan to stay, and agree to any conditions the owner makes, such as requiring a waiver.
2. Understand the regulations for use of public land and heed them. Disregard of regulations results in restrictions on all hobbyists.
3. Be sure to extinguish any fire, a campfire, a cigarette, and be especially careful to avoid starting a grass fire.
4. If you are camping or picnicking, clean up before you leave. Bury garbage and metal cans or take them away with you. Leave the landscape as you found it, and leave behind a good name for rockhounds.
5. Don't foul creeks or wells.
6. Stay away from farm animals and cattle. They may take alarm and injure themselves. Fill in any hole you dig; a range steer or horse could break a leg in it.
7. Gates should be left as you found them, open or closed.
8. Don't drive across fields of growing crops or grasslands. Stay on the roads in farm country.
9. When collecting on farms, in quarries, or elsewhere, stay away from machinery. Nothing infuriates an owner more than to find his equipment has been damaged. Also, stay away from workers; they are being paid to

produce, not to assist you. Never pull a loose wire in a rock quarry. You may set off a blast and lose your life or a limb.

10. For your own protection, report any hazards or vandalism you discover.
11. Carry and use firearms and explosives only if you have permission, know how to use them, and have a reason to do so.
12. Collect only for your own use. Collecting to sell is turning your hobby into a business and is an imposition on the property owners who allow you to take away their material.

The cheapest way to get rocks home is to put them in burlap sacks and send them by rail as freight. This will involve picking up the sacks at the freight depot, but it may be less troublesome in the long run than trying to drive home in an overloaded car.

Most clubs organized in the United States and Canada to bring together persons interested in the earth sciences have paid more attention to lapidary work, silvercraft, and mineral and fossil collecting than to rocks and physical geology. Just as these interests have organized themselves over the years, so a rock-swap organization might become the nucleus of a national group for rock collectors. Advertisements and articles in hobby magazines might call attention to this underemphasized aspect of the earth sciences. Such a movement might also enlist the help of professional geologists, whose activities are more closely akin to it than to the craft groups.

The spirit and values of the hobby and its associations are summed up in a bit of rhyming culled from a mineral club magazine years ago:

Some people search for diamonds;
Some people search for gold;
Some people only pick up rocks,
At least that's what we're told.

The diamonds make you famous;
The gold you have to spend;
The rocks just bring you pleasure
And a host of happy friends.

5. our many-splendored continent

The hills are shadows and they flow
From form to form, and nothing stands.
Tennyson

Geologists are explorers at heart, explorers who are always asking questions and seeking answers in the rocks. As they gain new insights, they begin to see a certain logic and order in nature, a rhythm that raises mountains and wears them down, a balance between creation and destruction. Rocks are not scattered at random, as would sometimes appear; a cycle of change dictates when and where they will appear.

Nature works slowly, eon after eon, piling grain on grain. As his friend and pupil John Playfair remarked to the geologist James Hutton while they stood looking at the ancient rocks at Siccar Point, Scotland, "The mind seems to grow giddy by looking so far into the abyss of time." No life or generation survives long enough to perceive even minor change; nevertheless change goes on relentlessly in the mountains, valleys, and on the coastlines. So geologists must literally dig the history of our continent and the forces that have shaped it from the rocks themselves.

No part of the primeval surface of the earth is known to exist. African sedimentary rocks and metamorphic gneiss from Minnesota and Greenland have been dated as more than 3 billion years old, and both kinds of rocks presuppose the existence of older rocks from which they were formed. The Appalachians are comparatively young at 250 million years, the Grand Canyon a mere infant at 2 million years. In a geological yesterday, 8,000 years ago, our continent lost its glacial overcoat.

With such a genealogy, the earth's past and the basic forces of physical geology that have shaped that past can be understood only by patient observation and brilliant generalizations based on the painfully gathered facts. Louis Agassiz's glacial theory, which did so much to explain the shaping of the continents, is an example. Such theories go far beyond academic exercises; they define the conditions under which life must be lived as well as providing an enlightening introduction to the magnificent North American landscape. For the rock collector, knowledge of the geological past dignifies and enriches the meaning of the hobby.

North America's scenery is probably more spectacular and varied today than at any previous period in the history of the continent. Rugged mountain chains bracket fertile plains, great rivers, and lakes; climate runs from arctic snows to rain forests to forbidding deserts. All of these phenomena have meaning for the satisfaction of human needs, material and aesthetic, and what is more vital, for their bearing on a fundamental question: whether we are to be the servants, the partners, or the masters of nature.

The Canadian Shield

From an artificial satellite, North America would look like an inverted saucer or, more elegantly, a shield, with a rim of mountains. The shield, nearly 2 million square miles in area, rises in the center to a gentle boss, or dome, which slopes down as far as Greenland and Labrador, west over much of Manitoba and Saskatchewan, east over Ontario and Quebec, down into the Adirondacks in New York, and across Lake Superior into Wisconsin, Minnesota, and Michigan. This area, usually called the Canadian Shield, forms the strong, stable platform of the continent, buttressed by mountains against the sea.

Glaciers have stripped much of the center of the shield down to bare rock, exposing gold, iron, nickel, and copper ores. Major iron deposits exist near Hudson Bay; the mines of the Ironwood and Marquette areas of Wisconsin and Michigan and the Mesabi Range in Minnesota have supplied American needs

Chalk formations in Smoky Hill River valley between Oakley and Scott City, Kans. They are known as Monument Rocks or Kansas Pyramids. (Kansas Dept. of Economic Development)

for nearly a century. From the Keweenaw peninsula and Ontonagon in Michigan came the copper that made possible the age of electricity. Sudbury, Ontario, of course, is the major source of the world's nickel.

The Canadian Shield with its ancient rocks and its treasures has particular interest for the rock collector, especially in the Grenville province, which is 200 to 300 miles long and lies just north of the St. Lawrence River, except where it dips into the Adirondacks, which are mountains carved from a batholith. The Grenville province is rich in nepheline syenite and marble, and holds the continent's principal deposit of anorthosite, which is nearly 90 percent feldspar, particularly labradorite. A good place to collect it is in the east central part of the Adirondacks close to Mount Marcy, highest peak in the range. All of these rocks were formed by metamorphosis of ancient sediments deposited in a broad valley.

The folded granites and gneisses of the shield, laced with basaltic lavas and coarse graywacke, speak from the past of ancient mountains faulted, eroded, and contorted by igneous intrusions. The rocky slopes exposed south of Hudson Bay and northeast and northwest of Lake Superior preserve rocks estimated to be as much as 2.5 billion years old.

After showing its bare face in Canada, the shield goes underground as the foundation for the heartland of the United States. It also undergirds the western Canadian provinces drained by the Mackenzie and Nelson rivers.

Over much of the central United States, sedimentary strata formed while the region was covered by a series of sea invasions. They lie on top of the ancient rocks of the shield. Later, glaciers grinding down from Canada blanketed the strata with rock fragments and soil. The basement rocks extend deep into the heart of Texas, underlie the Rocky Mountains and the Colorado Plateau, and form a firm foundation for Ohio and much of New York and Pennsylvania.

Sea and land fought over millions of years for possession of the central plains, as well as many other parts of the continent. At no time were the rocks far below the waves, perhaps at most a few hundred feet. At each encroachment, the seas sorted out the sand and deposited it on beaches, spread the mud farther out, and dropped limy sediments in deeper water. These became

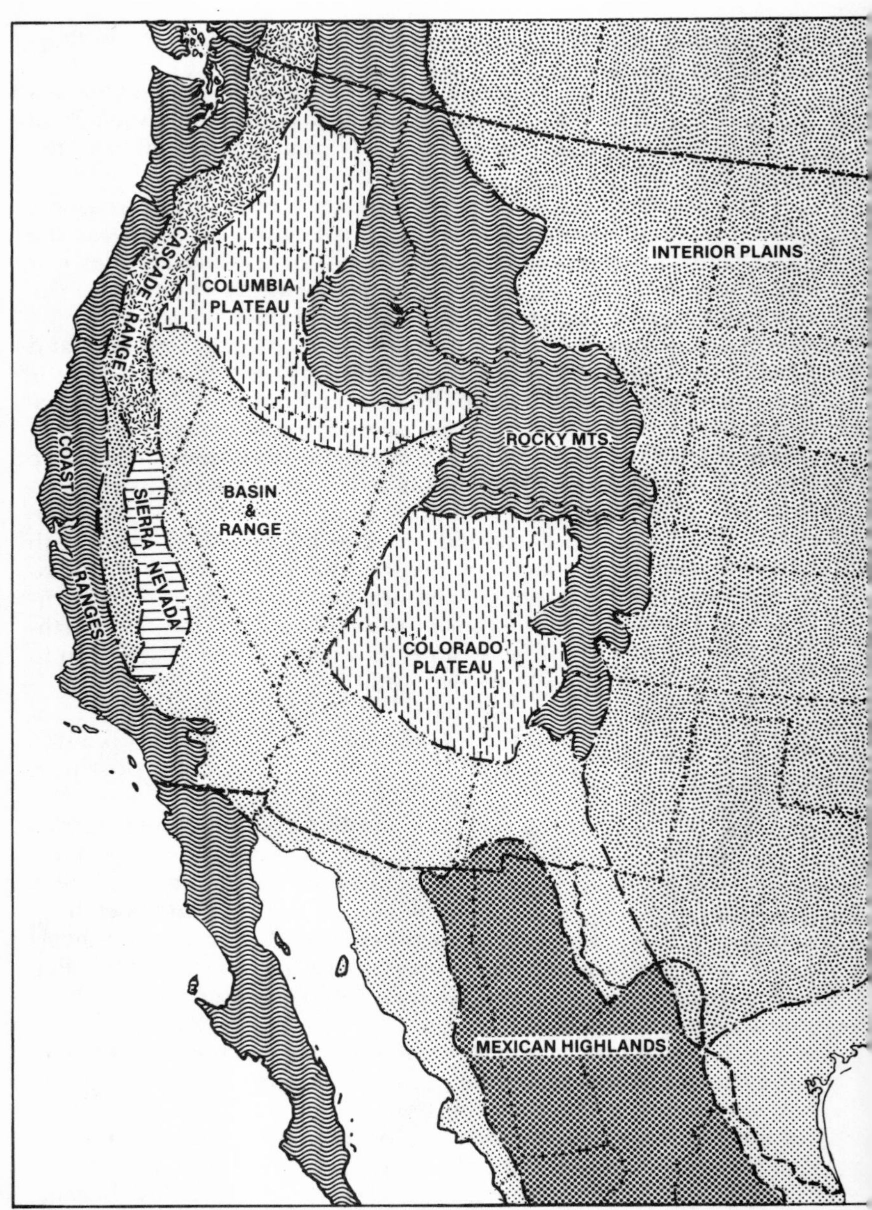

Geological divisions of the United States.

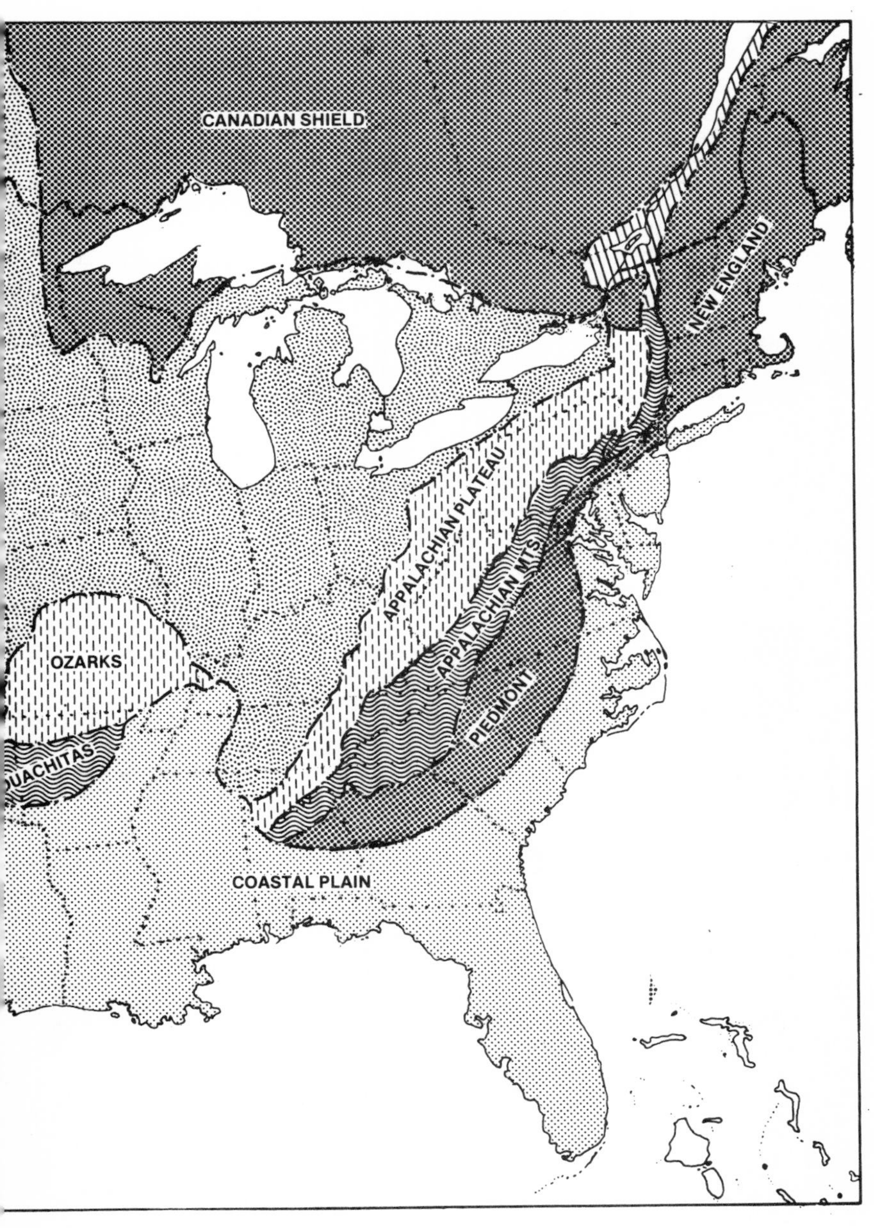
CANADIAN SHIELD
NEW ENGLAND
APPALACHIAN PLATEAU
APPALACHIAN MTS.
APPALACHIAN
PIEDMONT
OZARKS
OUACHITAS
COASTAL PLAIN

sandstone, shale, and limestone. If the warfare of sea and land were ever again to be renewed, depression of the continent only about 500 feet would make Cincinnati a seaport and leave a few skyscrapers as island monuments to drowned coastal cities. Some grasp of the wide extent of a single sea's dominion is gained from a limestone deposit that can be traced from Alabama to Quebec and that is extensively quarried in Illinois, Indiana, Wisconsin, and Michigan.

The central plains or, as they are often called, the stable interior, have more variety of landscape than these quiet names might suggest. The Cincinnati arch, and its related Findlay arch, rise from north-central Ohio down beyond Kentucky. Nashville, Tennessee, lies in a basin surrounded by cliffs that were once the sides of a now-eroded dome. Where Ohio arches, weathering has exposed the oldest strata at the top, with the successively younger strata fringing them. Farther south, the Ozark dome has been eroded clear down to the ancient crystalline basement.

Much of Michigan rests in an extensive basin where trapped seawater deposited gypsum and salt. Lakes Michigan and Huron frame the basin. They and the other Great Lakes dwell in former river valleys deepened by glaciers and depressed by the burden of mile-thick ice. Another basin cradles much of Illinois south to the Ohio River and the foothills of the Ozarks. From the sandstones and shales deposited in the basin, Illinois has drawn a wealth of oil and coal.

Work of the Glaciers

What the seas had begun, ice completed in shaping the center of the continent. From the Hudson Bay region came four massive glacial invasions in the last million years. The marks of the last one are still fresh on the landscape.

A glacier forms where more snow falls than melts away. This can happen through a moderate decline of five or six degrees in the average yearly temperatures and even from a change in the direction of the prevailing wind. The weight of the accumulating snow turns the mass into ice. When the ice becomes thick enough, it begins to flow. Glaciers existing today in mountainous regions demonstrate this movement as well as their

Limestone strata, Kentland, Ind. Warped and upended by powerful earth forces, presumably the impact of a large meteorite.

power as they carve U-shaped, steep-walled channels, called cirques, in the sides of the peaks.

The continental glaciers, however, a mile thick and armed with boulders as their teeth, rode roughshod over all obstacles. The Ohio and Missouri rivers drained the melting ice. Their channels today mark the limits of the advances of the ice into the Midwest. Eastward, the glaciers invaded New York, Pennsylvania, all of New England, and part of the east coast. Westward, they reached from Great Falls, Montana, along a strip south of the Canadian border clear to the Pacific.

The ice stripped central and eastern Canada to bedrock, scooping beds for countless lakes in what is now a popular resort country. Minnesota's Mille Lacs (thousand lakes) are a domestic example.

The glaciers picked up rocks and soil as they advanced, and dropped their spoils as they began to retreat. Over much of the Midwest, this material, called till, is spread evenly as much as 100 feet thick. In addition, hilly lateral moraines formed along the sides of the glacial tongues, and terminal moraines where they halted. Moraines consist of unsorted rock fragments and soil.

Besides moraines, the glaciers left such unique souvenirs as drumlins, which are long, oval hills where the ice, overriding an obstacle, shaped the till around it. Bunker Hill is perhaps the most historic example. There are several other drumlins near Boston. A kame is a hillock formed of sand and gravel deposited where a block of glacial ice melted, dropping its spoil; and a kettle is a depression where a block of buried ice melted. Occasionally a stream of meltwater running within the ice piled up a long, snakelike ridge of sand and gravel, sorting it well in the process. Such a deposit, called an esker, often becomes a profitable source of building material. A sand plain—another glacial creation—marks the site of a meltwater pond.

These formations, where they have not been leveled by man or natural erosion, are fairly common throughout the central region and in the East. As has been mentioned, one area where they can be seen in all their glory and variety has been set aside by Wisconsin northwest of Milwaukee.

Besides what they did to the land, the glaciers upset its whole system of drainage. Meltwater escaped at various times through the Wabash River in Indiana, the Illinois River, and later

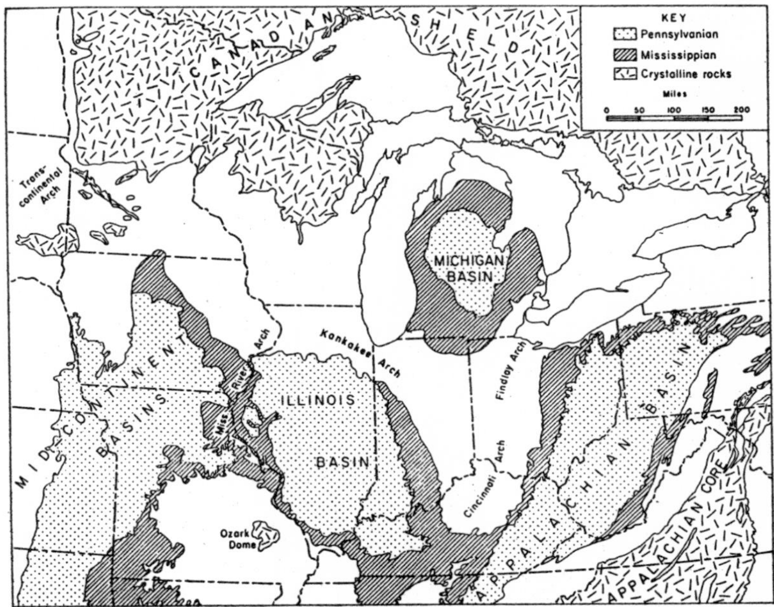

The Mississippi Valley and adjacent areas: Principal structural features and distribution of Mississippian and Pennsylvanian sediments.

eastward. In the process it laid the pattern for Niagara Falls. Most extensive of these creations, however, was Lake Agassiz, 800 miles long, larger in extent than all the present-day Great Lakes. Its former basin is now fertile farmland in North Dakota, Minnesota, and Manitoba.

As the glacial till dried, winds picked up the dust and piled it into deep beds. This soil of minute rock fragments, tightly interlocked, has the strange property of standing up to wind and rain like solid rock. It is called loess from the German word for light (pronounced officially *lów-ess* or, more properly, *lerse*). Cliffs of it can be seen at Vicksburg, Mississippi, and Council Bluffs, Iowa.

One small part of the central plains escaped leveling by the icy plow. This driftless area in southwestern Wisconsin and lapping over into nearby Iowa, Illinois, and Minnesota gives some idea, with its limestone cliffs and rugged valleys, what the Midwest once looked like. Lead and zinc have long been mined here;

galena gave its name to the principal town; and similar deposits are still being exploited in unglaciated Missouri farther south.

The Great Plains

From the central plains it's all uphill to the Rocky Mountains. Beyond the Iowa cornlands, from about the 100th meridian in Kansas and Nebraska, the Great Plains slope upward until they are a mile high at Denver. To the south they reach to the Pecos River and the Rio Grande, and to the north through Canada close to the Arctic.

This gigantic wedge of sediments is built largely of clay, sand, and gravel eroded from the Rocky Mountains region. Rugged and often arid, the Great Plains include the South Dakota Badlands, now a national monument. The Badlands demonstrate dramatically the processes that laid down these broad sheets of shale, clay, and volcanic ash, and how even in a land of little rain downpours can sculpture the barren rock into turreted ridges, spires, and sharply cut valleys. These marvels of erosion call to mind Providence Canyons, near Lumpkin, Georgia, where a small gully grew into acres of canyonland. Part of Nebraska is occupied by the dunes and dry basins of the Sand Hills region. Farther south, the Great Plains include the lava dikes and mesas around Raton, New Mexico, and Trinidad, Colorado, and exposed crystalline rocks near Burnet, Texas.

A map of Kansas tinted to distinguish the geological age of the formations where the state is crossed by Interstate 70 illustrates how the Great Plains grew. The eastern fourth of the state is printed in blue where it is covered by sediments of the Pennsylvanian period, like the level Midwest to the east. But then another quarter is Jurassic, a deep third is Cretaceous, and in the west, red fingers of much younger rocks reach out to illustrate the most recent arrival of the deposits from the Rockies. The state's surface chronicles the geological history of the Great Plains.

The Appalachian System

From these plains it is necessary to look eastward to the Appalachians before returning to the Rockies. The Appalachian system of ridges, valleys, plateaus, and mountains frames the central plains on the east. This historic region extends from

Newfoundland clear into Texas, and it demonstrates well the dynamic processes that shape the surface of the earth.

These processes that fold the crust, wrinkle it like a rug, and raise it into mountains have a terminology all their own. A folded ridge is an anticline, from the Greek words that mean leaning against, and the downfolded valley is a syncline, from the Greek words for leaning together—alluding to their shapes.

When James Hall, one of the greatest American geologists, traversed the region from Iowa to New York State and Pennsylvania in the 1850s, he observed that the sedimentary rocks grew thicker, like a wedge, toward the place where the Appalachians had risen. From this observation and the conclusions drawn from it by another famous American geologist, James D. Dana, grew the theory that sediments had accumulated in a long trough there and later had risen from it as mountains. Dana called this a geosyncline.

According to this theory, material eroded from highlands farther inland as well as volcanic lava and ash from islands offshore kept the trough full as it sank slowly under its own accumulated weight. Sometimes the surface was above water; then swamps formed, trees grew, fell, and were buried in mud, an environment like that existing today in the Great Dismal Swamp of Virginia and North Carolina. Ripple marks made on the beaches of that ancient sea are preserved in the rocks. The buried vegetation became the source of the coal, oil, and natural gas of Pennsylvania and West Virginia.

The trough, 2,000 miles long and 300 miles wide, filled and sank until the sediments were 40,000 feet thick. Compressed deep within the crust, the mass grew hot, shale turned to slate and schist, graywacke to schist, and quartz sand to quartzite. Granite was injected from the mantle, and as if the earth were weary of carrying it, the heavy load was thrust out of the trough as a great ridge or highland.

In present-day geological thinking, the classic geophysical theory has been modified to reconcile it with plate tectonics. The accumulation would be placed offshore on the continental shelf, the foredge of the continent, where it would be subject to volcanic deposition, igneous intrusion, and metamorphism from the intense pressures generated where the Atlantic plate supports the American continent.

For one reason or another, highlands did rise along the Atlantic coast. Some geologists attribute this dramatic development to a "fender-bender" impact of Africa with the American continent. Rock is hard, and it is brittle, but it yields slowly under pressure like a plastic. It may wrinkle like a rug. Sometimes the wrinkles turn into folds and even flop over into recumbent folds. Under sharp pressure, the fold may break and create a fault. In a normal fault one side, called the hanging wall, drops down, increasing the length of the space the two faulted pieces occupy. In a thrust fault, however, the hanging wall is thrust up, shortening the length of the formation. In many places, notably the Cumberland plateau in Tennessee and the Carolinas, faulted crust segments were thrust for miles over existing rocks.

The Appalachian highlands, bulging up and under stress, were riven by faults and glaciated into sharp peaks. Brought low, as all high places must be, they remain today as igneous and metamorphic stumps that underlie the rolling Piedmont region from Alabama to the Hudson River. The Fall Line, a sharp declivity, marks off the foundations of the ancient Appalachians from the coastal plain. Sediments are piling up on the plain and its shelf into the Atlantic, possibly the mountains of the future. Perhaps Will Rogers was wrong when he said: "Put your money into land; they ain't making it anymore."

Blue Ridge and Great Smoky Mountains

Behind the Piedmont, with its Stone Mountain in Georgia and the andesite sill of the Palisades of the Hudson River as monuments of a vanished glory, the Blue Ridge and Great Smoky Mountains rise on roots of the older range from Georgia until they adjoin New England's own highlands. Mount Mitchell (6,684 feet) north of Asheville, North Carolina, in the Blue Ridge, Clingman's Dome (6,643 feet) in the Smokies, and a number of other peaks nearly as high dominate this region. Mount Washington (6,288 feet) towers above both New Hampshire's White Mountains and Vermont's Green Mountains. Spurs of these ranges extend into Newfoundland, New Brunswick, and Nova Scotia. Nearby are the Berkshires of Massachusetts and Connecticut.

The Blue Ridge province is separated from the plateau farther west by a series of valleys 1,200 miles long. Among them are the Tennessee, Shenandoah, Cumberland, Hudson, and Champlain valleys, collectively known as the Great Valley. Through these highlands the Delaware, Susquehanna, and Potomac rivers have cut watergaps on their way to the sea. Several gaps also exist where streams once flowed before they were the victims of piracy by the Shenandoah River, a tributary of the Potomac. The Shenandoah did this by cutting its channel quickly in weak rock while the other streams were struggling with harder rock beds. By getting there first, it drained off their headwaters, and their channels dried up.

The Poconos, Catskills, and Adirondacks stand above the Great Valley's western slope, with the Taconics and Green Mountains on the east. Between lies Lake Champlain. Farther south, the sheer face of the Allegheny escarpment rises from the valley. Near Altoona, Pennsylvania, the railroad conquers this obstacle by its famous Horseshoe Bend route.

Above the Great Valley on the west stands a province of parallel ridges and valleys, like the surface of an old-fashioned washboard. This curious formation appears at its best in Pennsylvania, where pressure from the southeast wrinkled much of the region smoothly. The tops of the ridges, all about the same height, are hard sandstone, the valleys limestone and shale. Limestone is soluble in a moist climate, and shale is friable. The sandstone has survived erosion as ridges; the other rocks remain only in the downfolds. This same solvent action has made the Shenandoah valley a region of caves, such as the Luray and Endless caverns. Elsewhere, Mammoth Cave's vast system and New Mexico's Carlsbad Caverns owe their existence to the same circumstances.

Like the railroad, the Pennsylvania Turnpike had to find its way through the ridges and valleys. Tunnels and bridges helped it conquer a country that long delayed the westward march of pioneer Americans. South of the James River, especially in Tennessee, the forces that created the Ridge and Valley province acted more violently, thrusting great masses of sedimentary rock for miles over their neighbors.

Lofty plateaus from New York to Alabama mark the western extent of the Appalachian region. Here the sandstones, conglomerates, and shales have been weathered into rounded highlands such as the Catskill, Allegheny, and Cumberland mountains, and steep-walled valleys. Extensive coal deposits are mined from the plateau in Pennsylvania, West Virginia, and Kentucky. Metamorphosis of sediments by faulting and earth movements in this region created the slate deposits commercially worked in Pennsylvania, the marble quarried in Tennessee, and the beds of iron ore in Alabama.

Glaciation in the East

The continental glaciers that shaped the surface of so many other parts of North America also left their mark on the plateau as well as on New England and the east coast. The Finger Lakes in upper New York State were spooned out by the ice. In New England, ice stripped sediments from the mountains, exposed the granite and marble resources of Vermont, excavated basins and created lakes by damming river valleys. Saranac Lake in the Adirondacks and Lake Schoharie in the Mohawk valley are examples. Boulders brought from the north by the ice were left to litter the land.

The White Mountains in New Hampshire were overridden by the ice, even 6,288-foot Mount Washington, and scarred by cirques cut in their granite sides. The Green Mountains of Vermont, a complex of rocks from many ages and crucibles of nature, like the Blue Ridge were extensively glaciated, and so were the Adirondacks.

New England's coastal valleys became inlets and her hills islands as the sea rose in postglacial times, and the newly freed waters cut sea cliffs wherever they could attack the shore. This effect is most striking in Maine, less so farther south. Near Boston, glacial drumlins became offshore islands, and sand sorted by the waves from glacial till was deposited as beaches. Cape Cod, Sandy Hook, and New Jersey's island beaches thus owe their existence to the mighty forces of ice and water. Chesapeake Bay acquired its frayed coastline when the rising ocean drowned the valleys of streams draining the land.

The ocean attained this mastery over its shores, of course, because the glaciers that had absorbed so much of the world's supply of water restored it to the seas when they melted, and ocean levels rose.

The most conspicuous monument of the retreat of the ice is Long Island. A huge terminal moraine where the glacier dumped its load forms the north side of that populous New York suburb. The rest of Long Island is an outwash plain from the moraine. Staten Island and Nantucket Island have similar histories.

North of Cape Cod, the coastal plain dips beneath the waves. But to the south the plain sweeps past Florida, a limestone block raised from the sea floor, and the Keys with their coral fringes. Westward it rests on deeply buried remnants of the basement of the old Appalachians as far as the Mississippi River delta. The continent's greatest river has built this delta all the way from Cairo, Illinois, to the Gulf, where the deposit is 40,000 feet thick.

The plain wraps itself around Louisiana and southern Texas and the Gulf as far as Yucatan in Mexico. Salt domes dot the coast. These pillars of salt, as much as 6 miles across and reaching as far into the earth, are tapped for petroleum and mined for sulfur deposits in their caps. Other areas here, particularly in Texas, have been heavy producers of oil.

Resemblances of rock formations have been interpreted to mean that the basement rocks of the Appalachians come to the surface again in the Ozarks of Missouri and the Ouachita Mountains of Arkansas and Oklahoma. Erosion has stripped sedimentary rocks from the St. Francois Mountains in the Ozark dome to expose Precambrian rhyolite porphyry. The diamond-bearing volcanic pipes near Murfreesboro, Arkansas, Magnet Cove with its many rare minerals, quartz crystals in the mountains west of Hot Springs, Arkansas, and the novaculite deposits lie in the Ouachita region.

The Rocky Mountains

More than halfway across the continent, a massive complex of peaks, basins, valleys, and plateaus—the Rocky Mountains—extends from Alaska deep into Mexico. Like the Appalachians, the Rockies stand where the seas repeatedly inundated a geologically restless region. The Pierre shale of the Dakotas, the Dakota sandstone, and the Niobrara chalk so well displayed in Kansas bear witness to these floodings. Uplifted, faulted, folded, the complex system of mountains was carved, as is the way with high places, by ice and water until it was reduced to a plain, its substance spread across the Great Plains.

Subsequently the Rockies were raised again in such a diversity of ways that geologists usually divide them into southern, middle, and northern ranges. The southern group includes the Sangre de Cristos in New Mexico and southern Colorado, the San Juans east of the Colorado Plateau, the Front Range towering above Denver, and the Sawatch Range behind it, as well as the Laramie and Medicine Bow mountains in Wyoming.

Of these, the Front Range, facing boldly to the plains, is by far the best known, the picture postcard Rockies. Pikes Peak and Longs Peak in the Front Range are two of a number that rise more than 14,000 feet, solid granite, gneiss, and schists uplifted through such sandstones as can be seen in the Garden of the Gods outside Denver. The range has been carved from a massive uplift that contrasts with the downwarped basins of North and Middle Park.

Although less prominently placed, the Sawatch Range contains the highest peak in the Rockies, Mount Elbert (14,431 feet), and several more only a few feet lower. The picturesque Sangre de Cristos to the south are folded sedimentary rocks on metamorphic cores. Just west of the Sangre de Cristos, intense volcanic activity created a plateau of lava and tuff that glaciers carved into the rugged San Juan Mountains. The Million Dollar Highway along the mile-deep canyon of the Animas River and the well-named Needles, where mountaineers show their skills, expose ancient schists, conglomerate, and pink granite. Ash from the San Juans spread as far north as Gunnison and south into Arizona. Nearby in New Mexico's Jemez Mountains a violent eruption created the Valles caldera, a domed depression 15 miles in diameter ringed with lava cones.

The Southern Rockies continue north into Wyoming as the Laramie Range and, behind it, the Medicine Bow Mountains, which have been extensively molded by glaciers. Wyoming can show some of the most spectacular mountains on the continent, but most of the state is basin country. Emigrants to the Far West took the Oregon Trail through Wyoming primarily because its

Devil's Tower National Monument, northeast Wyoming. The Tower is a pillar rising 865 feet above its wooded base and composed of jointed, vertical columns of volcanic rock. (National Park Service)

small uplifts and sediment-filled basins offered fewer obstacles than the more rugged country to the south. Although the Oregon Trail led them over the Continental Divide, the watershed between the Atlantic and Pacific oceans, its gentle slopes resembled those of the Great Plains their wagon trains had traversed and with which they were familiar.

East of Wyoming stands an outlying block of the Rockies, the Black Hills. These striking granite monoliths in the plain had their beginnings in a dome, 125 miles long and nearly as wide, raised through the limestone strata and red soil that now rim the Black Hills. Harney Peak (7,216 feet) is the highest of these misnamed hills, but Mount Rushmore is the tourists' favorite because of the busts of four presidents carved in its massive face.

The Middle Rockies

The Middle Rockies comprise a medley of mountains in northeastern Utah, Wyoming, and Montana. Among these, the Uintas are unique; they run east and west to break the pattern generally true of American ranges. Like the other Rockies, however, the Uintas have lowlands at their feet. Kings Peak, highest in the range, towers at 13,500 feet above the Uinta basin that lies just north of the Colorado Plateau. To the east are beds of oil shale north of Grand Junction, Colorado, with their potentialities as a national resource for energy.

North of the Uintas, across the Green River basin, the bold Wind River Mountains, like the Uintas, exhibit glacier-cut sawtooth profiles to the lowlands to the east. Both ranges are sandstones and shales on cores of granite and schist.

The Tetons and Yellowstone National Park bring double glory to northwestern Wyoming. The spectacular mountain landscape of the Tetons was created by earth forces that thrust up a 30-mile-long block of the crust, then tilted it down on the west. The eastern face above downwarped Jackson Hole has been extensively carved by ice, exposing intrusive granites, pegmatites, and metamorphic rocks.

Yellowstone National Park, a plateau of rhyolites, fused tuffs, obsidian cliffs, petrified trees, geysers, and hot springs, gives notice daily that hot rocks lie close beneath the surface. A federal government geologist recently reported that a huge plume of magma, 30 to 50 miles deep, probably exists under

The Grand Tetons, one of the nation's most striking fault-block group of mountains. The range was uplifted along a great fault, then eroded into its present jagged profile towering more than a mile above Jackson Hole, Wyoming. (National Park Service)

Yellowstone. The park sits in a volcanic crater in a geologically unstable belt subject to hundreds of small earthquakes a year.

The Big Horn, Beartooth, and Absaroka mountains form a crescent around Yellowstone Park to the north and east. The first two, lying close together on the Wyoming–Montana line, are young mountains, their sedimentary surfaces scarred down to the granite by ice. The Absarokas, like Yellowstone, top a plateau of volcanic rocks.

The Northern Rockies

The Northern Rockies occupy a vast territory from Montana to the Brooks Range above the Arctic Circle in Alaska. They have been likened to the Ridge and Valley province of the Appalachians because pressure eastward toward the interior has crumpled the rocks into parallel ranges trending north and rising above steep valleys cut in sedimentary rock. Some are fossil reefs formed when the area was under the invading seas. These now yield oil, salt, and potassium salts.

In Montana, however, the Little Belt and Big Belt mountains are uplifted domes of igneous and metamorphic rocks fringed by hogbacks of sediments, more like the Middle Rockies than those of the north. Nearby, the Crazy Mountains are sediments cut by igneous dikes and sills. West of them the Bitterroot Mountains define the border with Idaho, and the Lewis and Clark ranges rise northward toward their full glory in Glacier National Park on the border with Canada.

Glacier National Park owes much of its spectacular scenery to the classic Lewis Fault that thrust Precambrian rocks eastward 14 miles. This great fault block, lying above younger rocks, has been fashioned by living glaciers into jagged peaks carved into cirques and deep valleys where the history of the region is written in the strata presented to view on towering walls. Far out in the plain stands Chief Mountain, crumbling limestone outlier of the fault thrust.

The Northern Rockies continue across the Canadian border into Waterton Lakes National Park. Farther up, Banff and Jasper national parks, with such impressive peaks as Mount Robson, Mount Edith Cavell, and Assiniboine Peak, and Lake Louise cradled in a mountain valley, attract thousands of tourists every year.

Pillow lava on northwest shore of Ingot Island, Prince William Sound, Alaska. (U.S. Geological Survey, F. H. Moffit)

The Colorado Plateau

Throughout the whole Rocky Mountain province, rivers have had to battle to survive wherever the land was uplifted. They had to deepen their channels or die. The Arkansas River with its Royal Gorge, the Gunnison with its Black Canyon 2,800 feet deep, the Rio Grande in its long route to the ocean, and the Snake River met the challenge. But the Colorado River with the Grand Canyon, the river's "road to glory," has been the most celebrated if not the stoutest warrior, and in the process has made the Colorado Plateau famous as a geological wonderland.

The plateau is shaped like a gigantic breakfast muffin, and its surface is like that of a muffin that has been opened with a fork —flat but roughened by peaks and depressions. So it is with this canyonland shared by Colorado, New Mexico, Utah, and Arizona where they meet at the Four Corners. With its canyons, mesas, bright-hued cliffs, and natural bridges it is a hard but beautiful land. To the geologist it is the classic example of erosion, of the power of water and wind.

Successively flooded and uplifted, the plateau is a towering pile of sedimentary rocks. The Grand Canyon, in the southwest

Mount Gould, Glacier National Park, Montana. High on the mountain appears a dark sill of diorite bracketed by two layers of marble, product of the metamorphism of the limestone by the diorite intrusion.

corner of the plateau, displays on its mile-deep sides a billion and a half years of the earth's history. History begins here with the dark Vishnu schist, at the bottom in the narrow inner gorge. Resting on this ancient metamorphic rock sit beds of sandstone, shale, and limestone that record the sequence of deposition and erosion that shaped the plateau. Strata existing elsewhere show that sediments nearly 2 miles thick once lay above the present Grand Canyon rocks but have been weathered away.

The canyon and the Kaibab Plateau it traverses lie at the crest of the uplift. From this crest the strata dip away to the north. As erosion attacks an uplifted surface, it first removes the top stratum, the youngest layer, then the others in succession. As the surface becomes flatter, the youngest stratum will eventually be farthest away from the crest of the uplift, and the others will become successively older toward it. Like a slice across an onion, the rings radiate out from the center with the newest growth on the outside. Those strata that radiate from the Kaibab Plateau face it as cliffs looking south.

Thus the Petrified Forest National Park lies in the Chinle formation; the Painted Desert in the Chocolate Cliffs Shinarump conglomerate; 3,000 vertical feet of the Vermilion Cliffs and White Cliffs in Wingate and Navajo sandstone at Zion Canyon; the Rainbow Bridge in Navajo sandstone; the Gray Cliffs in a Cretaceous formation; and the Pink Cliffs at Bryce Canyon and Cedar Breaks in the Wasatch formation, the youngest.

The Uinta basin at the foot of the mountains of the same name, with the Book Cliffs along the Green River, marks the northern extent of the plateau. Close by is San Rafael Swell, a severely dissected anticline chiefly remarkable for a steep escarpment, the Reef. Below the San Rafael Swell stand the Henry Mountains, laccoliths and volcanic stocks, and the Circle Cliffs, where 9,000 feet of strongly flexed beds of the uplift are on view. Such a sight emphasizes that the plateau is the creature of the power of water to build and destroy. Running from the high places, streams have cut canyons, using pebbles and sand as tools as they race through the sedimentary beds, themselves laid down by water and wind. In a level place, the stream meanders, and in such a place as Natural Bridges National Monument, near Moab, Utah, undercuts walls of limestone to open a shortcut that the viewer can enjoy as a natural bridge. Torrents, flash flooding, and wind-driven rain cut back the strata at the base of a mesa, ultimately reducing it to a pinnacle such as the desolate examples in arid Monument Valley.

The Mogollon Rim and the San Francisco peaks mark the junction of the plateau's southern limits with Arizona's Sonoran Desert, which is in another geological province. Sunset Crater National Monument outside Flagstaff, a large and symmetrical cinder cone, and lesser examples testify to the volcanic activity associated with the rise of the San Francisco Mountains, now much eroded. So does Shiprock, to the northeast in New Mexico, a tower of lava with radiating diabase dikes that plugged the throat of a now-vanished volcano.

Meteor Crater, near Winslow, Arizona, belongs to another world, for it was formed by the impact of a huge nickel-iron meteorite mass. The meteorite blasted a pit 4,000 feet across and more than 500 feet deep. Across the line into Colorado, ancestors of the Pueblo Indians used the limestone cliffs as a refuge where they built the dwellings now preserved as Mesa Verde National Park. Farther east, near Alamosa, Colorado, in the valley between the San Juans and the Sangre de Cristos, the Great Sand Dunes National Monument vividly testifies to the power of the wind. Here quartz grains eroded from the mountains have been shaped and swept into an American Sahara with dunes several hundred feet high.

The Basin and Range Province

On its west side, the Colorado Plateau merges almost imperceptibly into its neighbor, the extensive Basin and Range province. This province stretches north to the Columbia Plateau and the Snake River and south through Idaho, Nevada, southeastern California, Arizona, and New Mexico into Texas almost to the Pecos River. In Mexico it is bounded by the Sierra Madre Occidental.

The province takes its name from the small isolated mountain ranges 3,000 to 5,000 feet high and the valleys at their feet that are its characteristic geological feature. These ranges are fault blocks, pieces of the crust that have been elevated, then tilted in a pattern that has been likened to "an army of caterpillars crawling northwestward out of Mexico." Geologists call such

Shiprock, Navajo reservation, northwestern New Mexico. This jagged rock rising 1,640 feet above the plain is the remains of the lava in the neck of a volcano. (New Mexico Commerce & Industry Dept.)

blocks horsts and the downwarped blocks grabens, taking their terms from German. A horst typically has a steep face and a gentle backslope shaped like a lectern. The graben gathers eroded material and occasional storm waters in this arid country; most of the time it is a playa, a dry sandy or salty depression.

The Wasatch Mountains in Utah, a huge tilted block like the Tetons, 180 miles long, exemplify the pattern of the Basin and Range province and could be counted within it. Great Salt Lake northwest of the Wasatch Range is a saline remnant of Lake Bonneville, which was once the size of present-day Lake Michigan. When its waters covered much of the Basin and Range province its waves cut terraces still visible on the Wasatch Mountains.

Few grabens attract visitors, but Death Valley in southeastern California is the exception. In this national monument appears the lowest land surface, 280 feet below sea level, in the Western Hemisphere. This is at Badwater, near the center of the valley. By contrast, only a few miles away, Telescope Peak rises 11,049 feet high in the volcanic Panamint Range on the valley's western edge. The valley's own volcanic history is represented by Ubehobe Crater and several cinder cones. Death Valley once held a lake, known today by the salt deposits on its bed of pebbles and sand. The search for gold drew settlers to this region, but later the valley became the first major source of borax, long merchandised under the Twenty-Mule Team label.

The long trough from the Salton Sea up the Coachella Valley past mountain-cradled Palm Springs, California, is a graben. Farther east in Arizona and New Mexico, numerous small ranges and basins dominate the landscape with the Guadalupe Mountains as the most prominent. From the range to its west, gypsum crystals have weathered into the Tularosa basin, creating the dunes of the unique White Sands National Monument. At one margin a relatively recent, narrow lava flow, jagged and inky black, contrasts strongly with the gypsum dunes.

The Sierra Nevada

Near Death Valley, only 75 miles away, rises Mount Whitney in the Sierra Nevada. Here extremes meet, the lowest land surface and the highest within the contiguous United States, for

Mount Whitney's 14,495 feet tops the highest of the Rockies and Cascades. The Sierra Nevada (Spanish for Snowy Sawtooth Range) stands like a wall along much of the eastern border of California. Its tilted, 400-mile-long block of granite has been described as not only the world's largest batholith but also the most magnificently sculptured block mountain range on earth. The eastern face, rising sheer thousands of feet above the down-dropped Owens valley, and the gently sloping western face down to the Central Valley have both been modeled by glaciers. Toward its northern end, the batholith lies buried under lava, ash, and tuff from volcanoes. The Mono Craters standing in a row along a valley fissure, and the Devils Postpile, with its hexagonally jointed basalt columns, are relics of lively eras in the Sierra's past. Far off in northeastern Wyoming is a like formation, the Devils Tower National Monument, its clustered basalt columns rising 865 feet from a broad base.

The Sierra Nevada batholith was forced upward, perhaps in several stages, through shale, quartzite, and limestone still evident on its east slope, and graywacke, slate, and volcanic deposits on the west. The Mother Lode gold was derived from west slope metamorphic rocks. Lake Tahoe occupies a graben in the mountain mass, and Yosemite valley's heavily glaciated walls and the deep canyon of the Kings River bare the granite core of the range.

The Cascades

From northern California into British Columbia, the Cascades carry on the pattern of mountain majesty set by the Sierra Nevada. The Cascades are a range of volcanoes with Mount Rainier (14,408 feet), Mount Shasta (14,161 feet), Mount Hood (11,253 feet), and Mount Baker (10,750 feet) as some of their giants. They have built their magnificent cones of layers of andesite, ash, fragmental lava, and pumice and wear snow covers with dignity. Although mostly quiet now, they are part of the Pacific Ring of Fire, that belt of volcanoes and earthquake-prone regions that surrounds the world's largest ocean. Mount Shasta still fumes, and Lassen Peak in California's Lassen Volcanic National Park was active as recently as 1914 and continues to be restless.

Cinder cones in Craters of the Moon National Monument, Arco, Idaho. (National Park Service)

Crater Lake National Park near Medford, Oregon, brings vividly to life the volcanic past of this whole range, as well as displaying one of the continent's most exciting and beautiful mountain landscapes. The ancient Mount Mazama, once as big as Mount Shasta is today, erupted about 6,000 years ago, scattering ash, pumice, and cinders over hundreds of square miles, then collapsed into its caldera. Sky-blue Crater Lake, 5 miles across and 4,000 feet deep, now fills the caldera, with Wizard Island, a small volcano, rising from its surface. Pumice needles from the mighty blast formed beds in the park that have been eroded into fantastic pinnacles.

The Columbia Plateau

The mightiest work of the earth's internal fires was not the Cascades but the ocean of lava that created the Columbia Plateau. Here where the Cascades march northward, basalt, andesite, and rhyolite welled from fissures over 200,000 square miles, burying the land with lava as much as 2 miles thick. On the east the plateau is bounded by the Idaho and Butte batholiths with their Clearwater, Salmon River, and Coeur d'Alene mountains, from which silver and other metals are mined. On the south, the plateau abuts on the Basin and Range province.

Through this formidable barrier the Snake and Columbia rivers have cut their way. The Snake runs in a basalt canyon 200 miles long that is a mile deep where the river breaches the Seven Devils Mountains at Hells Canyon in Idaho. Near Idaho Falls the Craters of the Moon National Monument reminds the visitor that Yellowstone's fires burn not far away. The monument's cinder cones, lava caves, and acres of aa (two syllables), the blocky, rough lava, and pahoehoe (five syllables), which is ropy or even pillow-shaped lava, look like the setting for a moon exploration movie. A similarly unearthly landscape has been set aside as the Lava Beds National Monument near Tulelake, California.

The Columbia River's masterwork was Grand Coulee, an alternate channel the river cut 1,000 feet deep down to the granite basement when glacial ice forced it out of its normal course. Close at hand are the Scablands, 2,000 square miles of rock scalped bare by the runoff from the glaciers.

Peaks of Alaska and Hawaii

A thousand miles of North America's most majestic peaks carved from batholiths stretch through British Columbia to the Panhandle of Alaska. Mount St. Elias (18,000 feet), Mount Logan (19,850 feet), and 20,320-foot Mount McKinley, monarch of them all, wear active glaciers on their granite sides and are crowned with arctic snows. At their feet, plateaus on the interior side collect glacial sediments and carry away the meltwater. The ranges break their northward course and turn west to their anchor peak, Mount McKinley. Between them and the Arctic Circle rises the Brooks Range of folded sedimentary rocks, which is the terminus of the Rockies.

Volcanoes such as Mount Katmai and Mount Wrangell carry the Pacific Ring of Fire deep into Alaska. The former broke loose in 1912 with one of the major eruptions of modern times. Ash from its eruption floated around the world, and the internal fires created a region of fumeroles known as the Valley of Ten Thousand Smokes. Most of the vents have become inactive over the years.

America's volcanic west took in one of its own kind when Hawaii became the fiftieth state. The eight major Hawaiian islands are the summits of volcanoes raised, according to plate tectonics theory, successively as the Pacific plate moved over a hot spot in the earth's mantle. This would account for their remarkable alignment northwestward. Hawaii—the Big Island—appropriately is the site of the world's biggest mountain, Mauna Loa. This active volcano sits on the bottom of the Pacific Ocean 15,000 feet below the waves and raises its massive dome 13,680 feet above them. It is 60 miles long and 30 miles wide. Kilauea, its major vent, lies on the southeast slope. Haleakala, in a national park on the island of Maui, was active as late as the eighteenth century. Oahu and the capital city of Honolulu sit atop two extinct volcanoes. Diamond Head is a cone of one of them.

The lava from Hawaiian volcanoes is a thin, fluid type that forms dome mountains, unlike the explosive ones such as Mount Mazama. Pele's tears and Pele's hair, named for a Hawaiian goddess, are eagerly collected shreds and drops of hardened lava found on the island of Hawaii.

The Coast Ranges

The Coast Ranges, the face that the continent turns to the Pacific Ocean, run in the United States from the Olympic Mountains of Washington through Oregon and California to the Transverse Ranges in southern California. They are interrupted in a few places, such as the drowned valley through which the Columbia River hurries to the sea, and San Francisco Bay.

The Olympics, rising 7,000 feet from the sea and wearing fifty glaciers on their sides, might well be called the American Alps. Principally, they are uplifted metamorphic slates and greenstones.

The California Coastal Ranges, as might be expected in a region dominated by the San Andreas and Garlock faults, are built of much-faulted graywackes, shales, limestone, and lavas cut by serpentines and other metamorphic rocks on a basement of crystalline rocks. The Santa Ynez, Santa Monica, San Gabriel, and San Bernardino ranges make a saintly march into the sea near Los Angeles and also rise eastward toward Arizona. Southward, the Peninsular Ranges extend across the border into Baja California. The Sierra Nevada and the Coast Ranges bracket such fertile regions as California's Central Valley, which lies on five miles or more of sediments eroded from the mountains.

Battering by the Pacific Ocean's waves has carved the coastal rocks into headlands, sea stacks, and bold cliffs. Particularly in the south, the coast rises in terraces that were once at ocean level. At Palos Verdes, for example, a whole series of such terraces indicates that the land has risen 1,300 feet. The San Diego metropolitan area is built on terraces cut into hills by rivers flowing into the sea.

Mountain Making

Much of this brief and necessarily generalized look at the geological history of North America has been concerned with mountains. Someone has well said that mountains are where the action is, and that is true for collectors as well as for geologists. They have inspired some of the science's most exciting theories about mighty but little-understood natural forces. For both these reasons it is in order to recapitulate some current geological thinking about mountains, even though it has already been mentioned.

Mountains are not all alike. The Alps and the Himalayas, for example, appear to have been carved from masses of the crust forced up by pressure from the African plate on the Eurasian one, and of the Indian plate as it forced its edge under Asia. Similarly, the Andes appear to be rising where the Pacific plate is driving its edge beneath the South American continent.

Some theorists believe that all mountain chains owe their origin to plate movements. They trace the existence of most of the North American continent's west coast ranges to forces generated where the continent is overriding the Pacific plate, and the Basin and Range province faults to tension at plate borders. On the other side of the continent, rocks have been found that are believed to be part of a chain of mountains running from the Ukraine through Norway, the Hebrides, Greenland, Canada, and New England to Duluth and Virginia that were separated from their European counterparts when the American plate moved away from Europe. Likewise, the Appalachians and the foundations of several of the eastern United States are linked with a hypothetical encounter with the African plate some 100 million years ago. Offshore islands with volcanoes and geosynclinal activity are all embraced in these theories.

Truly, geology is an exciting science as it wrestles with all the mysteries hidden in 4.5 billion years and with such a question as a popular songwriter posed in "Blowin' in the Wind":

How many years can a mountain exist
Before it's washed to the sea.

Time alone—the vast abyss of geological time—has room for seemingly fantastic geological theories. Anything can happen in billions of years. Meanwhile, we can enjoy the rich harvest of rocks that nature in her own inscrutable ways has provided for the collector to enjoy and study on this great continent.

6. the collector and the craftsman

Let us then be up and doing.
Longfellow

Millions of tons of rock are quarried each year to meet the needs for cut stone used in the construction of buildings, crushed stone and gravel for paving roads, raw materials for the manufacture of cement, and for a number of other purposes. Small in size but important otherwise are the few tons that find places in hobby collections, in colleges and museums, and as ornamental objects.

Rock has long played a part in the economy. As an extreme example, more than a century ago the territorial governor of Oregon collected pieces of flint discarded by Indian arrowhead makers near Oregon City, pasted paper labels on them bearing a date and a value, and accepted them as currency at his general store.

Today's collector values rocks for their beauty or rarity and displays them for their own sake. Specimens brought back from vacation trips may also be fashioned into lamp bases or carved into vases and ashtrays.

Many homeowners assemble their trophies as facings for a fireplace. As they sit before it in the flickering light, they can recall incidents of collecting trips or some agreeable memory associated with one of the rocks before them. Facing a brick fireplace and chimney with stone is a relatively simple cementing process, provided the foundation is sound. Placing the slabs and stones so that they create a pleasing pattern affords an outlet for the decorative instinct that every homemaker has. Here Pikes Peak granite can rest beside slate from Pennsylvania, and sandstone from the Colorado Plateau may nudge a Lake Superior boulder. One outstanding specimen can be made the focus and centerpiece of the fireplace. A cabin at Eagle Harbor, Michigan, displayed in this way a huge mass of native copper from the mines over the hills a few miles away. This fireplace's mantel was a wood slab supported by steel angle irons, in keeping with its rustic setting.

Architects often use much the same technique to emphasize the doorway to a home with an arch of rock slabs embedded in the stucco wall.

Gardening with Rocks

Rock gardens contrast the massive strength of solid stone with the passing show of flowers and the green velvet of moss and ground-cover plants. High art lies behind creating such a garden, as the Japanese, with their genius for finding beauty in simple objects, have demonstrated. A number of excellent books describe the steps in building such a garden and its maintenance as well as the choice of ground-hugging plants and carefully placed flowering species. In general they advise that the rocks should constitute less than two-fifths of the area and that they should not be lost among the vegetation. A terraced structure on a base of well-drained sand is natural for slabs and boulders alike. The rock ledges should lie in both shady and sunny areas and afford moist as well as drier spots to accommodate the growing preferences of the plants. Crushed granite or marble walks harmonize with a rock garden, and so do stone walls draped with vines. Some books suggest that the rock collector may appropriately gather wild plants as well as stones and bring them together again in the garden, each rock resting comfortably amid its native vegetation.

The usefulness of rocks within the home is limited only by the ingenuity and imagination of the householder. A few colorful pebbles or lava fragments dramatize the beauty of a potted houseplant and serve to brace the stems of the blossoms spread above them. Tumbled beach pebbles with their polish and variegated patterns are especially effective for this use.

Flagstones brought back from a trip to a quarry are ideal material for walls around a house, for terraces and walks. For the latter uses, the stones should be split smoothly along strata or parting planes, so that they are no thicker than 1 to 2 inches. They are laid on a bed of sand that has been tamped and leveled. The slabs may be laid as steppingstones or as a walkway with narrow spaces between the slabs so that a fringe of grass can grow and embrace the stones into the garden. Slate, thin-bedded quartzite, gneiss, granite, or well-hardened sandstone are the preferred materials. All are durable, and most of them offer a choice of pleasing colors.

Stone walls are among the venerable monuments of New England village life that draw visitors back to this historic and picturesque region and to others like it. Many of the walls that have weathered the snows of centuries are what are known as dry walls, built of stones ingeniously fitted together without cement. As the colonists cleared their fields, they had ample material to build walls that bounded their fields and marked the roads. These pioneers developed high skill in splitting fieldstone with wedges and heavy hammers and then precisely fitting the pieces together for barn foundations and fences. Large key slabs inserted at intervals tied together the smaller stones.

Interest in this craft has grown in recent years. Some instruction in dry-wall building has appeared in print, such as *Historic Preservation* magazine (April–June 1975), and some prime examples of modern work exist, especially in the eastern United States. An outstanding demonstration is at the estate named Opus 40, the home of sculptor Harvey Fite, at Woodstock, New York.

Besides being used to surround or prop up houseplants, rocks find many appropriate niches and nooks as doorstops, corner ornaments, or mounted display pieces. Brightly pebbled conglomerate or curiously textured pegmatite can find a place on a mantelpiece or side table.

Slabbing and Polishing Rocks

Some carbonate rocks, such as marble, travertine, and calcite, or sulfates, such as gypsum, can be readily worked with simple tools. Such stones are soft (Mohs 2 and 3), reasonably compact, and take a good polish. All can be cut into slabs or other shapes with a hacksaw, but the lapidary's diamond-bladed saw saves much time and effort. The saw's circular blade, with an edge in which diamond grit is embedded, rotates against the rock, which is moved against it while locked in a vise. Blades run in diameter from 4 to 24 inches and larger, but the 10- to 18-inch sizes are usually adequate.

Slabs and blocks cut by the saw can be shaped with hand tools or a power trim saw, against which the rock is maneuvered by hand. Silicon-carbide grinding wheels take up the task of further shaping. Then the work can be completed with sanding cloth and polishing wheels. Marble mills polish slabs with oxalic acid, a mild and slightly poisonous acid, and such an abrasive as putty powder or rottenstone. Most amateurs polish with tin or aluminum oxide powder on a dampened, cloth-covered polishing buff.

Square and circular slabs for lamp bases are not difficult to prepare, and they can be pierced with steel drills for attachment to the rod that holds the lamp together. Marble and onyx vases, lamp standards, and candlesticks are turned commercially on lathes with hard carbide or diamond-tipped tools. The amateur can do quite as well with silicon-carbide power wheels and sanding cloth. Stone should be wet while it is worked to avoid filling the air with dust, which can cause serious lung damage. Marble and calcite onyx can be decorated by etching with hydrochloric (muriatic) acid. The design is exposed to the acid while the rest of the surface is protected with a coat of wax or varnish.

Ashtrays and penholder bases are popular smaller projects. After the rock slab has been shaped, a shallow depression is ground in it with a silicon-carbide wheel, and the face of the ashtray is sanded and polished. Pens with metal sockets can be purchased that are designed to be cemented to the rock base.

Bookends made of rock are popular because their weight holds the volumes securely while they contribute their own color to the row of gaily hued book jackets. The rock collector who is also a craftsman can either invest in a diamond saw and other power tools or else find a dealer in rocks and minerals or an amateur lapidary who will saw rocks for him. Nearly every museum or university has such equipment; thousands of amateurs are scattered across the United States; and some of the dealers

Bookends made by cutting a rounded boulder in two and flattening the base. The face is polished and the inside faces are covered with leather.

who advertise in rock hobby magazines will do custom sawing. Many of the thousand mineral- and gem-collecting clubs in the United States have workshops, and a number of cities offer lapidary instruction in their parks programs.

Crystal-lined geodes, septarian nodules, attractive breccia and conglomerate, marble, red granite, and its black relatives are among the many materials that will richly repay the effort of fashioning a pair of bookends.

Smaller geodes, such as the crystal-lined "coconuts" from Mexico, form attractive pairs when the geode is sawed, the faces polished, and the pair mounted on plastic or wood mounts.

Tumbling Pebbles

Pebbles, especially beach stones that are already rounded and smoothed by wave action, can be tumbled. The beach is the place to appreciate the beauty of common stones because it is most apparent when they are wet. Tumbling polishes the stones, so that they again appear as beautiful and colorful as they were in the surf.

Tumbling is done in a barrel or drum. The stones, selected so that they are about alike in hardness and size, are placed in the drum with some smaller stones, silicon carbide of 60 or 80 grit size, and water. The cover of the drum is fastened securely, and the device revolves slowly on an axle or driving wheels. As it does so, the stones rise up the side, slip back, and abrade one another. After several days or weeks, depending on the device, the drum is opened, cleaned, the stones washed, and they are tumbled again with a finer grit. When satiny smooth, they undergo a similar polishing process with tin oxide or some other material. Tumbling, like flower-growing, is something of an art as well as a routine, and the process must be varied to get the best results with differing types of load and machine.

The brightly gleaming stones from a successful tumbling episode can be used to fill a decorative vase, be displayed in a hollow glass lamp column, or be arranged around houseplants. Children love to play with a handful of smooth, polished stones, which divert them while their elders talk and visit.

Stones as soft as the calcified corals known as Petoskey stones and some other fossils can be tumbled successfully. Three or four days with coarse grit and the same length of time with fine grit should bring them to the polishing stage. They can be polished with tin oxide, a small amount of oxalic acid, and plastic pellets obtainable from mineral dealers. A final washing of several hours in the tumbler with detergent and water completes the treatment.

Rounded pebbles of all types can be shaped and polished, or polished on one face, by rubbing the stone smooth on wet silicon-carbide wet-or-dry paper cushioned on a pad of cloth or newspaper. Prepare the surface in several stages with 180- to 600-grit paper and then polish with tin oxide on dampened velvet or some similar cloth.

Slabbed stones can also be tumble-polished. The drum is filled with slabs to about 1 1/2 inches from the top. A few small, rounded beach pebbles are mixed with the slabs to improve the tumbling action. Some amateurs do not change grit; they let it wear finer during prolonged tumbling and thus prepare the stones with a satisfactory prepolish surface. In a small tumbler, this shortcut is not really effective; a change of grit is advisable.

Tumblers vary in more than size; some have a vibrating as well as a tumbling action. This presumably shortens the time required to complete the cycle. The manufacturer's recommendations and the amateur's own experience are the only reliable guides.

Carving and Sculptures

Colorful pebbles can be assembled with wire supports or glued together with such adhesives as epoxy resins into attractive groups that some practitioners describe as sculptures. Cavemen painted on stone walls; this practice is cited as a precedent for craftsmen who paint rocks. Let the shape of the rock and any discernible patterns stimulate your imagination and tell you what to paint, they say. The results, as shown in recent books, are astonishing for the variety of subjects and the media used to portray them. Some rocks appear decorated like Easter eggs; some are enameled; some are in the realm of decoupage; and some are etched with a vibrating tool. One widely known artist in the Midwest has painted many of the *Oz* book characters on flat pebbles picked up along Lake Michigan.

Emulating Roman mosaic artists, modern craftsmen have developed skill in creating designs with pebbles and broken pieces of stone. A Sunday school class of youngsters spent a busy and happy summer making such a decoration for a hallway in their church. A book describing the techniques for making mosaics is listed in the section "For Further Reading."

Soapstone, a relative of the mineral steatite and talc, is a favorite material for carving. It ranges in color from pearly gray to yellow, and is often translucent. African wonderstone, a dark gray material that takes a satiny polish, is also popular among craftsmen. Both can be carved with a sharp knife or sawed with any woodworking tool. Rasps and files are used to shape details of the design.

When the carving is completed, scratches are rubbed out with 200-grit sanding cloth, and 400-grit paper prepares the surface for polishing with 600-grit paper used under running water. The carving is dried, rubbed with wax or boiled linseed oil to improve the color, and burnished with a paper towel or a soft cloth.

Travertine and gypsum alabaster have been mentioned above as easily worked materials. Some noted sculptors, unable to afford costly marble, have executed works that won acclaim in limestone and even common fieldstone. Several have carved bas-reliefs in slate or pierced the slabs and assembled them into intricate, three-dimensional abstract patterns.

The development of powered lapidary machinery under the stimulus of the demand from amateurs interested in gem-cutting has given the rock sculptor new tools for his hobby. Some have created charming small sculptures of animals from Petoskey stones and the spotted mineral bauxite, and some have challenged the professionals with carvings and sculptures in agate and jade.

Carvings of eggs, cubes, and spheres in both hard and soft rock materials have long been produced both commercially and in home workshops. A diamond saw will quickly shape a cube, which is then sanded and polished. An egg starts as a rectangular block from the diamond saw. This is further shaped on a power trim saw and grinding wheels. A sphere starts as a sawed cube; the corners of the cube are sawed off, and the sphere takes shape between a rotating cup on the end of a pipe and a short piece of pipe held by hand against it. Abrasive in the pipes rounds the rock as it rotates against them. It is sanded and polished with the same machinery.

Books on rock gardens, rock sculpture and crafts, and lapidary procedures are listed in the section "For Further Reading," at the end of this book.

The Systematic Collector

Craftsmanship with rocks is an outlet for the creativity and dexterity of the rock collector. It is one side of human interest in things of the world. The other side is the province of the systematic collector, who sees rocks as the fabric of the science of physical geology. For such a collector, the rocks themselves and their study lie at the heart of his or her interest. The classic focus of that interest is a cabinet of shallow drawers where specimens are assembled and stored. Each specimen is trimmed to size, such as 3 × 4 inches and about 3/4 inch thick, and each occupies its own numbered and labeled cardboard tray. Hundreds of such sets of rocks, each often numbering two hundred or more pieces, have been sold by supply companies over the years. Among the most active have been Ward's Natural Sci-

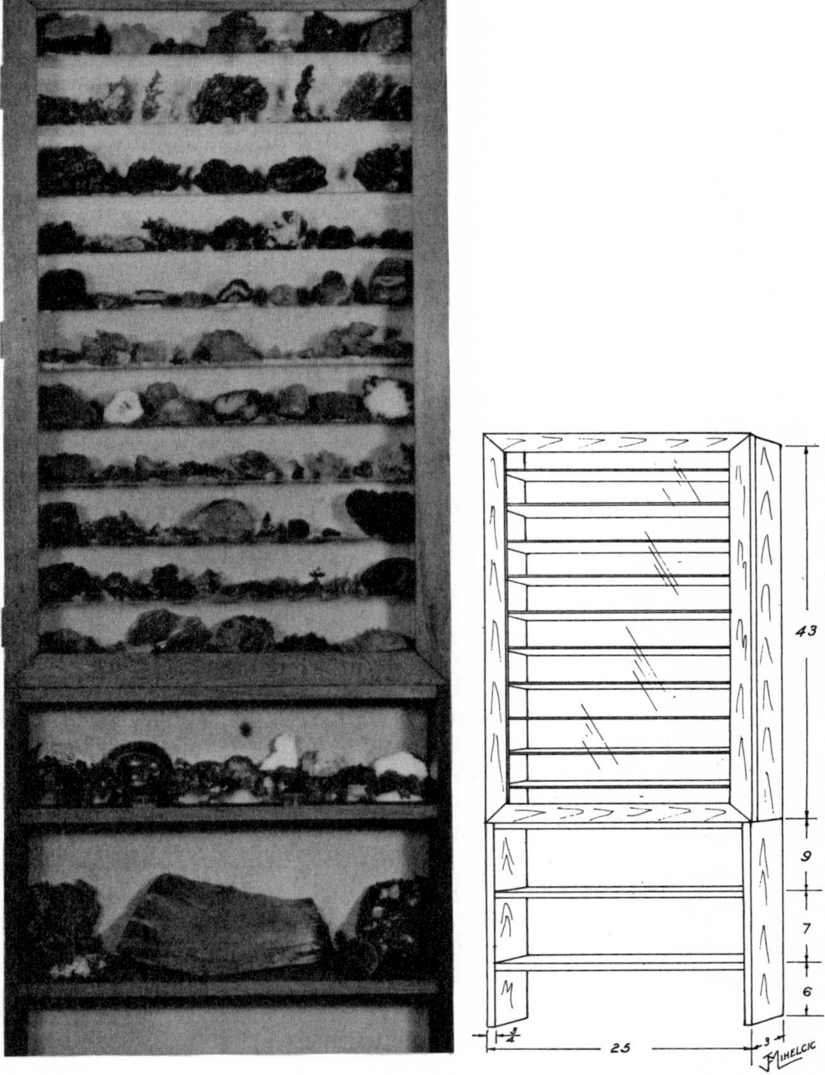

Tall narrow case for rocks with drawing of construction details. It provides space for both large and smaller specimens.

ence Establishment in Rochester, New York, and such dealers as F. Krantz, in Bonn, Germany. The sets were designed primarily for instructional purposes and came housed in handsome oak cabinets. Occasionally an old one will appear for sale as a university or museum cleans house. They can still be purchased from several dealers.

Years ago rock specimens for these sets were chipped into a pillow shape by hand, but rising labor costs and a preference among purchasers for more natural-looking examples caused suppliers to take them out of production.

With practice a collector could develop the skill to fashion specimens into such a uniformly sized collection. The collector could even make shaped specimens for swapping with others. Hydraulic rock-trimmers, geode-crackers, powerful slab-nippers, and diamond saws and tools have made preparation much less punishing than it was a half century ago. Some rocks, such as aragonite and calcite formations from caves, should not, of course, be trimmed. Their value lies in their native form.

Housing the Collection

Many types of cabinets suitable for holding a collection are on the market or can be improvised by the use of a little ingenuity. House sales and secondhand furniture stores may yield an old or an unfinished chest of shallow drawers, an architect's blueprint cabinet, or a discarded dental cabinet. Choice specimens can gleam from the top of such a cabinet, while others are grouped by type inside. Building a cabinet precisely engineered for specimens is not beyond the capabilities of many home craftsmen.

An old china cabinet, a corner cupboard with glass doors, or a bookcase is excellent if the collector's principal interest lies in display rather than storage. Arrangements will depend, of course, on the individual and on the space available. In only one respect are all collections alike: they increase to the limits of space and then overflow it. In extreme cases, rocks may be found under the beds.

If the collector has a storeroom or workshop, specimens can be stored on wall shelves in the flat cardboard trays in which cans of beer are delivered, or in shallow wooden boxes. Containers are regularly discarded at liquor, grocery, and hardware stores,

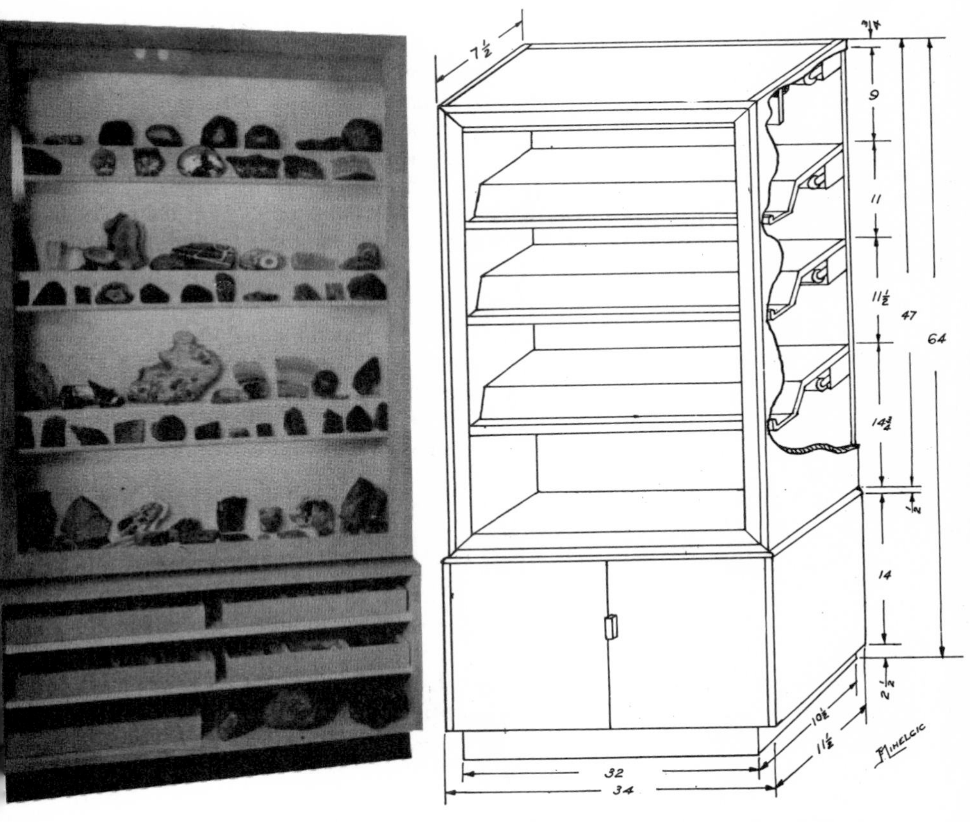

Cabinet with stepped shelves to increase display space and conceal lighting fixtures beneath the back parts of the shelves. There is also a cabinet below for specimens in loose cases. (From 1948 annual of Michigan Mineralogical Society)

and often arrangements can be made with the store owner to save certain types of boxes and trays. Pebbles and small specimens can be made comfortable in egg cartons.

A workroom with a sturdy bench, a strong vise, and good lighting facilitates preparation of specimens. A prospector's pick, a mason's hammer, and several chisels, such as a 1-inch flat blade and a pointed one, are the basic tools for splitting layered sedimentary and metamorphic rocks. Smaller chisels suffice to trim other rocks to cabinet size. Adventures into the lapidary and sculptural treatment of stone will call for power tools that have been mentioned above and are further described in books listed in the section "For Further Reading."

Cataloging the Specimens

A catalog housed in a durable file box is the key to the collection. It should contain a card for each specimen. The 3 × 5-inch card is filed according to the number assigned to each specimen. The numbers usually run consecutively in the order in which the specimens are cataloged. On the card should also appear a description of the rock—granite, limestone, and so on—and a notation of when and where it was found. This information should also be obtained for a specimen acquired by purchase, swapping, or gift, for in it lies the geological significance of the rock. A rock without a pedigree is an orphan, and there are no orphanages for rocks.

If the geological formation from which the specimen came is known, its name should also appear on the catalog card along with names of other rock types associated with the specimen in the formation.

On the specimen will appear the number by which it is listed in the catalog. A small spot of white enamel painted in an inconspicuous spot can be marked with the number in India ink and fixed when the ink is dry with a dab of colorless lacquer. Some collectors make a small label with number, rock type, and location, and glue it to the specimen; others place such a label in the tray with it. Even if labeled, each specimen should be represented by a card in the catalog.

For convenience, rocks should be arranged systematically. This can be done by catalog numbers, or by grouping rock types, such as granites, together. Each system has its advantages: ease of locating a specimen by its number, or easy comparison of related specimens. Some hobbyists form a third type of collection, which groups rocks by locations, such as Colorado Springs or Idaho. A collection of this sort is useful for the study of physical geology and for advising someone who wishes to know what to hunt for on a vacation trip.

Order and cleanliness are as important in a collection as in a home or office. Specimens should be washed or brushed occasionally, and the display should be varied periodically by adding new specimens and changing the groupings.

The Literature of Rocks

The nature and extent of their interests keep rock hunters close to the earth and to its gospel embodied in physical geology. For this reason, many collectors develop an interest in reading about the regions where they have hunted. A magnificent literature of this sort exists in such publications as the professional papers series of the United States Geological Survey. These are available in major libraries, and those still in print can be purchased from the Superintendent of Documents, Government Printing Office, Washington, D.C.

Many hobbyists enjoy collecting books about geology as much as they do the specimens in their collections. Hundreds of titles are in print, usually well-illustrated and competently written. Through them the reader can meet the great geologists, learn of their adventures and triumphs, and share with them the vistas that the collector may never have suspected were present on the horizon of the science.

Geologic History of the Yosemite Valley, by Francois E. Mattes, a U.S.G.S professional paper, and the same author's *The Incomparable Valley* well represent the best in research and literary distinction among books on geology. Also outstanding is Kirtley E. Mather's *The Earth Beneath Us.* Charm and a mastery of the broad sweep of his subject are apparent in every sentence by this retired Harvard geologist, and he has supported his text with delightful illustrations. Even textbooks, such as *Down to Earth* by Carey Croneis and William C. Krumbein, can be read for pleasure as well as instruction. Geology is fortunate in its spokesmen.

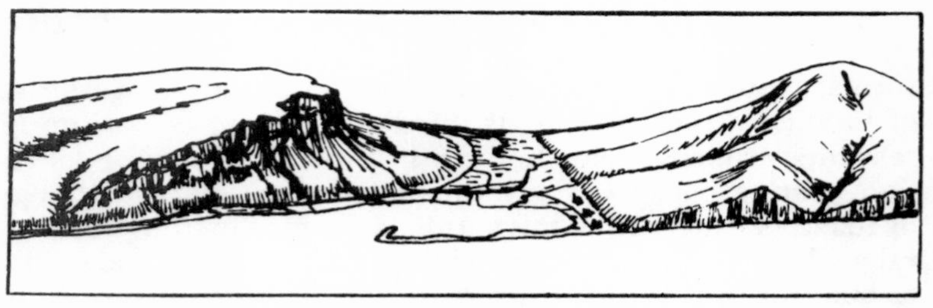

Drawing of a river valley and adjoining hills. River flows into a bay, with terraces along its banks. Hill at right is gradual, hill at left rises steeply to a tableland. Below is a topographical map of the same area. It represents elevations by contour lines, 20 feet apart. (From U.S. Geological Survey Topographical Maps)

Swapping and Other Activities

An important form of outreach lies in swapping. No arm can stretch to the distant borders of North America. But swapping brings those borders closer and permits building a representative collection by the exertions of many arms in many places. Books can familiarize the collector with what is found throughout the continent, and often exchanges of specimens can be arranged at the numerous mineral shows that are held annually throughout the United States and Canada. Dates of these shows are listed in the annual April issue of the *Lapidary Journal,* which is published in San Diego, California. This publication can be found on the racks of many public libraries and is sold in rock shops and magazine stores.

Swapping can be done in person or by mail (the usual way). Many rock shows have an area set aside for swappers to place tables for their specimens and bargain with their neighbors. Swapping by mail has its own etiquette. The person who initiates the swap should offer to send certain specimens in exchange for what is wanted from the other person. If the reply is favorable, the first collector mails a parcel. Whether swapping continues after the first exchange will, of course, depend on whether both parties are satisfied. If they are, the swap may have as a bonus the beginning of a lasting and mutually enjoyable friendship.

Several of the mineral hobby magazines accept swapping advertisements, and occasionally a whole club will arrange a swap with an individual or another club. Such exchanges have begun to cross national borders as sister club arrangements and publications broaden these opportunities.

The rock collector has several advantages in swapping over the gem and mineral collector. Specimens are less fragile, as a rule; they should be well packed and clearly labeled for sending by mail or the United Parcel Service, but there are unlikely to be discouraging losses or damage to rocks. Furthermore, questions of value often raise barriers in mineral swapping, but with rocks the interest is more in diversification than in financial gain.

Fortunately, the rock collector's rewards are the knowledge gained from specimens, from study of the literature of geology, and in the wholesome recreation enjoyed in the pursuit of the hobby. The collector is not only curator of a personal collection of beautiful natural objects but also an active and informed spectator of the wonders of a wonderful world.

There are also widening opportunities for the collector to serve as a volunteer in the field work of a university or museum, as an instructor for the geology merit badge of Scout groups, as a lecturer before school and club groups, and as a member and leader of local geological and mineralogical clubs. An abiding interest in geology exists; it is never difficult to find an audience.

7. locations for the rock collector

North America counts its people in the hundreds of millions, its broad extent in the millions of square miles, and if they were counted, its rock exposures in comparably large figures. The amplitude of the exposures allows room for a vast diversity of rock types, such as have been described in the preceding chapters.

The lists by states that comprise this chapter make no pretense at being complete; they are intended to be representative of the wide variety available for the rock collector. The listed locations have been culled from a number of sources believed to be reliable. But the national eagerness to cover the face of the earth with concrete highways, shopping centers, and condominiums may have buried some or made others difficult to find for such reasons as rerouting of roads and changes in local names.

Some states appear here with relatively few listings; others, which have a wide variety of rock types or which represent a major geological event in the history of the continent, are more generously described. Furthermore, many locations could not be included because they were not specific enough or could not be pinpointed by reference to an easily identified place, such as a city or mountain.

National parks and monuments of interest for their geological features are briefly described in connection with the states in which they are located. It must be emphasized that collecting in such places is forbidden. Yet often the rocks of these places are well described in the literature; they can be living textbooks for the collector. Many state and privately-owned resorts and parks offer similar advantages.

No attempt has been made to include the names of formations, such as the Niagara limestone or the Coconino sandstone. Geologists frequently differ about formation names to such a degree that the names themselves become a source of confusion to the amateur. A collector who wishes to obtain the precise formation names for any specimens should consult the section on Sources of Information.

A listed location will often offer more than one type of rock. An igneous inclusion may appear in a listed sedimentary rock exposure; granite, gneiss, and pegmatite are often found together. Look around and enrich your knowledge as well as your collection.

Listings below appear alphabetically by states and by rock types within the states.

Arizona

- AGGLOMERATE: Buell Park.
- ANDESITE: Red Mountain, Patagonia, Santa Cruz County.
- ANDESITE PORPHYRY: Ash Peak district, Luckie mine, Greenlee County.
- ARAGONITE: Castle Hot Springs, Yavapai County.
- ARAGONITE: Warren district, Cochise County, as flos ferri in caverns.
- ARAGONITE AND DOLOMITE: Bisbee, Copper Queen mine, Cochise County.
- BASALT: West of Perkinsville, Yavapai County.
- BASALT: Comstock Hill, Tombstone district, Cochise County.
- BASALT PORPHYRY: Iron King mine, Big Bug district, Yavapai County.
- BRECCIA: MGM claims northeast of Wickenburg, Yavapai County.
- BRECCIA: Garbet Ridge, Monument Valley, Navajo County.
- CONGLOMERATE WITH BASALT AND RHYOLITE: Mammoth mine, Tiger, Pinal County.

- DACITE: Picket Post Mountain, near Superior, Pinal County.
- DACITE: Sugarloaf Bluff, 5 miles west of Quartzsite, Yuma County.
- DIABASE: Old Dominion mine, near Globe, Gila County.
- DIABASE AND LIMESTONE: Along Salt River, north and northeast of Globe, Gila County.
- DOLOMITE: Double Standard mine, Patagonia district, Santa Cruz County.
- DOLOMITE: East of Agua Fria, near Castle Hot Springs, Maricopa County.
- DOLOMITE: Lakeshore mine, Pima County.
- GLAUCONITE: Near Wickieup, Mohave County.
- GNEISS: Ajo district, Pima County.
- GRANITE: Estrellas Mountains, southwest of Phoenix, Maricopa County.
- GRANITE PORPHYRY: Inspiration mine, Globe, Gila County.
- GRANITE PORPHYRY: Chase Creek canyon, Greenlee County.
- GRANITE PORPHYRY: Morenci, Greenlee County.
- GRANITE PORPHYRY: Palmetto district, Santa Cruz County.
- GRANODIORITE: Tombstone, Cochise County.
- GYPSUM: Mammoth claim, 60 miles southeast of Kingman, Mohave County.
- HORNFELS: Christmas mine, Banner district, Gila County.
- KIMBERLITE: Monument Valley, Navajo County.
- LIMESTONE: 79 mine, Banner district, Gila County.
- MARBLE: Southeast of Dragoon Station, Cochise County.
- MARBLE: 6 miles north of Helvetia, Pima County.
- PEGMATITE: Kingman quarry, Greenwood Mountains, near Signal, Mohave County.
- PEGMATITE: White Picacho district, Yavapai County.
- PEGMATITE: Quarry northwest of highway camp on White Spar Road, near Yarnell, Yavapai County.
- PEGMATITE: 7U7 ranch near Bagdad, Yavapai County.
- PEGMATITE: Virgin Mountains, Hummingbird claims, Mohave County.
- PEGMATITE: Near San Domingo Wash, northeast of Wickenburg, Maricopa County.
- PERLITE AND OBSIDIAN: Ray and Superior, Pinal County.
- PORPHYRY: Mineta Ridge on east flank of Rincon Mountains, Cochise County.

- QUARTZ MONZONITE: With arkose at Castle Dome mine, Gila County.
- QUARTZITE: Diamond Butte area, Gila County.
- QUARTZITE: Sierra Ancha Mountains, Gila County.
- RHYOLITE: 3 miles west of Morristown on west side of Hassayampa River, Maricopa County.
- RHYOLITE BRECCIA: Humboldt mine, Patagonia district, Santa Cruz County.
- SANDSTONE: Monument Valley, Navajo County.
- SCHIST: Canyon Station Wash in Cerbat Mountains, Mohave County.
- SCHIST: Santa Maria Mountains, near Camp Wood, Yavapai County.
- SCHIST: Ajo, Pima County.
- SKARN: Twin Buttes district at Twin Buttes mine, Pima County.
- TUFF: Along San Simon River, Cochise County.
- TUFF: On northeast slope of Vulture Mountains, 15 miles southeast of Aguila, Maricopa County.
- TRAVERTINE: Havasupai Falls, Coconino County.
- TRAVERTINE: 20 miles south of Canyon Diablo, Coconino County.
- TRAVERTINE: Big Bug Creek area near Mayer, Pima County.

National Parks and Monuments

- *Grand Canyon National Park:* Northwest of Flagstaff, Arizona. Usually ranked as the continent's greatest natural wonder. Here the Colorado River has cut a mile-deep canyon through 2 billion years of the earth's history, creating a matchless display of color and erosive power.
- *Sunset Crater National Monument:* A few miles from Flagstaff, Arizona. A 900-year-old cinder cone stained with vivid colors against the background of the beautiful San Francisco peaks.
- *Petrified Forest National Park:* Holbrook, Arizona. Miles of desert, strewn with fossil logs of jeweled jasper and agate. Nearby the varicolored Painted Desert.
- *Chiricahua National Monument:* Southeast of Willcox, Arizona. Rocky spires of lava broken by earth movements

and shaped by erosion into a fantastic landscape.

- *White Sands National Monument:* Just west of Alamogordo, New Mexico. The world's largest area of gypsum sand, shaped into giant dunes by the wind, a memorable fantasy of nature.
- *Capulin Mountain National Monument:* Near Raton in northeast New Mexico. Until a few thousand years ago, Capulin was an active volcano. Today a 1,000-foot cinder cone, one of the most perfect in the world, recalls its violent past.

Arkansas

- CALCITE: Kimsey Calcite quarry in Magnet Cove, 12 miles east of Hot Springs, Garland County.
- CHALK AND MARL: Near intersection of Arkansas 26 and 51, west of Arkadelphia, Clark County.
- CHERT: On east side of U.S. 52, 1/4 mile north of Busch, Carroll County.
- COAL: In bank along road, 1/5 mile north of its junction with Arkansas 109, north of Subiaco, Logan County.
- DOLOMITE: At Monte Cristo and other mines near Rush, Marion County.
- GRAVEL: In pits south of Wynne, Cross County.
- GYPSUM: At quarry just north of Highland, Pike County.
- GYPSUM (SELENITE): In road ditch 3 miles south of Dierks, Howard County.
- KIMBERLITE: At Crater of Diamonds State Park, 2 1/2 miles south of Murfreesboro on Arkansas 301.
- LIMESTONE (CRINOIDAL): With shale at quarry 1 mile south of Leslie, Searcy County, on U.S. 65.
- LIMESTONE: In Ben Hogan quarry north of Black Rock, Lawrence County, and east of U.S. 53.
- LIMESTONE: In cliffs just south of Boxley, Newton County, and at quarry 3 miles north and west of Arkansas 43.
- MARL: Along road to Saratoga Landing on Millwood Lake from Arkansas 32, south of Saratoga, Hampstead County.
- NEPHELINE SYENITE: In west and south rims of Magnet Cove, 12 miles east of Hot Springs, Garland County,

particularly in Diamond Jo quarry in south rim.

- NEPHELINE SYENITE: In road ditch 100 yards west of underpass on Arkansas 183, south of Bryant, Saline County.
- NEPHELINE SYENITE: Near south side of bridge abutment on west side of Cove Creek on U.S. 270, west of Magnet, Hot Springs County.
- NOVACULITE: In ridges along U.S. 270, north of Interstate 80, Hot Springs County.
- PHONOLITE (PORPHYRY): In old titanium mine on north rim of Magnet Cove, 12 miles east of Hot Springs, Garland County.
- PHOSPHATE ROCK (BLACK NODULES): In ditch 2/3 mile east of East Lafferty Creek, west of Cushman, Independence County.
- QUARTZ (IN SANDSTONE): Coleman's mine at Blue Springs, just north of Hot Springs, Garland County.
- SANDSTONE: At lead mines west of Arkansas 43 and north of Ponca, Newton County.
- SANDSTONE (WITH QUARTZ CRYSTALS): In bluff on south side of U.S. 270, west of Crystal Springs and 1/3 mile east of the Montgomery–Garland county line.
- SHALE: Near Crystal Springs, just south of Lake Ouachita, Garland County.
- SOAPSTONE: In pits south of Ferndale, Saline County.

National Park

- *Hot Springs National Park:* In the city of Hot Springs, Arkansas. A spa grown up around 42 hot springs rising from a fault in the rocks.

California

- ANORTHOSITE: Soledad Canyon between Land and Ravenna, Los Angeles County.
- APLITE: Bloom Valley, east of El Cajon, San Diego County.
- BRECCIA (JASPER): Ocean cliffs near Trinidad Head, 20 miles north of Eureka, Humboldt County.
- PILLOW BASALT: Point Bonita, north of the Golden Gate, Marin County.
- BRECCIA: Jubilee Pass, Death Valley National Monument.

- BRECCIA: 9 miles southeast of Capistrano Beach at San Onefre, Orange County.
- CALCITE (BLUE): Crestmore quarry, Riverside, Riverside County.
- CALCITE (ONYX): Aquarius mine, 15 miles north of Trona, San Bernardino County.
- CALCITE (ONYX): Yucca Valley, 15 miles northwest and above Pipe's Canyon Camp, San Bernardino County.
- CONGLOMERATE: Point Lobos State Park, Monterey County.
- CONGLOMERATE: East end of Panoche Pass in the Diablo Range, Monterey County.
- CONGLOMERATE: Along Highway 58, east of Bakersfield, Kern County.
- CONGLOMERATE: Point Reyes, Marin County.
- CONGLOMERATE AND SHALE: 8 miles north of Redding turn off Highway 299 on Dry Creek Road, along Dry Creek, Shasta County.
- DIATOMITE: Near Point Dume along Highway 101 on south side of Santa Monica Mountains, Ventura County.
- DIATOMITE: Near Twenty-Nine Palms, San Bernardino County.
- DIATOMITE: Casmalia and Lompoc, Santa Barbara County.
- DOLOMITE: Natividad mine, 2 miles east of Salinas, Monterey County.
- DOLOMITE: Kaiser quarry south of Salinas near Highway 101, Monterey County.
- DOLOMITE: Galena Canyon, southern Panamint Mountains, Death Valley National Monument.
- DOLOMITE, QUARTZITE, AND SCHIST: Fremont Peak State Park, 11 miles from San Juan Bautista, San Benito County.
- GABBRO (ORBICULAR): Rough and Ready, Calaveras County.
- GNEISS (WITH PEGMATITE): Tule Mountain, north-northwest of Jacumba, San Diego County.
- GRANITE: Joshua Tree National Monument, south of Twenty-Nine Palms, San Bernardino County.
- GRANITE: Along Seventeen Mile Drive from Carmel to Monterey, Monterey County.
- GRANITE: Hiriart Hill, Pala, San Diego County.
- GRANITE: At Castella, 1 mile west in Castle Crags State Park, Shasta County.

- GRANITE: Quarries at Raymond, Madera County.
- GRANITE: Quarries at Rocklin, near Sacramento, Sacramento County.
- GRANITE AND DIORITE: On flanks of mountain just south of Twenty-Nine Palms, San Bernardino County.
- GRANITE AND DIORITE: San Gabriel Mountains west of Little Tujunga Canyon, Los Angeles County.
- GRANITE PORPHYRY: Spiller Canyon, Tuolumne County.
- GRANITE, RHYOLITE, AND SCHIST: Along Highway 80 between Soda Springs and Donner Lake, Sierra County.
- GRANODIORITE: Along the road from Lake Arrowhead to Bear Lake, San Bernardino County.
- GRAYWACKE: 10 miles northwest of Weed and beyond toward Yreka, Siskiyou County.
- GRAYWACKE AND SCHIST: Angel Island, San Francisco Bay, San Francisco County.
- GREENSTONE (ALTERED BASALT): 1 1/2 miles west of Redding on Highway 299, Shasta County.
- LAVA: Caps on plateaus northeast of Kernville, Kern County.
- LAVA: In Cajalco Canyon, southwest of Corona, Riverside County.
- LAVA: Caps on hills near Jacumba, San Diego County.
- LAVA: Between Ludlow and Newberry, San Bernardino County.
- LAVA: South of Big Pine in the Owens Valley, Inyo County.
- LAVA (VOLCANICS): Just east of Broadway Tunnel in Berkeley Hills, Contra Costa County.
- LAVA WITH CINDERS: Just west of Amboy, San Bernardino County.
- LAVA AND TUFF: 13 miles southeast of Cima in the Mojave Desert, San Bernardino County.
- LAVA AND TUFF: Red Rock Canyon, 20 miles north of Mojave, Kern County.
- LAVA AND VOLCANICS: 8 miles southwest of Jamestown, Tuolumne County.
- LAVA, OBSIDIAN, AND PUMICE: Mono Craters, south of Mono Lake, Mono County.
- LIMESTONE: Butte Valley in the Panamint Mountains, Inyo County.

- LIMESTONE: Near Winchester in the Peninsular Mountains, Riverside County.
- LIMESTONE: In Palm Canyon, south of Palm Springs, Riverside County.
- LIMESTONE: Marble Mountains in the eastern Mojave Mountains, south of Needles, San Bernardino County.
- LIMESTONE: Quarry east of Interstate 5, 10 miles north of Redding, Shasta County.
- MARBLE: In the Sidewinder Mountains northeast of Victorville, San Bernardino County.
- OBSIDIAN: Along Bottle Rock Road, 2 1/2 miles east of Kelseyville, off Highway 29 and farther east on Soda Bay Road and at Cold Creek.
- OBSIDIAN: Glass Buttes, Siskiyou County near Modoc County border.
- PUMICE: Coleman mine, Clear Lake Highlands, Lake County.
- QUARTZITE: Lemoncove, 3 miles north on north side of the ravine, 1/3 mile northeast of Kaweah River and 1 mile east of Ward ranch, Tulare County.
- QUARTZITE AND MARBLE: Along the highway near Big Sur, Monterey County.
- RHYOLITE: Ubehebe Crater at north end of Death Valley National Monument.
- RHYOLITE: Along Highway 101, just northwest of Pismo, San Luis Obispo County.
- RHYOLITE BRECCIA: Soledad Mountain, north of Rosamund, Kern County.
- RHYOLITE TUFF: Chimney Rocks near Surprise Siding, Modoc County.
- SALT: Death Valley National Monument, at the Devil's Golf Course.
- SANDSTONE: East of Randsburg, Kern County.
- SANDSTONE: Painted Canyon, east of Mecca, Riverside County.
- SANDSTONE: 10 miles north and northwest of Needles, San Bernardino County.
- SANDSTONE: South flank of Susana Mountains, Los Angeles County.

- SANDSTONE: Atascadero, along road at north edge of town, San Luis Obispo County.
- SANDSTONE (BITUMINOUS): Quarry on west slope of Ben Lomond Mountain, Santa Cruz County.
- SANDSTONE AND CONGLOMERATE: Foothills of the Cascade Mountains from east of Chico to Redding, Butte County.
- SANDSTONE AND CONGLOMERATE: Along the Mulholland Highway north of Beverly Hills, Los Angeles County.
- SANDSTONE AND CONGLOMERATE: Mount Diablo and Mount Hamilton, Marin County.
- SANDSTONE AND SHALE: Along Highway 5 between Castaic and Gorman, Los Angeles County.
- SANDSTONE AND SHALE: Highway 49 near Bagby, Mariposa County.
- SANDSTONE AND SHALE: Point San Pedro, San Mateo County.
- SCHIST: Along Walker's Creek at Bakersfield, Kern County.
- SCHIST: Chowchilla River near Chowchilla Crossing on the Fort Miller road, Madera County.
- SCHIST: Along Highway 80 on approach to Auburn, Nevada County.
- SCHIST: 2 miles north of Murphy's, Calaveras County.
- SCHIST: In the Orocopia Mountains southeast of Indio, Riverside County.
- SCHIST (CHLORITIC GREENSTONE): Along Highway 49 from Mariposa to Jacksonville, Mariposa County.
- SCHIST: Near Weaverville, along Highway 299, Trinity County.
- SCHIST: In Bouquet Canyon southwest of the Reservoir, Los Angeles County.
- SCHIST: North and northwest of Julian, San Diego County.
- SCHIST: South of Corona in the Santa Ana Mountains, Riverside County.
- SCHIST AND DIORITE: Road cut in southern San Felipe Valley, San Diego County.
- SCHIST AND JADEITE: Clear Creek, San Benito County.
- SCHIST AND QUARTZITE: Placerita Canyon and Lower Lytle Canyon in the San Gabriel Mountains and also in Dry Morongo Canyon, Los Angeles County.

- SCHIST AND TUFF: 12 miles northeast of Victorville, San Bernardino County.
- SERPENTINE: Petaluma, 5 miles southwest on the east side of Massa Hill, Marin County.
- SERPENTINE: Mile north of San Luis Obispo along Highway 101, San Luis Obispo County.
- SERPENTINE: Middletown, 1 1/2 miles east on the road to Lower Lake, Lake County.
- SERPENTINE: Along Indian Creek north of Happy Camp, Siskiyou County.
- SERPENTINE: Porterville, 8 miles east and 1/2 mile south of Deer Creek, Tulare County.
- SERPENTINE: 4 miles south of New Idria in Clear Creek, San Benito County.
- SERPENTINE AND DIORITE: 2 miles north of Coulterville, Mariposa County.
- SERPENTINE, PERIDOTITE, AND JADE: Cape St. Martin, Monterey County.
- SLATE: Moore's Flats, 12 miles south of Mariposa, Mariposa County.
- SLATE: In Lower Merced River canyon, west of entrance to Yosemite, Maricopa County.
- SLATE: Sepulveda Canyon north of Beverly Hills, Los Angeles County.
- TRAVERTINE: Northwest side of the Salton Sea in cliffs, Riverside County.

Yosemite Park Area

- APLITE: West of Pohono Trail and Chinquapin Road.
- GABBRO: On Wawona Road north of Inspiration Point.
- GABBRO: At El Portal.
- GRANITE PORPHYRY: In cirque north of Gray Peak in Clark Range.
- GRANITE PORPHYRY: In Tuolumne Meadows.
- GRANITE PORPHYRY: Valley of Bridalveil Creek.
- GRANODIORITE: Walls of Yosemite Valley, Kings River Canyon, and Kern River Canyon.
- GRANODIORITE: Lower Coulterville Road.
- HORNBLENDE GABBRO: Near mouth of Upland Valley of Bridalveil Falls.

National Parks and Monuments

- *Yosemite National Park:* Due east of San Francisco near the Nevada border. A magnificent landscape in the heart of the Sierra Nevada that records in its inspiring valley the work of mighty glaciers.
- *Devils Postpile National Monument:* In the high Sierra near Yosemite. Here, deep in the rugged mountains, a great mass of basalt parted as it cooled into slender columns that form a sheer wall 60 feet high, shaped like a giant pipe organ.
- *Sequoia and Kings Canyon National Parks:* East of Fresno, California, these two parks enshrine the tallest mountain, Mount Whitney (14,495 feet), in the contiguous United States, and the mightiest trees, groves of giant sequoias. Kings Canyon is 8,000 feet deep.
- *Death Valley National Monument:* East of Kings Canyon Park on the Nevada border. A workshop of geological forces where faulting of the earth's surface created the lowest spot in North America.
- *Lassen Volcanic National Park:* West of Susanville in northeast California. The park encloses a group of sleeping volcanoes, of which Lassen Peak is the most recently active. Steam and smoke betray the restlessness of the region; Hot Lake is a good laundry temperature.
- *Lava Beds National Monument:* At Tulelake on the Oregon border. This area has been described as a museum example of lava cones, tubes, and other volcanic phenomena. In addition, the monument has 300 caves, one of ice.
- *Pinnacles National Monument:* South of Hollister, California. Earth movements and erosion transformed a volcanic mountain into a landscape of rocky spires, caves, crags, and canyons.
- *Crater Lake National Park:* Northeast of Medford, Oregon. Second only to the Grand Canyon as a sublime spectacle of nature's handiwork, this blue lake tucked snugly in a volcanic caldera charms rather than overwhelms the human visitor.

Colorado

- ALABASTER: Bear Creek, southwest of Golden, Jefferson County.
- ALABASTER: Quarry at Owl Canyon, north of Fort Collins, Larimer County.
- ALABASTER: Colorado Alabaster Company quarry, 30 miles south of La Junta, Otero County.
- ALABASTER: Old barite mine across Dolores River at Gateway, Mesa County.
- ALABASTER: 15 miles east of Delta, Delta County.
- AMPHIBOLITE: Sedalia mine, 4 miles north of Salida, Chaffee County.
- ANDESITE: Race creek, 11 miles south of South Fork station on D. & R.G. station, Rio Grande County.
- ANHYDRITE AND GYPSUM: Iron Nellie mine, 2 miles north of Gypsum, Eagle County.
- ANTHOPHYLLITE (ASBESTOS): West of Cree Camp, Chaffee County.
- APLITE: Jamestown, Boulder County.
- ARAGONITE: 9 miles northwest of La Garita.
- ARAGONITE: In caves at Manitou, El Paso County.
- ARAGONITE: Pagosa Springs, Archuleta County.
- BRECCIA: Gloryhole, 4 miles south of Central City, Gilpin County.
- BASALT: 3 miles north of Hartsel, Park County.
- BASALT: La Jara Creek, 19 miles northwest of Antonito, Conejos County.
- DACITE: Ward, Boulder County.
- DOLOMITE: Gilman district, Eagle County.
- DOLOMITE: Aspen district, Pitkin County.
- DOLOMITE AND ANKERITE: Bull Domingo mine, Silver Cliff district, Custer County.
- FELDSPAR: 4 miles north of Cotopaxi, Fremont County.
- FELDSPAR: Burroughs mine, Kerr Gulch, Jefferson County.
- GABBRO: Mount Sneffels, 5 miles southwest of Ouray, Ouray County.
- GABBRO: Near Ignacio Reservoir, La Plata County.
- GABBRO: Iron Mountain, 12 miles southwest of Canon City, Fremont County.

- GNEISS: Grape Creek, 2 miles southwest of Canon City, Fremont County.
- GRANITE: Mount Antero, Chaffee County.
- GRANITE: St. Peters Dome, Teller County.
- GRAPHITE: North Italian Mountain, Gunnison County.
- GYPSUM: Calhan, 3 1/2 miles northeast on Paint Mine Road, El Paso County.
- GYPSUM: Perry Park, 10 miles northwest of Palmer Lake, El Paso County.
- HORNFELS: Monarch district, 1 mile east of Boss Lake, Chaffee County.
- JET: Trinidad, 34 miles southeast at Wet Mountain Valley in Trincherea Valley, Las Animas County.
- LATITE: Near Victor, Teller County.
- LAVA: Table Mountain, east of Golden, Jefferson County.
- LIMESTONE: Curio Ridge, 7 miles south of Canon City, Fremont County.
- MARBLE: Southwest of Steamboat Springs on the Yampa River, Routt County.
- MARBLE: Yule Creek, at Marble, Gunnison County.
- MONZONITE: Italian Mountain, north of Gunnison, Gunnison County.
- MONZONITE PORPHYRY: Breckenridge district, Summit County.
- ORTHOCLASE FELDSPAR (SANIDINE): West Sugarloaf Mountain, Boulder County.
- PEGMATITE: Pine Creek, 11 miles west of Sedalia, Douglas County.
- PEGMATITE: Take U.S. 50 from Royal Gorge Road 1 1/3 miles toward Buckskin Joe to quarry on road. Others nearby, Fremont County.
- PEGMATITE: Clora May mine, east of Buena Vista, Chaffee County.
- PEGMATITE: Pine Ridge, 7 miles north of Cotopaxi, Fremont County.
- PEGMATITE: Spruce Grove Campground, 13 miles northwest of Lake George, Park County.
- PEGMATITE: Devils Hole, 6 miles north of Texas Creek, Fremont County.
- PEGMATITE: Ohio City, Gunnison County.

- PEGMATITE: 5 miles northwest of Canon City, Eight Mile Park area, Fremont County.
- PEGMATITE: Along Railroad Gulch, near Turret, Chaffee County.
- PEGMATITE: Crystal Mountain, 45 miles west of Fort Collins, Lake County.
- PEGMATITE: Trout Creek Pass, 10 miles east of Buena Vista, Chaffee County.
- PEGMATITE: Crystal Park, 2 miles southwest of Manitou Springs, El Paso County.
- PEGMATITE: Crystal Peak, 4 miles north of Florissant, Teller County.
- PEGMATITE: Santa Fe Mountain, 3 miles southeast of Idaho Springs, Clear Creek County.
- PHONOLITE: Beacon Hill near Cripple Creek, Teller County.
- PHONOLITE AND RHYOLITE: Grouse Hill, Cripple Creek, Teller County.
- PITCHSTONE: Specimen Mountain, Poudre Lakes area, 31 miles west of Estes Park, Larimer County.
- QUARTZITE WITH LIMESTONE: At Italian Mountain, Gunnison County.
- RHYOLITE: Ragged Mountain, Gunnison County.
- RHYOLITE: Castle Rock area, Douglas County.
- RHYOLITE: Ruby Mountain, near Nathrop, Chaffee County.
- SANDSTONE: Between Hartsel and Fairplay, Park County.
- SANDSTONE: McElmo Creek valley, Montezuma County.
- SANDSTONE: Opal Hill, near Fruita, Mesa County.
- SANDSTONE: Placerville, San Miguel County.
- SCHIST (WITH MARBLE AND GNEISS): Homestake and Calumet Iron mines, near Turret, Chaffee County.
- SCHIST: Idaho Springs area, Gilpin County.
- SCHIST: Sedalia Copper mine, north of Salida, Chaffee County.
- SCHIST: Thompson Canyon district, Larimer County, especially in Poudre Canyon, 18 miles northwest of Fort Collins.
- SCHIST: Railroad cut west of Victor, Teller County.
- SYENITE: Golden Cycle mine, Victor, Teller County.
- TUFF: Buffalo Peaks, Chaffee County.
- TRACHYTE: Mineral Hill, Cripple Creek, Teller County.

- TRAVERTINE: Antero Junction, Park County.
- TRAVERTINE: 3 miles up Taylor Gulch from Wellsville, Fremont County.
- VERMICULITE: Gem Park mine, on Custer–Fremont county line.

National Parks and Monuments

- *Rocky Mountain National Park:* Headquarters in Estes Park, Colorado. The majestic wall of the Front Range of the Rockies displays the handiwork of volcanoes, glaciers, and rivers, and the slow forces that raised the mountains from the plain.
- *Black Canyon of the Gunnison National Monument:* Montrose, Colorado. Here the Gunnison River, struggling to survive as the Rockies were raised, displayed its power by carving a canyon through 2,500 feet of many types of rock. The canyon gets its name from the shadows in its narrow depths and the black rocks and shrubs that form its sides.
- *Great Sand Dunes National Monument:* Near Alamosa, Colorado. Mountain torrents that have crumbled the Sangre de Cristo Mountains to sand and the winds that sweep the San Luis Valley have turned this land into Saharalike dunes, the most striking display on the continent.

Connecticut

- AMPHIBOLITE: East of Saybrook Highway and south of road from Chester to the railroad station, Middlesex County.
- AMPHIBOLITE: West of Nut Plains, town of Guilford, New Haven County.
- APLITE: Millstone quarries, Waterford, New London County.
- ARKOSE (BROWNSTONE): Middletown, Middlesex County, at Old Brazos quarry.
- ARKOSE AND SCHIST: Southington, Hartford County.
- BASALT: Saltonstall Crescent just east of New Haven, New Haven County.

- CONGLOMERATE: South end of Lake Quassapaug, New Haven County.
- CONGLOMERATE AND QUARTZITE: Along road northwest from Madison Center across railroad, New Haven County.
- DIABASE: Dike in highway just east of Higganum, town of Haddam, Middlesex County.
- DOLOMITE: Northwest corner of North Stonington, New London County.
- GABBRO: Sweet Hill, Lebanon, New London County.
- GNEISS: Quarry at Arnold, town of Haddam, Middlesex County.
- GNEISS: Quarries at Sterling, Windham County.
- GNEISS: East River station, Madison, New Haven County.
- GNEISS: Quarry 1/2 mile south of Naval Station, Groton, New London County.
- GRANITE: Flatrock and Goos quarries, New London, New London County.
- GRANITE: Lantern Hill, North Stonington, New London County.
- GRANITE AND QUARTZ: Redstone Ridge, Stonington, New London County.
- GRANITE PORPHYRY: Railroad cut at Dudley.
- LIMESTONE AND SCHIST: Old Silver mine, Connecticut State Hospital, Middletown, Middlesex County.
- PEGMATITE: Cobalt, 5 miles south of Hurd Park Road, Middlesex County.
- PEGMATITE: McCurdy quarry on Duck River near Lyme Village, New London County.
- PEGMATITE: Walden Farm, 5 miles northeast of Portland, Middlesex County.
- PEGMATITE: 1 mile northwest of Goshen Point, Waterford, New London County.
- PEGMATITE: Andrews quarry east of state highway from Portland to East Hartford, Middlesex County.
- PEGMATITE AND GNEISS: Hale quarry and Collins Hill (Strickland) quarry at Portland, Middlesex County.
- PHYLLITE: South of Harrisville, Windham County.
- PHYLLITE: 1 mile north of Pomfret Street Village on road to South Woodstock, Windham County.

- QUARTZ: Swanton Hill, North Stonington, New London County.
- QUARTZITE: Quarries at Chaffee's Place in Stafford, Tolland County.
- QUARTZITE: Near county line north of Rockland, town of Durham, Middlesex County.
- SCHIST: Along road from East Haddam Bridge to Moodus, Middlesex County.
- SCHIST: Near Bolton, Tolland County.
- TONALITE: Killingworth, Middlesex County.

Florida

- CONGLOMERATE: In Caloosahatchee River, upstream from mouth of Banana Creek, Hendry County.
- DOLOMITE: Along Ancilla River north of bridge on Highway 257, Jefferson County.
- FULLER'S EARTH: Mine at Quincy, Gadsden County.
- GYPSUM: 3 miles east of Christmas, Orange County.
- LIMESTONE: Quarry at Crystal River, Citrus County.
- LIMESTONE: 3 miles northeast of Lamont, also below Lamont to Nutall Rise along the Ancilla River, Jefferson County.
- LIMESTONE: Big Blue Spring on the Wacissa River, Jefferson County.
- LIMESTONE: Along Lloyd creek, north of Lloyd, Jefferson County.
- LIMESTONE: Hillsborough Bay area, Tampa, Pinellas County.
- LIMESTONE: Along the Apalachicola River in Jackson, Godsden, and Liberty counties.
- LIMESTONE: Sand Key to Loggerhead Key, Key West.
- LIMESTONE: Ocala, Marion County.
- LIMESTONE: Pits at Inglis, Levy County.
- LIMESTONE: Along Tamiami Trail, in Collins and Monroe Counties, such as at Sunniland Limestone Company, Sunniland.
- LIMESTONE: Blowing Rock, north of Boca Raton, Palm Beach County.
- LIMESTONE: Siesta Key, near Sarasota, Sarasota County.

- LIMESTONE AND COQUINA: Crystal River, Citrus County; Newberry, Polk County; Kedrick, Marion County; Reddick, Marion County; Martin, Marion County; S.M. Wall quarry, Alachua County; Williston Shell Rock Company quarry, Alachusa County; Suwanee Limerock Company quarry, Suwanee County; along Suwanee River, especially at Ellaville, Falmouth Springs, near Live Oak and Crystal River; 2 miles south of Crawfordsville, Wahulla County; Alum Bluff, Liberty County; Oak Grove on Yellow River, Okaloosa County; Brooks Sink, Bradford County.
- OOLITIC LIMESTONE: Le Jeune and Sunset roads, Coral Gables, Dade County.
- MARL (WITH LIMESTONE): Along the Caloosahatchee River between Fort Thompson and Ortona Locks, Hendry County.
- MARL: At Alum Bluff on Apalachicola River 4 miles north of the bridge, Liberty County.
- MARL: Red Bay, Walton County.
- PHOSPHATE ROCK: Quarries in Gilchrist County.
- PHOSPHATE ROCK: Camp Phosphate Enterprise, south of Dunnellen, Marion County.
- PHOSPHATE ROCK: Quarries near Bartow, Polk County.

Georgia

- CONGLOMERATE AND SCHIST: 1 mile east of Canton in south fork of Town Creek, Cherokee County.
- DIORITE: 3 miles northwest of Jefferson, Jackson County.
- DOLOMITE AND SCHIST: Quarries to north of Whitestone, Gilmer County.
- GABBRO: 8 miles southeast of Elberton, and 13 miles east of Elberton at Bethlehem Church, Elbert County.
- GNEISS: Along southeast side of the Chattahoochee River in quarries in Atlanta, Fulton County.
- GNEISS: 3 miles northeast and 4 miles east of Jasper, Pickens County.
- GNEISS: Near Burton, Rabun County.
- GNEISS (AUGEN): West of Dallas, Paulding County.
- GNEISS (BIOTITE): East of Cherry Log, Gilmer County.

- GNEISS (BIOTITE): Tiger Creek, at Lakemont, Rabun County.
- GNEISS (EPIDOTE): 5 miles east of Phinizy, Columbia County.
- GNEISS (HORNBLENDE): 1 1/2 miles north of Toccoa, Stephens County.
- GNEISS (HORNBLENDE): 3 1/2 miles south of Dennis, Putnam County.
- GNEISS AND GRANITE: Athens, Clarke County.
- GRANITE: Near Villa Rica, Paulding County.
- GRANITE: Stone Mountain, Atlanta, DeKalb County.
- GRANITE PORPHYRY: South of Palmetto, Fulton County.
- GRANITE AND GNEISS: Near Lithonia, DeKalb County.
- GRAYWACKE: Quarries near Dawsonville, Dawson County.
- MARBLE: Old copper mine 1 mile south of Canton, Cherokee County.
- MARBLE: 2 miles south of Gainesville, Hall County.
- MARBLE AND GNEISS: Quarries in Long Swamp Valley at Tate and at Marble Hill, Pickens County.
- MYLONITE: 1 1/2 miles north of Neel's Gap, Union County.
- PEGMATITE IN GNEISS: At Rudicil Mill, 4 miles south of Orange, Cherokee County.
- PHYLLITE: Hamburg, Washington County.
- PHYLLITE: Belair, Richmond County.
- QUARTZITE: Terrell property northeast of Gainesville, Hall County.
- QUARTZITE: Conley quarry, Fulton County.
- QUARTZITE: Along Highway 108 east of Jasper to Ellijay, Rickens–Gilmer Counties.
- QUARTZITE: 12 miles north of Cartersville and east of U.S. 411 just north of Bartow County line in quarry at Dripping Spring, Gordon County.
- QUARTZITE: In Weisner quarry on east side of U.S. 411, 12 1/2 miles north of Cartersville, Bartow County.
- QUARTZITE: Gorge of Tallulah River, Rabun County.
- QUARTZITE: Sweetgum, Fannin County.
- SANDSTONE: Cloudland, Chattooga County.
- SANDSTONE WITH RHYOLITE AND TUFF: Graves Mountain, Lincoln County.
- SCHIST: Near Covington, Newton County.

- SCHIST (MICA): Consolidated and Findley mines near Dahlonega, Lumpkin County.
- SCHIST (MUSCOVITE): Between Vanna and Hartwell and in quarries at Hartwell, Hart County.
- SCHIST (PYRITIC): In brick company quarry 2 miles south of Emerson, Bartow County.
- SLATE: Quarry at Mineral Bluff, Fannin County.
- SLATE: 3/4 mile north of Hopewell Church, Cherokee County.
- TALC: Holly Springs, Cherokee County.
- TALC: Chatsworth, Murray County.

Hawaii

- BASALT: Puhi quarry, Kauai.
- BASALT: Kualapuu quarry, Molokai.
- BASALT: Kailua, quarries at Hilo, Hawaii.
- LIMESTONE: West of Kekaha, Kauai.
- LIMESTONE (CORAL): Quarries near Haleiwa and Waimanalo, Oahu.

National Parks

- *Hawaii Volcanoes National Park:* On the island of Hawaii. The newest state brought into the Union two of the world's mightiest active volcanoes, Mauna Loa and Kilauea. Facilities of the park provide unique opportunities to see at first hand the fiery forces of nature at work.
- *Haleakala National Park:* Near Kahului, on the island of Maui. Here a great crater can be explored on foot, set in a junglelike rain forest growing in the fertile volcanic soil.

Idaho

- ANDESITE: Crystal Butte, 18 miles north of St. Anthony, Fremont County.
- ARAGONITE: Along west bank of Wood River between Bellevue and Hailey, north of mouth of Mammoth Gulch, Blaine County.
- BASALT: Near Moscow, Latah County.

- BASALT: 5 miles below Glenns Ferry, along the Snake River, Elmore County.
- BASALT: Warm Spring Creek, northwest of Hailey, Blaine County.
- BASALT: East of Boise, Ada County.
- BASALT: Bluff on banks of Snake River near King Hill, Elmore County.
- BASALT (LAVA TUNNELS): 6 miles northeast of Dubois, Clark County.
- BASALT (WITH NEPHELINE): 24 miles east of Blackfoot, on ridge on north side of Wood Creek, Bingham County.
- CONGLOMERATE: Moonlight mine near Pocatello, Bannock County.
- DIABASE: Post Falls, Kootenai County.
- DOLOMITE (AND ANKERITE): Mines around Kellogg and along Pine Creek, Shoshone County.
- DOLOMITE (AND MARBLE): At Lakeview on the south shore of Lake Pend d'Oreille, and at Bayview on the west shore, Bonner County.
- GEODES (IN LAVA): In upper valley of Big Lost River, Custer County.
- GNEISS: At head of Wildhorse Canyon on east side of Hyndman Peak, Custer County.
- GRANITE: Deadwood Gulch just off the road from Oro Grande to Elk City, Idaho County.
- GRANITE (AND SLATE): On Beauty Bay Creek near Beauty Bay, Lake Coeur d'Alene, Kootenai County.
- GRANODIORITE: At head of Minnie Gulch near Hailey, Blaine County.
- GYPSUM: 3 miles east of Montpelier on the east side of Montpelier Canyon, Bear Lake County.
- LIMESTONE: Fort Hall mine, Fort Hall (on Indian reservation), Bingham County.
- LIMESTONE (AND GRANITE): West of Hailey, Blaine County.
- MARBLE: Yellow Pine, Valley County.
- MARBLE: In mines of the Seven Devils Mountains, Adams County.
- MARBLE (WITH DIOPSIDE): On west side of Hyndman Peak at head of east fork of Wood River, Blaine County.

- MONZONITE: Near Gem, Shoshone County.
- MONZONITE: Along Eightmile Creek, 12 miles west of Leadore, Lemhi County.
- MONZONITE (PORPHYRY): Along Lieberg Trail on southwest side of Chilco Mountain, south of Lake Pend d'Oreille, Kootenai County.
- PEGMATITE: In mica mines, 3 to 6 miles north of Avon, Latah County.
- PEGMATITE: Shafer Creek, Idaho City, Boise County.
- PERLITE: Spencer opal mines, near Spencer, Clark County.
- PHOSPHATE ROCK: Waterloo mine, Montpelier, Bear Lake County.
- PHOSPHATE ROCK: As pellets at Soda Springs, Caribou County.
- PORPHYRY: On ledge paralleling Panther Creek 6 miles below its headwaters, May, Lemhi County.
- PORPHYRY (GRANITE): Mackay, Custer County.
- PORPHYRY (TRACHYTE): On Corral Creek near Soldier Mountain, Corral, Camas County.
- QUARTZITE (AND SLATE): Mine on Gorge Gulch 1 mile north of Burke, Shoshone County.
- SANDSTONE: 1 mile south of Salmon, Lemhi County.
- SANDSTONE: Along Moore creek, Idaho City, Boise County.
- SCHIST: Along Forestry Service road along Carpenter Creek upstream from St. Maries River, Benewah County.
- SCHIST (WITH ASBESTOS): 14 miles southeast of Kamiah, Lewis County.
- SERPENTINE: Queen of Hills mine, 1 1/2 miles west of Bellevue, Blaine County.
- SERPENTINE: North of Ashton, Fremont County.
- SLATE: Along Prichard Creek in mines east of Murray, Shoshone County.
- SLATE: Stanley mine, Burke, Shoshone County.
- SLATE (GRAPHITIC): On Trail Creek, Ketchum, Blaine County.
- SLATE (IN TALUS): Along Summit Creek at Ketchum-Mackay Road, Custer County.
- TUFF: 35 miles south-southeast of Bruneau, Owhyee County.

National Monument

- *Craters of the Moon National Monument:* Near Arco, Idaho. As its name implies, this area is a weird expanse of craters, cinder cones, lava fields, and tubes formed when molten rock welled from a great rift less than 1,000 years ago.

Iowa

- ANHYDRITE: Sperry, Des Moines County.
- CALCITE: Northwest of Central City, Linn County.
- CALCITE: Cresco, Howard County.
- CALCITE (SATIN SPAR): Pella, Marion County.
- CHERT: Quarries near Grant and Stennett, Montgomery County, and near Mount Pleasant, Henry County.
- COAL BALLS: Mines in Knoxville–Oskaloosa area, Marion and Mahaska counties.
- CONCRETIONS (CLAY IRONSTONE): Big Sioux River valley, on west Iowa line.
- CONE-IN-CONE: 5 miles north of Stratford, near Belle Mills Park, Hamilton County.
- CONGLOMERATE: Coburg, Montgomery County.
- DOLOMITE: Quarry at Keswick, Keokuk County.
- DOLOMITE: Quarry at Coralville, Johnson County.
- DOLOMITE: Southeast of Grand Mound, Clinton County.
- GEODES: Mudcreek, Henry County.
- GEODES: Des Moines River from Keosauqua to Farmington, Van Buren County.
- GEODES: Quarry north of Sandusky, Lee County.
- GEODES: Quarries around Chapin, Franklin County.
- GEODES: West Union, Fayette County.
- GEODES: Millville, Winneshiek County.
- GEODES (COLDWATER AGATE): Near Keswick, Ollie, and Harper quarries, Keokuk County.
- GRAVEL: At Sabula, Bellevue, Clinton, Muscatine, and Dubuque along the Mississippi River.
- GRAVEL: At Hawarden and Akron along the Big Sioux River and Cherokee on the Little Sioux River.
- GYPSUM: Mine at Fort Dodge, Webster County.

- GYPSUM: Centerville, Appanoose County.
- GYPSUM: Sperry, Des Moines County.
- GYPSUM: In shale along Highway 12, Plymouth County.
- GYPSUM (SELENITE): In shale at Mason City, Cerro Gordo County.
- LIMESTONE: Pint's quarry, Waterloo, Black Hawk County.
- LIMESTONE: With limonite at Iron Hill, northeast of Waukon, Allamakee County.
- LIMESTONE: Wendling quarry, Moscow, Muscatine County.
- LIMESTONE AND CALCITE: Farmington, Van Buren County.
- SANDSTONE: Bluffs near Lansing and New Albin, Allamakee County.
- SANDSTONE: 1 mile west of Lewis, Cass County.
- SEPTARIA: In coal strip mines in Marion, Mahaska, and Monroe counties.
- SHALE: In river bluffs at Sioux City, Woodbury County.
- SHALES: At quarry in Centerville, Appanoose County.

Kentucky

- CALCITE: Two Brothers mine, 5 miles west of Marion, Crittenden County.
- CANNEL COAL: Cannel City, Morgan County.
- CONGLOMERATE: Natural Bridge, Powell County.
- CONGLOMERATE IN SANDSTONE: Cumberland Falls, Whitley County.
- GEODES: Along Green River near New Bethel, Lincoln County.
- GYPSUM: New Providence formation, Marion County.
- PERIDOTITE: Mine north of View, Crittenden County.
- PERIDOTITE: Vein dike, 7 miles southwest of Marion, Crittenden County.
- PERIDOTITE: Northeast of Marion in bed of Claylick Creek, Crittenden County.
- PERIDOTITE: Near Caldwell, Crittenden, and Livingston counties.
- PERIDOTITE AND SERPENTINE: 1 mile southwest of Sheridan, Crittenden County.
- PERIDOTITE AND SERPENTINE: Sills and dikes along Ison Creek near Ison-Johnson School and between Ison

and Hambleton creeks, Elliott County.

- PERIDOTITE PORPHYRY IN LIMESTONE: Hutson Zinc mine 3 miles southwest of Salem, Livingston County.
- SANDSTONE: On Highway 927, 3 miles southwest of Parkers Lake, McCreary County.
- SERPENTINE: Dike 1 1/2 miles north of Bethany Church, Farmersville, Caldwell County.
- SERPENTINE IN LIMESTONE: Old Jim Dikes, 4 1/2 miles west of Marion, Crittenden County.
- SHALE: Along Highway 25, 10 miles east of Cumberland Falls, Whitley County.
- TRAVERTINE: Elk Lick Falls, Fayette County.

National Park

- *Mammoth Cave National Park:* Northeast of Bowling Green, Kentucky. The legendary cave with its 7 miles of easily accessible caverns in the limestone, a maze of underground lakes and rivers, fantastic cave formations, and huge underground chambers. All these can be enjoyed on federally guided tours.

Maine

- GRANITE: Quarries at New Limerick, Aroostook County; Brunswick, Freeport, Pownal, North Yarmouth, and Westbrook, Cumberland County; Jay and Phillips, Franklin County; Blue Hill, Brooksville, Dedham, Deer Island, Franklin, Long Island, Mount Desert, Orland, Sedgwick, Stonington, Sullivan, Swans Island, and Tremont, Hancock County; Hallowell, Kennebec County; Muscle Ridge, St. George, South Thomaston, and Vinalhaven, Knox County; Bristol, Waldoboro, and Whitefield, Lincoln County; Fryeburg, Oxford, and Woodstock, Oxford County; Hermon, Penobscot County; Guilford, Piscataquis County; Hartland and Norridgewock, Somerset County; Frankfort, Lincolnville, Searsport, and Swanville, Waldo County; Addison, Baileyville, Calais, Centerville, Jonesboro, Jonesport, Marshfield, and Milbridge, Washington County; Alfred, Biddeford, Hollis, North Kennebunkport,

South Berwick, Wells, and York, York County.

- CONGLOMERATE: Mouth of Great Works River, South Berwick, York County.
- PEGMATITES: Auburn, Minot, and Poland, Androscoggin County; Baldwin, Brunswick, Casco, and Pownal, Cumberland County; Township E, Franklin County; Vienna, Kennebec County; Warren and Cushing, Knox County; Edgecomb, Waldoboro, and Wiscasset, Lincoln County; Albany, Andover, Andover North, Andover West, Batchelders Grant, Buckfield, Canton, Denmark, Gilead, Greenwood, Hartford, Hebron, Hiram, Lovell, Mason, Mexico, Newry, Norway, Oxford, Paris, Peru, Roxbury, Rumford, Stoneham, Stow, and Waterford, Oxford County; Lakeville, Penobscot County; Bowdoin, Bowdoinham, Georgetown, Phippsburg, Topsham, West Bath, and Woolwich, Sagadahoc County; Lyman and Waterboro, York County.
- QUARTZITE: Along Piscataqua River, Kittery, York County.

National Park

- *Acadia National Park:* Bar Harbor, Maine. A group of islands and a bit of coastline that demonstrate vividly in their cliffs and inlets the effects of the continental glaciers on the remodeling of the Atlantic seaboard.

Massachusetts

- AMPHIBOLITE: East of Middleton, on Peabody Street, Essex County.
- AMPHIBOLITE: Quarry north of Danvers and west and east of Goodale Cemetery there, Essex County.
- AMPHIBOLITE: Leverett, Franklin County.
- ANDESITE AND DIABASE: Black Rock Island off Nautasket, Norfolk County.
- APLITE: Hill 2 miles south of Uxbridge, Worcester County.
- APLITE: 1 mile northeast of Westboro, Worcester County.
- APLITE: South Peru, Berkshire County.
- ARKOSE: Foxbrook, south of road over West Mountain, in Bernardston, Franklin County.

- ARKOSE: Leyden Glen, northwest of Greenfield, Franklin County.
- BRECCIA: Northwest of Harvard Village, Worcester County.
- CONGLOMERATE: Pondville station, Norfolk, Norfolk County.
- CONGLOMERATE: Dighton, Bristol County.
- CONGLOMERATE: Brookline, Norfolk County.
- CONGLOMERATE: Hill south of Dalton station, Berkshire County.
- DIABASE: Mount Tom, Hampshire County.
- DIABASE: 1/8 mile east of Louisville, Hampshire County.
- DIABASE: Smith Ferry, Hampden County.
- DIABASE: Northwest of Pierces Pond, Peabody, Essex County.
- DIABASE: Along the road from Milford to Hopkinton, Worcester County.
- DIORITE (QUARTZ): South of Howe, Essex County.
- DIORITE: 1 1/2 miles north of Beverly airport, and cut by basalt, diabase, and pegmatite dikes between Salem and Lynn, Essex County.
- DIORITE AND APLITE: 2 1/2 miles northeast of Belchertown, Hampshire County.
- FELSITE PORPHYRY: Marblehead, Essex County.
- GABBRO: Egg Rock, Nahant Bay, Essex County.
- GABBRO: 2 1/2 miles southwest of New Braintree, Worcester County.
- GABBRO AND DIORITE: Salem Neck, Salem, Essex County.
- GNEISS: Washington, Berkshire County.
- GNEISS: Uxbridge, Worcester County.
- GNEISS: Oak Hill, north of North Adams, Berkshire County.
- GNEISS: Alderman quarries, Becket, Berkshire County.
- GNEISS: East of Woodbury Point and along Beverly Shore, Essex County.
- GNEISS (AUGEN): U.S. 1 and State 144 intersection, Danvers, Essex County.
- GNEISS (AUGEN): Goodale and Sons of Jacob cemeteries, Danvers, Essex County.
- GNEISS (QUARTZ): Northwest corner of Washington, Berkshire County.

- GNEISS AND GRANODIORITE: Quarries at Monson, Hampshire County.
- GRANITE: North Common Hill, Quincy, Norfolk County.
- GRANITE: Quarry, Rockport, Essex County.
- GRANITE: South of Ruggles Creek, Quincy, Norfolk County.
- GRANITE: Rattlesnake Hill, Blue Hills, Norfolk County.
- GRANITE: Hill north of Spring Pond, Peabody, Essex County.
- GRANITE: Old quarry at South Lynnfield, Essex County.
- GRANITE: Endicott Junior College, Beverly, Essex County.
- GRANITE: Beverly airport, Danvers, Essex County.
- GRANITE: Ledge Hill, Pawtucketville, Lowell, Middlesex County.
- GRANITE: Ballard quarry, Worcester, Worcester County.
- GRANITE: Quarry east of Florence, Northampton, Hampshire County.
- GRANITE (PINK): Fayville quarries, Milford, Worcester County.
- GRANITE PORPHYRY: Indian Hill, east of Marlborough, Middlesex County.
- GRANODIORITE: At Topsfield School and in railroad cut east of fairgrounds, Topsfield, Essex County.
- GRANODIORITE: Along Endicott Road, Boxford, Essex County.
- GRANODIORITE: North of crossing of Nichols Brook by Old Copper Mine Road, Topsfield, Essex County.
- GRAPHITE: "Lead mine," Sturbridge, Worcester County.
- GREENSTONE (ALTERED BASALT) WITH SANDSTONE: Along Old Copper Mine Road in Topsfield, Essex County.
- GREENSTONE PORPHYRY (ALTERED BASALT): South end of ridge in bend of Ipswich River, 1/3 mile west of Middleton Colony, Middleton, Essex County.
- HEMATITE IN SANDSTONE: Along U.S. 1, 1/4 mile northwest of Hill Street and Rowley Bridge Road in Topsfield, Essex County.
- LIMESTONE: Northwest of Old Copper Mine Road and 1/3 mile north of Nichols Brook, Topsfield, Essex County.
- LIMESTONE: Quarries in Lee, Berkshire County.
- NEPHELINE SYENITE: Winter Island and Cat Cove, Salem Neck, Salem, Essex County.

- PEGMATITE: Hollow Ledge, West Chesterfield, Hampshire County.
- PEGMATITE: East shore of Mackerel Cove, Beverly, Essex County.
- PEGMATITE: At Barrus farm, 2 1/2 miles north of Goshen, Hampshire County.
- PEGMATITE: From New Salem Center into Orange, Franklin County.
- PEGMATITE: At Isinglass Hill, 1/2 mile east of West Chesterfield, Hampshire County.
- PEGMATITE: At iron bridge in South Windsor, Berkshire County.
- PEGMATITE: 1 mile north of Chester Village, Hampden County.
- PEGMATITE WITH APLITE: At Long Hill, Sterling, Worcester County.
- PHYLLITE: Quarries at Lancaster and Harvard, Worcester County.
- PHYLLITE (GARNET): Along road from Wendell to New Salem, Franklin County.
- PORPHYRY: Allen Head, Prides Crossing, Essex County.
- QUARTZITE: Quarry at Lowell City, Middlesex County.
- QUARTZITE: Southborough, Worcester County.
- QUARTZITE: Quarry at Haverhill, Essex County.
- QUARTZITE: Oakdale, Worcester County.
- RHYOLITE: Marblehead Neck, Essex County.
- SANDSTONE: East Longmeadow quarries, Hampden County.
- SERPENTINE: Old mine, Chester, Hampden County.
- SERPENTINE: Osborn's quarry, Blandford, Hampden County.
- SERPENTINE: Quarry at Westfield, Hampden County.
- SERPENTINE WITH TALC: Quarries at Windsor Falls, Berkshire County.
- SCHIST: Near Charlemont, Franklin County.
- SCHIST: East of Bare Hill Pond, Harvard, Worcester County.
- SCHIST: Ledges at mill at Whitmores Ferry, Sunderland, Worcester County.
- SCHIST (BIOTITE): North of Main Street, Marlborough, Middlesex County.

- SCHIST (CORDIERITE): Shumway Hill, Sturbridge, Worcester County.
- SLATE: Hoppin Hill, North Attleboro, Bristol County.
- SLATE: Wrentham, just north of Rhode Island line, Norfolk County.
- SLATE: Weymouth, Norfolk County.
- SLATE: Hayward creek, Quincy, Norfolk County.
- SLATE: Dorchester district of Boston, Suffolk County.
- SYENITE: Arlington Heights, northwest of Boston, Middlesex County.
- SYENITE AND DIABASE: Coney Island, Salem Harbor, Salem, Essex County.
- TONALITE: 1 mile northeast of Sciantic, Hampden County.
- TONALITE: Crossroad east of New Braintree, Worcester County.
- TONALITE BRECCIA: City quarry, Northampton, Hampshire County.
- TUFF: North and east of Smith Ferry, Hampden County.
- TUFF WITH RHYOLITE: Four Corners on Newburyport Turnpike, south of Glen Mills in Rowley, Essex County.
- VERMICULITE: Bramanville in Millbury, Worcester County.

Michigan

- ARKOSE: Near Norway, Dickinson County.
- BASALT: Most of the mine dumps in Ontonagon, Houghton, and Keweenaw counties in the Keweenaw peninsula, such as Mass and Rockland in Ontonagon County, South Range, Baltic, Painesdale, and Quincy in Houghton County, and Osceola, Ahmeek, Mohawk, Central, Cliff, Phoenix, and Copper Falls in Keweenaw County.
- BASALT: Porcupine Mountains State Park, Ontonagon County.
- BASALT: St. Ignace, Mackinac County.
- BRECCIA: Mackinac Island, Mackinac County.
- CONGLOMERATE: Dan's Point on lake west of Copper Harbor, Keweenaw County, and in many of the mine dumps of the peninsula, such as Allouez.
- CONGLOMERATE: Devil's Icebox, Quinnesec, Dickinson County.

- CONGLOMERATE: Port Austin and Grindstone City, Huron County.
- CONGLOMERATE (JASPER): Tawas, Iosco County.
- DOLOMITE: Quarry near Ozark, Mackinac County.
- DOLOMITE: Scofield quarry northeast of Maybee, Monroe County.
- DOLOMITE: North end of Mackinac Straits Bridge, Mackinac County.
- DOLOMITE: Quarries at Cedarville, Mackinac County.
- DOLOMITE: Quarries at Manistique, Schoolcraft County.
- DOLOMITE: Quarry 1/2 mile east of Metropolitan, Dickinson County.
- GRANITE: Near Republic, Marquette County.
- GRANITE IN DOLOMITE: Metrolite quarry, 2 1/2 miles east of Felch, Dickinson County.
- GREENSTONE (ALTERED BASALT): 7 miles west of Marquette, Marquette County.
- GYPSUM: Mines at Alabaster, Tawas City, and 1 1/2 miles south of National City, Iosco County.
- HEMATITE: Athens mine dumps, southeast of Negaunee, Marquette County.
- JASPILITE: Jasper Knob and in road cuts near Ishpeming, Marquette County.
- LIMESTONE: Quarries near Bellevue, Eaton County.
- LIMESTONE: Bluffs near Fayette, Garden Peninsula, Delta County.
- LIMESTONE: Quarries at Pigeon, near Bayport, Huron County.
- LIMESTONE: Quarries at Au Gres, Arenac County.
- LIMESTONE: Dundee, Monroe County.
- LIMESTONE: Quarry at Rogers City, Presque Isle County.
- LIMESTONE: Quarry at Rockport, Alpena County.
- LIMESTONE: Quarry 2 miles west of Petoskey, Emmet County.
- QUARTZITE: Quarry on U.S. 41, 3 1/2 miles southeast of Marquette, Marquette County.
- SANDSTONE: Stable Road 3 1/2 miles east of Laurium, Houghton County.
- SANDSTONE: Quarries near Napoleon, Jackson County.
- SANDSTONE: Along U.S. 41 between L'Anse and Baraga, Baraga County.

- SANDSTONE: Quarries at Ionia and Grand Ledge, Ionia County.
- SANDSTONE: Pictured Rocks on south shore of Lake Superior east of Munising, Alger County.
- SCHIST (CHLORITE): Mine dumps 1/2 mile east of Michigamme, Marquette County.
- SERPENTINE: Quarry northwest of Ishpeming, Marquette County.
- SHALE: Coldwater quarry near Union City, Branch County.
- SLATE: Quarries at Huron Bay and L'Anse, Baraga County.
- SLATE AND QUARTZITE: 2 1/2 miles east of Negaunee, Marquette County.

National Parks and Monuments

- *Isle Royale National Park:* An island reached by boat from Copper Harbor, Michigan. The largest island in Lake Superior, which is the largest body of fresh water in the world. Isle Royale is a scenic land of lava flows where a prehistoric people mined copper.
- *Pictured Rocks National Seashore:* North of Munising, Michigan. A region of lakeshore cliffs, caves, pillars, and strange formations eroded in sandstone, long famous for its color and dramatic landscape.

Nebraska

- ARAGONITE, DOLOMITE, AND SHALE: Quarries at Plattsmouth, Cass County.
- CALCITE: Louisville quarries, Cass County.
- CALCITE: Weeping Water and near Dunbar, Otoe County.
- CHALK: Niobrara, Knox County.
- CHALK: Franklin, Franklin County.
- CHALK: Alma, Harlan County.
- CHALK: Chadron, Dawes County.
- CHERT: Quarries at Weeping Water, Cass County.
- GEODES: Quarry near Wymore, Gage County.
- GEODES (CALCITE) IN SHALE: In creeks near Brock and Johnson, Nemaha County.
- GEODES (CALCITE) IN SHALE: Humboldt, Richardson County.

- GEODES (CALCITE) IN SHALE: Douglas and Burr, Otoe County, often with gypsum.
- GYPSUM: In Pierre shale and Niobrara chalk along Republican River in Franklin and Hardin counties.
- GYPSUM: Newcastle, Dixon County.
- LIMESTONE: Fort Calhoun, Washington County.
- LIMESTONE: Angora, 2 miles east of Angora Hill, Morrill County.
- LIMESTONE: Holmesville, Wymore, and Blue Springs, Gage County.
- LIMESTONE: Quarries at Garland, Seward County.
- LIMESTONE: Quarries at Fairbury, Jefferson County.
- LIMESTONE: Quarries at Hebron, Thayer County.
- SAND CRYSTALS: Orella, Sioux County.
- SAND CRYSTALS: Chadron and Crawford, Dawes County.
- SEPTARIA IN SHALE: 20 miles north of Chadron, Dawes County.
- SEPTARIA IN SHALE: Hay Springs, Sheridan County.
- SHALE: In Middle Creek, southwest of Pleasant Dale, Seward County.
- SHALE: Dubois, Pawnee County.
- SHALE: Brownsville, Nemaha County.
- SHALE: Denton and Lincoln, Lancaster County.
- SHALE: Valparaiso, Saunders County.

New Hampshire

- AMPHIBOLITE (HORNBLENDE): South of South Keene, Cheshire County.
- DIORITE: East end of Rock Road, Seabrook, Rockingham County.
- DIORITE AND APLITE: Intersection of U.S. 4 and Highway 108, Durham, Strafford County.
- DIORITE AND PEGMATITE: Gap Mountain, 3 miles southwest of Mount Monadnock, Cheshire County.
- GNEISS, SCHIST, AND AMPHIBOLITE: North Beach, and also at Farragut Hotel, both Rye, Rockingham County.
- GRANITE: Quarry 1 mile south of Marlborough, Cheshire County.
- GRANITE: North side of Webb Hill, Fitzwilliam Depot, Cheshire County.

- GRANITE: Quarries at Roxbury, Troy, and South Keene, Cheshire County.
- GRANITE AND GNEISS: In fluorite mines southwest of Westmorland, Cheshire County.
- GRANITE AND PEGMATITE: Breakfast Hills, Rye, Rockingham County.
- PEGMATITE: Moat Mountain, Carroll County.
- PEGMATITE: Globe mine, 2 miles northeast of Springfield, Sullivan County.
- PEGMATITE: Bala Colony and Porter quarries, Acworth, Sullivan County.
- PEGMATITE: Keene mine and Turner quarry, Alstead, Cheshire County.
- PEGMATITE: Ruggles quarry, Grafton Center, Grafton County.
- PEGMATITE: Chickering and Damasiak quarries, Walpole, Cheshire County.
- PEGMATITE: Fletcher and Palermo mines, Grafton County.
- PEGMATITE: Houghton Ledge, Sullivan, Cheshire County.
- PEGMATITE: Pinnacle and Bald Hill, west and northwest of Roxbury Center, Cheshire County.
- PEGMATITE: 1 mile north of Marlborough, Cheshire County.
- QUARTZITE: Cedar Point, Durham, Strafford County.
- QUARTZITE (RED) AND MICA SCHIST: Along road to Halfway House on Mount Monadnock, Cheshire County.
- QUARTZITE: Ashuelot River gorge, north of Troy, Cheshire County.
- SCHIST: Minnewawa Gorge, 1 mile east of Marlborough, Cheshire County.
- SCHIST: Near Bellamy River dam, Madbury, Strafford County.
- SCHIST (GARNET) AND QUARTZITE: Beech Hill near Dublin Lake, Cheshire County.
- SLATE: Lee Five Corners, Lee, Strafford County.
- SLATE: South bank of Cocheco River, east of Dover, Strafford County.

New Jersey

- ARGILLITE (HARDENED SHALE): North of Pittstown, Hunterdon County.

- BASALT: Dike at Flemington, Copper Hill, and Rocktown, Hunterdon County.
- BASALT: Between New Vernon and Green Village, Morris County.
- BASALT: Sand Hill on U.S. 1, east of Princeton, Mercer County.
- BASALT: Houdaille Materials Company quarry, Bound Brook, Somerset County.
- BASALT: Garret Mountain Reserve in First Watchung Mountain, Passaic County.
- BRECCIA (VOLCANIC): Libertyville, Sussex County.
- CONGLOMERATE: Green Pond, Morris County.
- CONGLOMERATE: Cliff along Delaware River north of Fredericktown, Hunterdon County.
- CONGLOMERATE: Bergen Hill, Hudson County.
- DIABASE: Palisades of Hudson River north from Fort Lee, Bergen County.
- DIABASE: Sourland Mountain, north of Hopewell, Mercer County.
- DUNITE: In central formation of cliffs along Hudson River at Fort Lee, Bergen County.
- GABBRO AND GNEISS: Trenton, Mercer County.
- GLAUCONITE MARL: Hornerstown, Monmouth County.
- GLAUCONITE MARL: Mullica Hill and Sewell, Gloucester County.
- GNEISS (IN BOULDERS): Near Montville, Morris County.
- GRAVEL: Between Frenchtown and Lambertville, along Delaware River, Hunterdon County.
- GRANITE: Dumps of old copper mines at Griggstown, Somerset County.
- HORNFELS: Near Princeton, Mercer County.
- LIMESTONE: Wallpack, Sussex County.
- LIMESTONE: Exposed along U.S. 46 in the Pequest Valley, Warren County.
- LIMESTONE: Limecrest quarry, Sparta, Sussex County; take Highway 15 for 2 1/2 miles west, then left 1 1/2 miles at quarry.
- LIMESTONE: Edison quarry, Rudeville, Sussex County.
- LIMESTONE: Near Clinton, Hunterdon County.
- LIMESTONE: Greenwood Lake, Hudson County.

- LIMESTONE: South of Belvidere, Warren County.
- LIMESTONE AND SHALE: Vernon on the New York line, Sussex County.
- LIMESTONE: Northwest side of the Minisink Valley north of Kittatinny Mountain and along the Delaware River, Sussex County.
- LIMESTONE AND SHALE: Phillipsburg, Warren County.
- LIMESTONE AND SHALE: In the Musconetcong Valley southwest of Hackettstown, Warren County.
- MARBLE: Franklin and Sparta, Sussex County.
- NEPHELINE SYENITE: Beemerville, Sussex County.
- QUARTZITE: Peapack, Somerset County.
- QUARTZITE: Trenton, Mercer County.
- QUARTZITE: Along the southeast edge of the Kittatinny valley and south of Highlands at Clinton, Hunterdon County.
- QUARTZITE: Along Kittatinny Ridge, Warren and Sussex counties.
- QUARTZITE AND LIMESTONE: As boulders along Highway 202 northeast of Pompton, Passaic County.
- SANDSTONE (RED): Quarries at Stockton on the Delaware River, Hunterdon County.
- SANDSTONE (YELLOW): Near Princeton, Mercer County.
- SANDSTONE: At Wallpack Ridge in the Wallpack Bend of the Delaware River, Sussex County.
- SANDSTONE: Quarries at Paterson, Passaic County.
- SANDSTONE: Quarries at Newark, Essex County.
- SANDSTONE AND CONGLOMERATE: On the northwest border of the valley at Califon, Hunterdon County.
- SANDSTONE AND LAVA: From Boonton, Morris County, to Stony Point.
- SANDSTONE AND LAVA: Between Peapack and Lebanon, Hunterdon and Somerset Counties.
- SANDSTONE AND SHALE: Along the Raritan River, New Brunswick, Middlesex County.
- SERPENTINE: Quarries at Phillipsburg, Warren County.
- SERPENTINE: Castle Point, Hoboken, Hudson County.
- SHALE: Quarries near Somerville, Somerset County.
- SHALE AND ARGILLITE: At 80th Street and Tonnelle Avenue, North Bergen, Hudson County.

- SLATE: Near Columbus on the Delaware River, Burlington County.
- SLATE: Outcrops along U.S. 46 as it follows the Delaware River on the way to Bridgeville, Warren County.
- TALC AND HEMATITE: At Andover Iron mine 1 1/3 miles east of Andover, Sussex County.

New York

- ANORTHOSITE: Near Keene, Essex County.
- CHERT: 1 mile west of Ghent and at Stuyvesant Falls, Columbia County.
- CONGLOMERATE: 1 1/2 miles north of Elizaville and east of road to Manorton, Columbia County.
- CONGLOMERATE: Rysedorph Hill southeast of Rensselaer, Rensselaer County.
- CONGLOMERATE: Just south of Claverack, Columbia County.
- DIABASE: Suffern, Rockland County.
- DIABASE: Palisades of the Hudson River.
- DOLOMITE: Lockport, Niagara County.
- DOLOMITE: East and south of Middleville, Herkimer County.
- GABBRO: East Hampton, Suffolk County.
- GNEISS: Sedgwick Avenue and 161st Street, Bronx, New York.
- GNEISS (AUGEN): Harrisville, Lewis County.
- GNEISS (LIT-PAR-LIT): Near Ausable Falls, Essex County.
- GRANITE: Van Cortlandt Park, Bronx, New York.
- GRANITE: Palmer Hill quarries, Clinton County.
- LIMESTONE: Wappinger Falls, Dutchess County.
- LIMESTONE: Cement quarries near Catskill and Hudson, Greene County.
- LIMESTONE: Port Ewan near Rondout, Ulster County.
- LIMESTONE: Banks of Genesee River, Rochester, Monroe County.
- LIMESTONE: Hailsboro quarries, St. Lawrence County.
- LIMESTONE: Fogelsanger quarry, 2 1/2 miles east of Buffalo, Erie County.
- LIMESTONE AND MARBLE SKARN: North of Pitcairn, south of Camp Trefoil, St. Lawrence County.

- LIMESTONE WITH QUARTZITE: Ridges in shale from Linlithgo, Columbia County, to Barrytown, Dutchess County.
- LIMESTONE AND SHALE: Ash Hill quarry on Mount Merino, south of Hudson, Columbia County.
- MARBLE: Edwards mine, Edwards, St. Lawrence County.
- MARBLE: Seaman Avenue and Isham Street, Manhattan, New York.
- MARBLE: At Finlay farm, near Pierrepont, St. Lawrence County.
- MARBLE AND FELDSPAR: Southwest of Rossie, St. Lawrence County.
- PEGMATITE: South of DeKalb Junction on Highway 11, take Highway 33 east 3/4 mile to dirt road to quarry, St. Lawrence County.
- PEGMATITE: Woodcock Mountain, east of Overlook, Saratoga County.
- PEGMATITE: 169th Street and University Avenue, Bronx, New York.
- PERIDOTITE: Numerous dikes near Ithaca, Tompkins County.
- PHYLLITE: Annsville, just north of Peekskill, Westchester County.
- PHYLLITE: Jackson Corners, Dutchess County.
- QUARTZITE: 1 mile southeast of Germantown, Columbia County.
- QUARTZITE: Poughquag, 15 miles south of Poughkeepsie, Dutchess County.
- QUARTZITE WITH HEMATITE: Mount Tom at Church Hill, near Hudson, Columbia County.
- QUARTZITE AND MARBLE: Mitchell farm, Richville, St. Lawrence County.
- SANDSTONE (GRIT): Troy, east of Lansingburg, Rensselaer County.
- SANDSTONE AND SHALE: Austin Glen at Catskill and in Broom Street quarry, Greene County.
- SANDSTONE WITH SHALE: Along New York Central Railroad south of North Germantown, Columbia County.
- SHALE AND CONGLOMERATE: Fister's quarry, 1 1/2 miles southeast of Germantown, Columbia County.
- SALT (ROCK SALT): Mined on Cayuga Lake and Retsof, Livingston County.

- SERPENTINE: Quarry at Natural Bridge, Lewis County.
- SERPENTINE: Staten Island, New York, at Slossan Avenue exit of expressway.
- SERPENTINE (IN MARBLE): Quarry 1 mile southeast of Thurman, Warren County.
- SCHIST: West side of Harlem River Drive, north of 155th Street exit and near 180th Street, Bronx, New York.
- SCHIST AND GNEISS: Just east of Alexander Hamilton bridge, New York.
- SCHIST AND GNEISS: Morningside Heights, 110th Street between Columbus and Manhattan Avenues, New York.
- TALC: Loomis mine on Highway 58, northwest of Fowler, St. Lawrence County.
- TALC: Talcville and Balmat, St. Lawrence County.
- TRAVERTINE (TUFA): Mumford, Monroe County.

North Carolina

- AMPHIBOLITE (WITH GNEISS): Near Ela along Tuckasegee River and along North Carolina 284 north of Dellwood, Haywood County.
- CONGLOMERATE (WITH SCHIST): 5 miles east of Cherokee, Swain County.
- DIORITE (ORBICULAR): U.S. 64 east from Fork 2 1/2 miles, then south of logging road 300 yards and north 100 yards, Davie County.
- DOLOMITE: Quarry at Woodlawn, McDowell County.
- DOLOMITE: Along north bank of French Broad River northwest of Montaqua Hotel, Hot Springs, Madison County.
- DUNITE: East side of Great Hogback, north of Oakland, Transylvania County.
- DUNITE: 1/4 mile west of Frank post office on U.S. 19-E, Avery County.
- GNEISS: Quarries 1/4 mile north of Penland, north of U.S. 19-E at Crabtree Creek, Avery County.
- GNEISS: 1/2 mile east of Crumpler on east side of north fork of New River, Ashe County.
- GNEISS (BIOTITE): From Saluda take U.S. 176 east 4 1/2 miles, then right on State Road 1102, 2 miles to outcrop at bridge, Polk County.

- GNEISS: Less than a mile north of Bat Cave on North Carolina 9, Henderson County.
- GNEISS: 1/2 mile north of Cherokee along river, Swain County.
- GNEISS (AND PHYLLITE): From Henderson take U.S. 158 north to State Road 1319, then north on it 5 miles, Vance County.
- GRANITE: Along Irvin Creek, 3/4 mile east of the U.S. 21 exit on Interstate 85, Mecklenburg County.
- GRANITE: Quarry 2 1/2 miles east from Wilton on North Carolina 56 and north on State Road 1625 and west a mile, Granville County.
- GRANITE (AND AUGEN GNEISS): Across the Pigeon River north of Cove Creek Gap, Swain County.
- GRANITE (UNAKITE): On Roaring Fork Creek above junction with Meadow Creek, less than 3 miles southwest of Bluff, Madison County.
- GRAPHITE: At Barrett Mountain, 5 1/3 miles southwest of Taylorville, Alexander County.
- GRAPHITE: North of Macedonia across U.S. 1 near Meredith College, Wake County.
- MARBLE: With iron mines near Murphy, Cherokee County.
- MARBLE (DOLOMITIC): Along the C.C.&O. Railroad a mile south of Roses Branch and the Toe River, Mitchell County.
- PEGMATITE: Just east of Penland at Deer Creek mine along North Toe River, Mitchell County.
- PEGMATITE: At Carson mine, 2/3 mile northwest of Deep Creek Church, and in formations running northeast to Franklin Grove Church, Swain County.
- PEGMATITE: At Duncan mine, 1 1/4 miles southwest of West Jefferson, Ashe County.
- PEGMATITE: 1 1/3 miles east of Earl along a branch of Buffalo Creek, Cleveland County.
- PEGMATITE: East of Farmington; take North Carolina 801, then go north of State Road 1485 a half mile, and east on State Road 1457 a half mile, Davie County.
- PEGMATITE: 1 1/2 miles west of Bessemer City at the southeast corner of the intersection of State Roads 1401 and 1402, Gaston County.

- PEGMATITE: 1/2 mile south of Semora on the east side of State Road 1559, Caswell County.
- PEGMATITE: 1 1/2 miles south of Petersburg near Bull Creek, Madison County.
- PEGMATITE: At Jones mine on State Road 1856, 1/2 mile east of Tuxedo, Henderson County.
- PEGMATITE: In roadcut on State Road 1554, 1/3 mile northwest of its intersection with State Road 1557, Caswell County.
- PEGMATITE: Just north of Highlands along U.S. 64-A, Macon County.
- PERIDOTITE: Along Buck Creek, north of U.S. 64, Clay County.
- PERIDOTITE: 2 miles southwest of Willits, Jackson County.
- PORPHYRY: 1 1/2 miles east of Charlotte at Belmont Springs, Mecklenburg County.
- QUARTZITE (AND SANDSTONE): 5 miles northwest of Bridgewater along State Road 1236, Burke County.
- SCHIST: At Sugarloaf Mountain, 1 mile southwest of Willits, Jackson County.
- SCHIST: Along U.S. 19-E at Liberty Hall Church near Estatoe, Mitchell County.
- SCHIST (BIOTITE): Southwest of Suttertown along U.S. 19 at Lake Junaluska, Haywood County.
- SCHIST (BIOTITE): Along North Carolina 90 just east of Little River, Caldwell County.
- SCHIST (AND GNEISS): At Raven Rock, Harnett County.
- SCHIST (MICA): North of Plumtree, Avery County.
- SCHIST (MICA): 3/4 mile southwest of Dudley Shoals along State Road 1746, Caldwell County.
- SCHIST (MICA): 3 miles northeast of Shooting Creek at Burell farm on U.S. 64, Clay County.
- SCHIST (MICA): 2 1/3 miles north on State Road 1128 from Ogden school in Brasstown, Clay County.
- SCHIST (MICA-GARNET): Along State Road 1922 north and south of Horse Creek, Wake County.
- SCHIST (SILLIMANITE): Along road 1/2 mile northeast of Carpenters Knob, Cleveland County.
- SCHIST (STAUROLITE): Near mouth of Land Creek west of Bryson City, Swain County.

- SERPENTINE (AND DIOPSIDE): South of Webster along Tuckasegee River, Jackson County.
- SOAPSTONE: Several areas near Bayleaf, Wake County.
- SOAPSTONE: 2 miles east of Newton and north of North Carolina 10, along McLin Creek, Catawba County.
- TALC: On hill near State Road 1328, 1 1/2 miles from its intersection with State Road 1335, Caldwell County.
- TALC: At Hitchcock mines, 1 1/2 miles north of Murphy and 4 miles southwest of Murphy on U.S. 64, Cherokee County.
- VERMICULITE: At Frank, Avery County, and Day Book, Yancey County.

Ohio

- CONGLOMERATE AND SANDSTONE: Hocking State Park, Hocking County.
- DOLOMITE: West of Jamestown, Greene County.
- DOLOMITE: West of East Liberty, Logan County.
- DOLOMITE AND CHERT: Hillsboro quarry, Highland County.
- FLINT: Flint Ridge State Park, Licking County; the flint deposits run from Newark to Zanesville.
- FLINT: West of Prattsville, Vinton County.
- FLINT: 2 1/2 miles southwest of Kachelmacher, Hocking County.
- GYPSUM: Port Clinton, Ottawa County.
- LIMESTONE: Medusa quarry, Sylvania, Lucas County; take Main Street south to Brint Street, then north to Centennial Street and north to quarry.
- LIMESTONE: Clay Center, 12 miles east of Toledo, Ottawa County.
- LIMESTONE: Evans quarry, Marion, Marion County.
- LIMESTONE: 1 mile southwest of Shannon, Muskingum County.
- LIMESTONE: Cambridge, Guernsey County.
- LIMESTONE: Pugh quarry, Custar, Wood County.
- LIMESTONE AND CHERT: South of bridge, Ohio Brush Creek, 1 mile southwest of Jacksonville, Adams County.
- LIMESTONE AND COAL: Delaware, Delaware County.
- LIMESTONE, COAL, AND SANDSTONE: Northwest of Ellis, Muskingum County.

- LIMESTONE WITH FLINT: Pine Creek, Moulton, Lawrence County.
- SANDSTONE: Berea, Cuyahoga County.
- SANDSTONE: South Amherst, Lorain County.
- SANDSTONE: Glenmont, Holmes County.
- SANDSTONE: Turkey Run, north of Bristol, Perry County.

Pennsylvania

- BASALT: Mile south of Jacksonwald, Berks County.
- BASALT AND RHYOLITE: Jacks Mountain, east of Charmian Station, Hamiltonban Township, Adams County.
- CONGLOMERATE: Gettysburg, Adams County, associated with diabase.
- CONGLOMERATE: Mauch Chunk, 3/4 mile north at Mount Pisgah, Carbon County.
- DIABASE: Quarries 1 mile south of Birdsboro, Berks County.
- DOLOMITE: Texas, Lancaster County.
- DOLOMITE: Avondale quarry, Chester County.
- DOLOMITE AND SERPENTINE: Cedar Hill quarry at Nottingham, Bucks County.
- FELDSPAR: Poorhouse quarry, West Bradford, Chester County.
- FELDSPAR: West Nottingham, Chester County.
- GNEISS: O'Neill's quarry, Overbrook, Philadelphia County.
- GNEISS: Dana's farm, northwest of Morrisville, Bucks County.
- GNEISS: Green's Creek, 1 mile southwest of Chelsea, Delaware County.
- GNEISS: Chestnut Hill, north of Easton, Northampton County.
- GNEISS: Burk's quarry, Ridley Creek, 1 mile northeast of Chester, Delaware County.
- GNEISS: Quarries 3/4 mile north of Dale, Berks County.
- GNEISS AND DIABASE: Wheatley mines, 2 miles south of Phoenixville, Chester County.
- GNEISS AND GABBRO: West side of Neshaminy Creek, 2 miles north of Neshaminy Falls, Bucks County.
- GNEISS (GRAPHITIC): 1/4 mile northeast of Gabelsville, Berks County.
- GNEISS PEGMATITE: Leiper's quarry, Avondale, Delaware County.

- LIMESTONE: Lehigh River valley north of Allentown, Lehigh County, to Nazareth, Northampton County.
- LIMESTONE: Cornwall iron mine, 5 miles south of Lebanon, Lebanon County.
- LIMESTONE: Quarries north of Lancaster, Lancaster County.
- LIMESTONE: Quarries near Hellam, York County.
- LIMESTONE: Pusey's quarry, 1 1/2 miles west-southwest of Willowdale, Chester County.
- LIMESTONE: General Trimble's mine, 3/4 mile northwest of Planebrook station, Chester County.
- LIMESTONE: Ruth mine, 3/8 mile south of Fritztown, Berks County.
- LIMESTONE: Mendenhall's quarry, 1 mile southwest of Chadds Ford, Chester County.
- LIMESTONE: Mount Union, Mifflin County.
- LIMESTONE: Bellefont, Center County.
- LIMESTONE: Quarries at Ballietsville, Lehigh County.
- LIMESTONE: Southwest of Reading, Berks County.
- LIMESTONE: Marietta, Franklin County.
- LIMESTONE AND DIABASE: Randenbush mine, 1 mile south of Oakland, Berks County.
- LIMESTONE AND DIABASE: Jones mine, 2 miles northeast of Morgantown, Berks County.
- LIMESTONE AND SANDSTONE: Boyertown Iron mine, 1/2 mile southwest of Boyertown, Berks County.
- PEGMATITE: Black Horse area, Delaware County.
- PEGMATITE: Avondale quarry, Delaware County.
- PEGMATITE: Trexler mica mine, Alsace Township, Berks County.
- PEGMATITE: Brinton's quarries, 3 miles south, and Osborn Hill, 2 1/2 miles south, of West Chester, Chester County.
- PERIDOTITE: Rodman's Run, west of Flushing, Bucks County.
- PERIDOTITE: Corundum Hill, 2 miles northeast of Unionville, Chester County.
- PERIDOTITE: Dixonville, Indiana County.
- PERIDOTITE: 1 1/2 miles northeast of Goshenville, Chester County.

- PERIDOTITE AND SERPENTINE: Line Pits, 2 miles south of Texas, Lancaster County.
- QUARTZITE: Flint Hill, 1 mile south of Bowers Station, Berks County.
- QUARTZITE: Quarries northwest of Coatesville, Chester County.
- SANDSTONE: East of Robinsonville, Bedford County.
- SANDSTONE: 4 miles southwest of Barclay, Bradford County.
- SCHIST: South of Littlestown, Adams County.
- SLATE: Pen Argyl as far as Bangor, Northampton County.
- SOAPSTONE: Northwest of Gladwyn Station, Montgomery County.
- TRAVERTINE: East of Chambersburg, Franklin County.

Rhode Island

- CONGLOMERATE: 1 mile west of Ashaway, Washington County.
- CONGLOMERATE: Premiser Hill, Woonsocket, Providence County.
- DIABASE: Spencer Hill, Warwick, Kent County.
- DOLOMITE: South Foster, Providence County.
- DOLOMITE AND STEATITE: Violet Hill quarry, Manton, Providence County.
- DOLOMITE: Fort Adams quarry, Newport, Newport County.
- FELDSPAR: Larson's quarry, Hopkinton, Washington County.
- FELDSPAR: Smith's quarry, Coventry, Kent County.
- FELDSPAR: Mooresfield quarry, town of South Kingstown, Washington County.
- FELDSPAR (ORTHOCLASE AND MICROCLINE): Gammon's quarry, Cranston, Providence County.
- GABBRO PORPHYRY AND PERIDOTITE: Iron Mine Hill, town of Cumberland, Providence County.
- GLAUCOPHANE: Beacon Pole Hill, town of Cumberland, Providence County.
- GNEISS: Kingston, Washington County.
- GRANITE: Graniteville quarry, Providence County.
- GRANITE AND APLITE: Redstone, Sullivan, and Westerly quarries, town of Westerly, Washington County.

- GRANITE AND RHYOLITE: Diamond Hill granite quarry, town of Cumberland, and outcrops on Beacon Pole Hill, Providence County.
- GRAPHITE: Mines near Cranston, Kent County.
- GRAPHITE: Tower Hill, town of South Kensingtown, Washington County.
- GREENSTONE: Violet Hill quarry, Manton, Providence County.
- LIMESTONE: Quarries, town of Lincoln, Providence County.
- LIMESTONE: Harris and Dexter quarries, Limerock, Providence County.
- PEGMATITE: Outcrops on shore at Narragansett from Fort Varnum to Bonnet Shores, Washington County.
- PHYLLLITE: Conanient Island, Jamestown, Washington County.
- QUARTZ: Diamond Hill, northwest of Cumberland Village, town of Cumberland, Providence County.
- SCHIST: West side of Sneech Pond, town of Cumberland, Providence County, and on Copper Mine Hill.
- SCHIST (CHLORITE): Violet Hill quarry, Providence, Providence County.
- SCHIST (ILMENITE): Near Natick, Kent County.
- SERPENTINE AND STEATITE: Dexter quarry, town of Lincoln, Providence County.
- SERPENTINE AND STEATITE: Indian Ledge, Cranston, Providence County.
- SERPENTINE: Tower Hill, Cojoot lead mine, South Kingston, Washington County.
- TALC: Manville Mine, Lincoln, Providence County.

South Dakota

- AMPHIBOLITE: Southwest of Glendale, Pennington County.
- ANHYDRITE AND CHLORITE SCHIST: Homestake Mine, Lead, Lawrence County.
- CALCITE: Wind Cave, 9 miles north of Hot Springs, Custer County.
- CALCITE (ONYX): 1 mile west of Pringle, Custer County.
- CATLINITE: East of Sioux Falls, Minnehaha County.
- CONCRETIONS IN SHALE: Elk Creek and Cheyenne River

junction and westward, Meade County.

- CONGLOMERATE: Dells of Sioux River north of Sioux Falls, Minnehaha County.
- CONGLOMERATE: In bluffs in Fairburn area, Custer County.
- FELDSPAR: White Elephant mine, 3 miles north of Pringle, Custer County.
- GEODES: Mouth of Medicine Root Creek, southeast of Imlay, Shannon County.
- GEODES (WITH ANHYDRITE): Whitewood Creek, 3 miles below Deadwood, Lawrence County.
- GEODES (GRANITE): Little Elk Creek, 4 miles north of Nemo, Lawrence County.
- GLACIAL BOULDERS: Near McIntosh on Indian reservation, Corson County.
- GRANITE (RED): Milbank, Grant County.
- GRANITE AND PEGMATITE: Beecher lode, 5 miles southeast of Custer, Custer County.
- GYPSUM: In red clays around the Black Hills in Hot Springs area, Fall River County.
- GYPSUM: With lignite at Mendenhall strip mine, 6 miles south of Reva Gap, Harding County.
- KAOLIN: Etta mine, Keystone, Pennington County.
- LEPIDOLITE: Hill City, Pennington County.
- LIMESTONE: Tepee Canyon, west of Custer, Custer County.
- MARBLE: Quarry on Needles highway, 5 1/2 miles northeast of Custer, Custer County.
- PEGMATITE: Hugo mine, 1 mile south of Keystone, Pennington County.
- PEGMATITE: Beecher Lode, 4 1/2 miles south-southeast of Custer, Custer County.
- PEGMATITE: Crown mica mine, 2 miles northwest of Custer, Custer County.
- PEGMATITE AND APLITE: High Climb mine, 6 miles north of Custer, Custer County.
- PEGMATITE AND SCHIST: Smith mine, 5 miles southwest of Custer, Custer County.
- PORPHYRY: Northwest of Twin Peaks, 5 miles west of Lead, Lawrence County.
- QUARTZ: Holy Terror mine, Keystone, Pennington County.

- QUARTZ (ROSE): Scott mine, 6 1/2 miles southeast of Custer, Custer County.
- QUARTZITE: East of Mitchell, Davison County.
- QUARTZITE (ROSY): North of Sioux Falls with slate, Minnehaha County.
- SANDSTONE: East of Hot Springs, Fall River County.
- SANDSTONE: Craven Canyon mines, Fall River County.
- SANDSTONE (WITH CONGLOMERATE AND VOLCANIC ASH): Badlands National Monument.
- SCHIST: Southwest of Rockerville near Tepee Gulch, Pennington County.
- SCHIST (GRAPHITIC): American Tungsten Company mine, 4 miles east of Hill City, Pennington County.
- SCHIST (MICA): Mount Rushmore, Pennington County.
- SERPENTINE: Minnie Mae mine in Ruby Creek, 2 1/2 miles northwest of Custer, Custer County.
- SHALE: In western South Dakota along the Cheyenne River.
- SLATE: Southwest of Rapid City, Pennington County.
- TALC: West of Nemo, Lawrence County.

National Monuments and Parks

- *Badlands National Monument:* Headquarters at Interior, South Dakota. An incredible region of white to vividly colored bluffs, ridges, spires, and canyons covering more than 170 square miles. These were carved in soft sedimentary deposits by wind and water.
- *Wind Cave National Park:* North of Hot Springs, South Dakota. A limestone cave with many subterranean rooms and passages, noted for fanciful drip-stone formations and for the air currents that give the cave its name.

Tennessee

- CALCITE (ONYX): 5 miles southeast of Jamestown, Fentress County.
- CONGLOMERATE: Along state line divide from Starkey Gap to Buckeye Gap, Sevier County.
- CONGLOMERATE: Between Tuckaleechee and Wear Coves on ridges near Pawpaw and Lemon Hollows, Sevier County.

- CONGLOMERATE AND SLATE: Southeast of Sevierville, on east end of Shield Mountain, Sevier County.
- DIORITE AND ANORTHOSITE: In valley on north slope of Clingman's Dome; sill in sandstone in headwaters of Little River, Sevier County.
- DOLOMITE AND LIMESTONE: Southeast of Sevierville at Hodsen bridge, 3 miles south, and Lambert Brothers quarry, east of west prong on Little Pigeon River, 1 1/2 miles south of Sevierville, Sevier County.
- LIMESTONE: Quarry 1/2 mile from Pigeon Forge, Sevier County.
- LIMESTONE: Near Lenoir City, Loudon County.
- LIMESTONE AND PHYLLITE: At Tennessee Highway 73 at Townsend entrance to Great Smoky Mountains National Park, Blount County.
- PERIDOTITE: Union County.
- PHOSPHATE ROCK: 40 miles south of Nashville, Maury County.
- PHYLLITE: Cades Cove Road on Laurel Creek above junction with west prong of Little Pigeon River, Sevier County.
- QUARTZITE: Northeast end of Chilhowee Mountain, Blount County.
- QUARTZITE: 4 1/2 miles southeast of Sevierville, at David's Knob, Sevier County.
- SANDSTONE (CRAB ORCHARD): At Crossville, Cumberland County.
- SANDSTONE: Southeast flank of Cove Mountain, west of Gatlinburg, Sevier County.
- SANDSTONE: In north part of Gatlinburg, Sevier County.
- SANDSTONE: Roadcuts along Pigeon River, south of Hartford, Cocke County.
- SANDSTONE AND ARKOSE: Near south fork of Ellijoy Creek, Sevier County.
- SANDSTONE CONCRETIONS AND SCHIST: Outcrops on U.S. 441 along the southwest base of Mount LaConte, Sevier County.
- SANDSTONE WITH CONGLOMERATE: On north and west slopes of Burnt Mountain, Elkmont, Sevier County.
- SANDSTONE, SHALE, AND PHYLLITE: South of Gatlinburg along LeConte Creek, and at quarry east of National

Park Service headquarters, Sevier County.

- SHALE (SILTSTONE): Near Waterville, along Pigeon River, Cocke County.
- SLATE AND SCHIST: Along state line divide west of Thunderhead Mountain and on north slope of Clingman's Dome, Sevier County.
- SLATE: At McCorksville, Sevier County.
- SLATE AND SILTSTONE: 4 miles north of Gatlinburg, near west prong of Little Pigeon River, Sevier County.
- SLATE AND SILTSTONE: Along U.S. 441, south of mouth of Caney Creek, Van Buren County.
- SCHIST (MICA): Quarry east of lower bridge on Little River, Blount County.
- SLATE: Along Cove Creek, at northeast end of Wear Cove, and near Cove Creek cascades, Sevier County.
- SLATE: Along Pigeon River, 1/4 mile east of Bluffton, and on Highway 32, 1 1/2 miles southeast of Cosby, Cocke County.

National Park

- *Great Smoky Mountains National Park:* Gatlinburg, Tennessee. Most impressive of the ancient Appalachians, a region of rounded peaks clothed in dense forests, where plants and animals retreated from the glacial ages. Clingman's Dome, most lofty of the Smokies, is 6,643 feet high, one of the highest peaks in the eastern United States.

Texas

- ANHYDRITE: Along Salt Fork of the Brazos River, Knox County.
- ASBESTOS: In northeast Gillespie County.
- BASALT: In Chisos Mountains, Brewster County.
- BASALT: In Van Horn Mountains, Culberson County.
- CALCITE: Caverns of Sonora, Sutton County.
- CALCITE: Longhorn Cavern State Park, Burnet County.
- CALCITE: Terlingua, Brewster County.
- CHALCEDONY: Near Freer, Duval County.
- CHALCEDONY: Shafter Lake, Andrews County.

- DOLOMITE: Fairland, Burnet County.
- GEODES (CALCITE): West of Austin, Travis County.
- GRANITE: Granite Mountain, west of Marble Falls, Burnet County.
- GRANITE: Fredericksburg, Gillespie County.
- GRANITE (LLANITE): 10 miles north of Llano, at quarry west of Highway 16; 15 miles south at Enchanted Rock; and west of Bayhead—all in Llano County.
- GYPSUM: Gyp Hill, south of Falfurrias, Brooks County.
- LIMESTONE: San Saba, in quarries to southeast, San Saba County.
- LIMESTONE: Guadalupe Peak, Culberson County.
- LIMESTONE: Georgetown, Williamson County.
- LIMESTONE: Hazel mine, northwest of Van Horn, Culberson County.
- PEGMATITE: Mica mine, 15 miles south of Van Horn, Culberson County.
- RHYOLITE: Freer, Duval County.
- RHYOLITE: 16 miles south of Alpine, Brewster County.
- SALT DOMES: Grand Saline, Van Zandt County, and Hockley, Harris County.
- SCHIST: Honey Creek, Packsaddle Mountain, Llano County.
- SERPENTINE: North of Oxford in quarry near Highway 16, Llano County.
- SERPENTINE: South of Beecaves, which is northwest on Highway 71 of Oak Hill, Travis County.
- SOAPSTONE: In mine at Willow City, Gillespie County.
- TALC: Allamore, just north of Highway 80, Hudspeth County.

National Parks

- *Big Bend National Park:* On the Mexican border, southwest of Presidio. Where ancient seas and earth movements had their playground, now stands a geological showcase of water-carved canyons and remote mountain fastnesses.
- *Carlsbad Caverns National Park:* On the Texas border at Carlsbad, New Mexico. A magnificent series of limestone caves deepened over the ages by lowering of the

water table until some chambers are 850 feet below the surface.

Utah

- BASALT: Sills in shatter zones, Mount Ellen, Henry Mountains, Garfield County.
- CALCITE (ONYX): Hatch, 1 1/2 miles south on Mammoth Creek, Garfield County.
- COAL: 2 miles northwest of Factory Bluff, Henry Mountains, Garfield County.
- COAL: Mine northeast of Cainesville, Wayne County.
- GYPSUM: East side of Capital Reef, Wayne County.
- KIMBERLITE BRECCIA: In east Monument Valley, San Juan County.
- LIMESTONE: Boulder Canyon, San Rafael Swell, Emergy County.
- LIMESTONE, SHALE, AND SANDSTONE: Cataract Canyon, east of Henry Mountains, San Juan County.
- OBSIDIAN: Milford, 30 miles north at Black Rock, Millard County.
- PORPHYRY: East side of Horseshoe Ridge, Mount Ellen, Henry Mountains, Garfield County.
- PORPHYRY: Table Mountain, south and east of Mount Ellen, Henry Mountains, Garfield County.
- PORPHYRY (DIORITE): North end of Wickiup Ridge between Granite and Bull Creeks, Mount Ellen, Henry Mountains, Garfield County.
- PORPHYRY (DIORITE): Mount Hillers in stock and shatter zone, Henry Mountains, Garfield County.
- PORPHYRY (MONZONITE AND APLITE): Stock of Mount Pennell, Henry Mountains, Garfield County.
- QUARTZITE: West flank of Mount Ellsworth and south side of Mount Hillers with hornfels, Henry Mountains, Garfield County.
- RHYOLITE: Castle Cliffs Station, to north in Beaver Dam Wash, Washington County.
- RHYOLITE: Thomas Mountains, Iron County.
- SANDSTONE (BUFF AND RED): Canyon of the Dirty Devil River, 2 miles above its junction with the Colorado River, Garfield County.

- SANDSTONE (WHITE): With gypsum in same canyon and in Glen Canyon, Garfield County.
- SANDSTONE: Muddy River at the Reef in San Rafael Swell, Garfield County.
- SANDSTONE: In Seven Mile Canyon, 1/2 mile above its mouth, Henry Mountains, Garfield County.
- SANDSTONE: Baker Ranch, lower valley of Halls Creek, Garfield County.
- SANDSTONE (SCENIC): Hurricane, Washington County.
- SANDSTONE, SHALE, AND GYPSUM: North end of Big Wild Horse Mesa, Emery County.
- SEPTARIA: Mount Carmel, Kane County.
- SHALE (RED), SANDSTONE, AND CONGLOMERATE: Along Boulder Canyon, Emery County.
- SHALE AND PETRIFIED WOOD: Mouth of Red Canyon, Henry Mountains, Garfield County.

National Parks and Monuments

- Utah abounds in national parks and monuments. Among them are Bryce Canyon, Zion, and Cedar Breaks national parks, east and south of Cedar City; Rainbow Bridge Monument on the Arizona line east of Page, Arizona; Canyonlands National Park, a huge area near Moab in east-central Utah, with Arches and Capital Reef parks and Natural Bridges Monument nearby. All these areas are remarkable for the brilliantly colored sedimentary formations as well as pinnacles, cliffs, gorges, and natural arches. Utah has the scenery.
- *Lehman Caves National Monument:* West of Baker, Nevada, near the Utah border. Water carved these caves in limestone formations now raised to 7,000 feet above sea level. Pools, a swamp, and a variety of fine cave formations in rainbow hues are among the geological attractions.

Vermont

- ASBESTOS: Ruberoid mine, Lowell, Orleans County.
- ASBESTOS AND SERPENTINE: Belvidere mine on Belvidere Mountain, Eden, Lamoille County.

- GRANITE: Numerous quarries at Barre, Washington County.
- GRANITE: Quarries at Montpelier, Washington County.
- GRANITE: Quarries at Woodbury, Washington County.
- GRANITE: Bethel, Windsor County.
- GRANITE: Craftsburg, Orleans County.
- MARBLE: Quarry southeast of Swanton, Franklin County.
- MARBLE: Numerous quarries in Rutland County—at Pittsford, Brandon, Proctor, West Rutland, Clarendon, and Danby.
- SCHIST: Near Rutland, Rutland County.
- SCHIST: North Pownal, Bennington County.
- SERPENTINE: Quarry north of Eden Mills, Lamoille County.
- SERPENTINE: Grafton, Windham County.
- SLATE: Poultney, Rutland County.
- SYENITE: Stamford, Bennington County.
- TALC IN SERPENTINE: Johnson, Lamoille County.

Virginia

- ASBESTOS: Chestnut Ford, Bedford County.
- ANORTHOSITE: Quarry east of Roseland, Nelson County.
- CALCITE: Paxton's Cave, Bolling Springs, Allegheny County.
- DIABASE: Goose Creek quarry, Belmont Station, Loudoun County.
- DIABASE: Manassas quarry, Manassas, Prince William County.
- DIABASE (TRAPROCK): Fairfax quarry, Centreville, Fairfax County.
- DOLOMITE: Lone Jack quarry, Glasgow, Rockbridge County.
- FELDSPAR: Amber Queen mine, northeast of Goochland, Goochland County.
- GLAUCONITE (GREEN SAND): Below mouth of Aquia Creek, Henderson Bluff, Stafford County.
- GRANITE: Bennington Mill, Grayson County.
- GRANITE: Trego quarry, southwest of Emporia, Greensville County.
- GRANODIORITE: Irish Creek, Rockbridge County.
- GRAPHITE: Massie's Mill, 2 miles southwest of Roseland, Nelson County.

- GREENSTONE (ALTERED BASALT): Lynchburg, Campbell County.
- GYPSUM: Plasterco, Washington County.
- GYPSUM: North Holston, Smyth County.
- LIMESTONE: New Market, Shenandoah County, and elsewhere in that county.
- LIMESTONE: Kimballton, Giles County.
- LIMESTONE: Quarry 1 mile east of Buchanan, Botetourt County.
- LIMESTONE: Myers-Copenhaven mines, west of Marion, Smyth County.
- MICA: Hewlett mine, Hewlett's Station, Hanover County.
- MICA: Harris Mica Mine Farm, 8 miles west of Highway 1 along Highway 738, Goochland County.
- NEPHELINE, SYENITE, AND GRAPHITE: Buck Mountain, 7 miles northwest of Parnassus, Augusta County.
- PEGMATITE: Hairston mine, 3 miles north of Axton, Pittsylvania County.
- PEGMATITE: Moneta, Bedford County.
- PEGMATITE: Edenton Mica mine, north of Mineral, Spotsylvania County.
- PEGMATITE: Farley mine, 3 miles northeast of Flatrock, Powhatan County.
- PEGMATITE: Numerous mines near Amelia, Amelia County, such as the Rutherford, Morefield, and Jefferson mines.
- QUARTZ: Porterfield quarry, Rich Valley, Smyth County.
- QUARTZ: Hampton mine, New River, Hampton Ford, Grayson County.
- SANDSTONE: Ashland, Hanover County.
- SCHIST: Sulfur mine, Mineral, Louisa County.
- SCHIST: Old Woman Creek and the Roanoke River, 8 miles upstream from Altavista, Pittsylvania County.
- SLATE: Esmont, Albemarle County.
- SLATE: Warrenton, Fauquier County.
- SOAPSTONE: Near Schuyler, Nelson County.
- SOAPSTONE AND TALC: Alberene, Albemarle County.
- TALC: Schuyler, Nelson County.
- TALC: King-Ramsey quarry, Henry, Franklin County.
- UNAKITE (AN EPIDOTE GRANITE): Along Highway 56 in road-

cuts, and in a quarry west of the Tye River Gap, near Vesuvius, Rockbridge County.

- UNAKITE: East of Skyline Drive and intersection with Highway 56, Willkie, Nelson County.
- UNAKITE: Outcrops along Highway 16, southeast of Troutsdale, Grayson County.

National Park

- *Shenandoah National Park:* Headquarters at Luray, Virginia. Preserving some of the granites of the ancient Blue Ridge Appalachians, as well as beautiful mountain scenery. Nearby are many celebrated caves, Dixie and Endless caverns, Luray and Grand caverns, and Shenandoah and Skyline caverns.

Washington

- AMPHIBOLITE: Washington mine, Cedonia, Stevens County.
- ANDESITE: Banks of White River, 11 miles east of Enumclaw, King County.
- ANDESITE: Raging River quarry, Preston, King County.
- ANDESITE: Along road west from Wellpinit, Stevens County.
- ANORTHOSITE: East of North Bend, King County, near Horseshoe Mountain.
- APLITE: On Fuller Mountain, near North Bend, King County.
- BASALT: 1 mile northwest of Mondovi, Lincoln County.
- BASALT: Mossyrock Dam, west of Morton, Lewis County.
- BASALT: Pioneer quarry, south of Bremerton, Kitsap County.
- BASALT: At mouth of Quartz Creek on Lewis River, northeast of Yale, Cowlitz County.
- BASALT: At Skookumchuck Dam near Bucoda, Thurston County.
- CONGLOMERATE: On Waldron Island, San Juan County.
- DACITE: Near Baring in Stevens Pass, King County.
- DIATOMITE: Southeast of Kittitas, Kittitas County.
- DIATOMITE: Northwest of Quincy, Grant County.
- DIORITE: On Deer Flat, near Index, Snohomish County.
- DOLOMITE: Minnie mine, Carlton, Okanogan County.

- DUNITE: In the Twin Sisters Mountains, northeast of Wickersham, Whatcum County.
- GABBRO: In Sultan Canyon north of Sultan, Snokomish County.
- GEODES: On shore of Lake Cle Elum, Kittitas County.
- GEODES: In Walker Valley, north of Arlington, Snohomish County.
- GRANITE: At Hatfield mine, 30 miles north of Winthrop, Okanogan County.
- GRANITE: West of Mazama at Cutthroat Ridge, Okanogan County.
- GRANODIORITE: In roadcut near Icicle Creek, 2 miles southwest of Leavenworth, Chelan County.
- GRANODIORITE: In railroad cut at Sunset Falls, near Baring, King County.
- GRAPHITE: At mine north of Disautel, Okanogan County.
- GYPSUM: At Tonasket, Okanogan County.
- GYPSUM (ON SANDSTONE): At Tibbetts Creek coal mines, Issaquah, King County.
- HORNFELS: At Sunday Lake, north of North Bend, King County.
- LIMESTONE: Read Iron mine near Fruitland, Stevens County.
- LIMESTONE (WITH DIORITE): In Maloney Mountain quarries at Skykomish, King County.
- MARBLE: In several quarries near Chewelah, Stevens County, such as one reached by taking Waits Lake Road west from Valley to Carr's Corner, then left 6 miles.
- MARBLE: At Copper Lake, northeast of Sultan, Snokomish County.
- MARBLE: East of Granite Falls, at Canyon Creek quarry, Snokomish County.
- MARBLE: At Stevens Pass Cut, near Baring, King County.
- MARBLE: At Coffee mine, Ione, Pend Oreille County.
- NEPHELINE SYENITE: On Ellenham Mountain, near Oroville, Okanogan County.
- NODULES: Along Highway 97 from Leavenworth south to Yakima, Chelan, and Yakima counties.

- PEGMATITE: At Cannon mine, northeast of Chewelah, Stevens County.
- PEGMATITE: At campground west of Lake Wenatchee, Chelan County.
- PEGMATITE: Northeast of Usk, at Skookum Lake, Pend Oreille County.
- PEGMATITE: Various places along Marten Creek, north of North Bend, King County.
- PERIDOTITE: On Cypress Island, Skagit County.
- PERIDOTITE: South of Darrington, at Jumbo Mountain, Snokomish County.
- PORPHYRY: In granite at Loon Lake, Stevens County.
- SANDSTONE: In coal mines near Wenatchee, Chelan County.
- SCHIST: Along Meadow Creek, west of Ione, Pend Oreille County.
- SCHIST: At Holden mine, Lucerne, Chelan County.
- SERPENTINE: At Van Epps mine and at Mount Hawkins, both north of Cle Elum, Kittitas County.
- SERPENTINE: Along Mill Creek, near Cashmere, Chelan County.
- SKARN: At the 48–55 mine, Vesper Peak, near Sultan, Snokomish County.
- TALC: Northeast of Sedro Woolley, Skagit County.
- TALC: 7 miles north-northwest of Mount Vernon, on southwest flank of Cultus Mountain, Skagit County.
- TALC: At quarry 3 miles northeast of Marblemount, and the Skagit quarry to the north—both in Skagit County.
- TUFF: West of Doty, Lewis County.
- VOLCANIC ASH: In Horse Heaven Hills near Prosser, Benton County.
- VOLCANIC ASH: In the Saddle Mountains, south of the highway from Beverly to Corfu, Grant County.

National Parks

- *Mount Rainier National Park:* Southeast of Tacoma, Washington. The home of the monarch of the Cascades and, at 14,410 feet, one of the nation's highest mountains. Mount Rainier is also one of the most symmetrical volcanic cones and a laboratory of glacial systems and glacial action. Some of the notable rock exposures in Mount Rainier National Park are: Andesite breccia—rock falls from north face of Little Tahoma Peak. Glacial moraine—1 mile southwest of Panhandle Gap, and at west end of bridge over Nisqually River, 3 1/2 miles northeast of Longmire. Landslide debris—just north of Ohanapecosh campground; nearby is travertine. Lava bombs and andesite—along highway in south Puyallup River valley. Mudflow—valley 1 1/2 miles west of White River campground. Pumice—in a cirque 1/4 mile southeast of Sluiskin Falls; fine yellow material at Crater Lake; coarse brown pumice on Mount Rainier; light buff, sandy material on Mount St. Helens. Pumice is also present in Paradise Park. Till—old drift with boulders of bedrock on north side of Glacier Basin. Talus —below the Palisades in northeast area of park; also on north side of Sunset Ridge.

- *Olympic National Park:* On the ocean, west of Port Angeles, Washington. Jagged, ice-laden peaks—the Alps of America—rising amid a dense, shadowy rain forest on the coast. A favorite place to view the peaks is at Hurricane Ridge.

Wisconsin

- ANDESITE AND PERIDOTITE: West of Rudolph, Wood County.
- ANDESITE (PORPHYRY): East of Bloomer, Chippewa County.
- BASALT: Bluffs near St. Croix Falls and at Dresser quarry, Polk County.
- BRECCIA: Tomahawk, Lincoln County.
- CONGLOMERATE AND CHERT: Powers Bluff, Wood County.
- DIORITE: Southeast of Rhinelander, Oneida County.
- DOLOMITE: Quarry 1 mile north of Darlington, Lafayette County.
- DOLOMITE: Prairie du Chien, Crawford County.
- DOLOMITE: Quarry, Racine, Racine County.
- DOLOMITE: Mineral Point and Dodgeville, Iowa County, and Shullsburg, Lafayette County.
- DOLOMITE: North of Oshkosh, Winnebago County.
- DOLOMITE: East side of Green Bay, Door County.

- GABBRO (BLACK GRANITE): Quarry at Mellen, Ashland County.
- GABBRO: Lohrville, Waushara County.
- GNEISS: West of Stevens Point, Portage County.
- GNEISS: Dunbar, Marinette County.
- GNEISS AND SCHIST: Black River Falls, Jackson County, with granite.
- GRANITE: Merrill, Lincoln County, and Berlin, Green Lake County, in Quarries.
- GRANITE: East of Marshfield, Wood County.
- GRANITE: Along Wolf River, Menominee County.
- GRANITE: Amberg, Marinette County.
- GRANITE (RED): Marathon and Wausau, Marathon County, and Redgranite, Waushura County, in quarries.
- GRAYWACKE: North of Wausau, Marathon County.
- GREENSTONE: Penokee Range, Iron County.
- HEMATITE: Mine dumps at Hurley and Montreal, Iron County, and Florence, Florence County.
- LIMESTONE: Quarry at Sussex, Waukesha County.
- MARBLE WITH CONGLOMERATE: South of Ashland, Ashland County.
- MARBLE: Quarry at Grand View, Bayfield County.
- PHYLLITE: Black River Falls, Jackson County.
- QUARTZITE: Devil's Lake, near Baraboo, Sauk County.
- QUARTZITE: Rib Mountain, Wausau, Marathon County.
- QUARTZITE: Near Rice Lake, Barron County.
- QUARTZITE: North of Lake Mills, Jefferson County.
- RHYOLITE: Mountain, Oconto County.
- SANDSTONE: Bluffs at Irvin Park, Chippewa Falls, Chippewa County.
- SANDSTONE: Dells of the Wisconsin River, Sauk County.
- SANDSTONE: Pierce, Kewaunee County.
- SANDSTONE (STRIPED): Alma Center, Jackson County.
- SCHIST: Athens, Marathon County.
- SLATE: Northeast of Wausau, Marathon County, with syenite porphyry.
- SLATE: Florence, Florence County.
- TALC AND SOAPSTONE: North of Milladore, Wood County.

Wyoming

- AMPHIBOLITE AND HORNBLENDE SCHIST: At head of Cottonwood Creek, 5 miles east of the railroad at Encampment, Carbon County.
- CALCITE: At Meta mine, 19 miles southwest of Saratoga, Carbon County.
- CALCITE WITH FLUORITE: 6 miles north of Sundance, Crooks County.
- DIORITE: Gold Crater mines, near Keystone, on branch of Douglas Creek, Albany County.
- DOLOMITE: 4 miles west of Cody, in Shoshone Canyon, Park County.
- DOLOMITE: Quarry at Guernsey, Platte County.
- DOLOMITE: 11 miles northeast of Laramie, Albany County.
- DOLOMITE: 20 miles south of Thermopolis, in the east end of Wind River Canyon, along Highway 20, Hot Springs County.
- GRANITE: Morrison-Knudsen pit in Granite Canyon, along Highway 30, Laramie County.
- GRANITE: Quarry in Sinks Canyon, southwest of Lander, in Washakie National Forest, Fremont County.
- GRANITE (RED), SCHIST, AND GNEISS: 23 miles west of Cheyenne and north of Granite Canyon, Laramie County.
- GYPSUM: Cement company quarry north of Como Bluff, near Medicine Bow, Albany County.
- GYPSUM: Interstate Chemical Company quarry near Cody, and Wyoming Mineral Products Company quarry southwest of Cody, Park County.
- GYPSUM: Pit 5 miles northeast of Laramie, Albany County. Earthy gypsum (gypsite) is abundant south of Laramie.
- GYPSUM: 3 miles north of Greybull, on the north side of Shell Creek, Big Horn County.
- GYPSUM WITH TRAVERTINE: In hot springs deposits, 2 1/2 miles west of Thermopolis, Hot Springs County.
- LIMESTONE: Horse Creek mine along the Colorado & Southern Railroad, 36 miles northwest of Cheyenne, Laramie County.

- LIMESTONE: Near South Redwater Creek, 6 miles north of Sundance, Crook County.
- LIMESTONE: At cement quarry just east of Laramie, Albany County.
- LIMESTONE AND FLINT NODULES: At Green Mountain Boy mine, 1/2 mile east of Guernsey, Platte County.
- LIMESTONE AND GRANITE WITH GRAPHITE AND GNEISS: 25 miles west of Wheatland and 30 miles north of Laramie in Halleck Canyon, Albany County.
- MARBLE (ONYX): Quarry near Cokeville, Lincoln County.
- MARBLE: 15 miles northwest of Wheatland, along the Laramie River, Platte County.
- NEPHRITE JADE WITH APLITE: North and northeast of Jeffrey City on cattle ranches, Fremont County.
- PEGMATITE: East side of Encampment River, near the mouth of Cascade Creek, Carbon County.
- PEGMATITE: 10 miles northeast of Guernsey, Platte County.
- PEGMATITE IN SCHIST: Dikes in Copper Mountain district, 15 miles north of Shoshoni, Fremont County.
- PHOSPHATE ROCK: At Leefe, 25 miles west of Kemmerer, near the railroad, Lincoln County.
- PHOSPHATE ROCK: Old quarry at Rocky Point, just east of Cokeville, Lincoln County.
- PUMICE: Superior Pumice Company mine, 3 miles northeast of Superior, Sweetwater County.
- QUARTZITE: Railroad quarry east of Guernsey, Platte County.
- QUARTZITE (PINK): Quarry north of Rawlins, Carbon County.
- QUARTZITE AND GABBRO: Mines on South Spring Creek, 3 miles northwest of Davis, Carbon County.
- QUARTZITE AND SCHIST: Silver Cliff mine in the west city limits of Lusk, Niobrara County.
- SANDSTONE: Quarries at Dietz, Monarch, Arno, and Absawkee Park, Sheridan County.
- SANDSTONE: Quarry south of Rawlins and 4 miles from the railroad, Carbon County.
- SANDSTONE: 6 miles east of Como, Albany County.
- SANDSTONE, LIMESTONE, AND SCHIST: 12 miles west and

south of Douglas, and northwest of La Prele reservoir, Converse County.

- SANDSTONE AND SHALE: Arizona Creek, 6 miles south of Yellowstone National Park and 3 1/2 miles east of Jackson Lake, Teton County.
- SERPENTINE AND ASBESTOS: Fire King deposit, 4 miles north of Atlantic City, Fremont County.
- SERPENTINE AND ASBESTOS: In granite, 5 miles south of Beaver Hill, Fremont County.
- SCHIST AND QUARTZ: 1/2 mile northeast of Atlantic City and 1 mile west of South Pass, Fremont County.
- SCHIST AND GRANITE: Deer Creek mine in Deer Creek canyon, 15 miles southwest of Glenrock, Converse County.
- SHALE WITH BENTONITE: West and southwest of Casper, Natrona County.
- SLATE AND SCHIST: On Miner Creek, 4 miles south of Encampment, Carbon County.
- SYENITE PORPHYRY: Hutchins Consolidated Gold Mining Company mine, 8 miles north of Sundance, in the Bear Lodge Mountains, Crook County.
- TALC AND MICA: 1 mile south of Encampment, Carbon County.
- TRAVERTINE: Near Thermopolis, along the Bighorn River, Hot Springs County.
- TRAVERTINE: 3 miles west of Cody, along the east side of Cedar Mountain, Park County.
- VERMICULITE: At Union Asbestos mine near Encampment River at Baggott Rocks, Carbon County.
- VOLCANIC ROCKS: In the Leucite Hills, mesas, necks, and cones near Rock Springs, Sweetwater County. (Leucite is a potassium aluminum silicate found in lavas; this is the world-famous source.)

National Parks and Monuments

- *Yellowstone National Park:* The northwest corner of Wyoming on the Idaho and Montana borders. Yellowstone was the first and is still the most widely known of the national parks, for its geysers, hot springs, and other manifestations of the earth's unrest, for its magnificent canyon and falls, and for a lesser-known petrified forest. Some of the notable rock exposures in Yellowstone National Park are: Granite, gneiss, and phyllite—in boulders 1 to 3 miles northwest of Boundary Trail, 3 miles north of Fox Creek patrol cabin. Gypsum—in south branch of the Snake River, 2 miles southeast of the mouth of Red Creek. Limestone—ravine crossing South Boundary Trail, 3 miles northeast of the south entrance to the park. Quartzite and shale—1/2 mile south-southeast of the mouth of Red Creek, at sharp bend in the Snake River. Sandstone and shale—at north end of Huckleberry Ridge, 2 1/2 miles east of the south entrance to the park. Shale (red) and sandstone—on north slope of Huckleberry Ridge, 1/4 mile west of Milepost 14 in the park. (Obsidian exposures and hot spring formations are well publicized.)

- *Grand Teton National Park:* Just south of Yellowstone Park. The rugged, snowy Tetons tower sheer above Jackson Hole in one of the world's most impressive examples of fault-block mountain-building.
- *Devils Tower National Monument:* In the northeast corner of Wyoming, near Sundance. A gigantic mass of basalt columns rising 865 feet from a broad base, like a tree stump of heroic proportions.
- *Glacier National Park:* In northwestern Montana on the Canadian line. Has few rivals for recognition as the finest mountain scenery in the United States. Here the great Lewis overthrust fault mass has been carved into valleys and cirques by ice and water.

Provinces of Canada

Alberta

- GYPSUM: North of Brule Lake, Jasper Park.
- GYPSUM: Along Peace River between the mouth of Jackfish River and Peace Point, a few miles below Boyer.

British Columbia

- AGGLOMERATE: On Savona Mountain, Ashcroft division.
- AMPHIBOLITE: Bonanza mine, 3/4 mile from mouth of Bonanza Creek.
- ANDESITE (PORPHYRY AND GRANITE): Brynnor mines, 3 miles north of Maggie Lake, near Ucluelet, Vancouver Island.
- ARAGONITE: 1 mile north of the south fork of the Salmon River on south slope of Staghorn Mountain.
- BASALT: Squilax Mountain, Squilax.
- BASALT: Salmon Creek, 7 miles from Westwold, around Vernon.
- BASALT: Canadian Pacific Railroad quarry, Prince George.
- BASALT (AMYGDALOIDAL): Near Nanaimo and on South Valdez Island.
- BASALT: Near Penticton.
- BRECCIA: On beach near Finlayson Point, Victoria, Vancouver Island.
- BRECCIA (DALLASITE): Home Lake, and at Big Tree Creek, 9 miles above Roberts Lake, Vancouver Island.
- DACITE: Tranquille Plateau, 25 miles northwest of Kamloops, on wagon road from Tranquille to Red Lakes.
- DIORITE: Red Rose mine near Hazelton.
- DIORITE (AND GREENSTONE): Harrison group claims, Tweedsmuir Park on north side of Lindquist Lake, Omineca area.
- DIORITE (WITH HEMATITE): Highland Valley mines east of Ashcroft.
- GABBRO (AUGITE): With amygdaloidal basalt at gravel pit 9 miles north of Seymour Narrows Lookout, which is 8 miles north of Campbell River.
- GRANITE: At the head of Salmon arm of Jervis Inlet and between the inlet and Howe Sound.
- GYPSUM: In bluffs 8 miles north of Canal Flats.
- LATITE: In pass at head of Beatty Creek, 1/2 mile east of Meszah Peak, Stikine River area.
- LIMESTONE: On McDame Creek, 1 mile east of Centreville.
- MARBLE: Quarry near Marblehead, 8 miles north of Lar-

deau, and quarry on south fork of Kaslo Creek, 5 miles from Kaslo.

- NEPHELINE SYENITE: Ice River, Beaverfoot River, and Kicking Horse River.
- PEBBLES: Island View Beach, Vancouver Island.
- PEGMATITE: On Clearwater Peak in Lillooet district.
- PEGMATITE: Just south of Midge Creek, 1 mile from Kootenay Lake.
- PERIDOTITE: East side of Bonaparte River valley, north of Ferguson Creek, Ashcroft district.
- PERIDOTITE: On summit of Timothy Mountain, Cariboo district.
- PERIDOTITE: Northeast end of Liza Lake, Bridge River area, Lillooet district.
- PORPHYRY (ANDESITE): On Hardscrabble Creek, 1 mile west of Canadian national line, near Pitman.
- PORPHYRY (GABBRO AND QUARTZ): Almost any beach on Vancouver Island, especially at Gordon, Island View, Miracle Beach, and Campbell River.
- PORPHYRY (GRANITE): Independence mine, 1 1/2 miles east of Coquihalla.
- QUARTZITE: Northeast of Deer Park.
- SANDSTONE (AND JASPER): Muir Creek and Gordon Beach, Vancouver Island.
- SERPENTINE: West side of Hobo Creek, 2 miles from Atlin Lake, and also on Goat Island in Atlin Lake.
- SERPENTINE: Near Highland Valley, Ashcroft area, and 20 miles north of Ashcroft at Chrome Creek, 1/3 mile above its mouth at Scottie Creek.
- SERPENTINE (ASBESTOS): Mine on northwest flank of Mount McDame, 3 miles north of Cassiar.
- SERPENTINE (AND TALC): Aurum mine, 1 mile north of Jessica.
- SCHIST: At Jordan River beach, Vancouver Island.
- SCHIST: Mouth of Grant Brook, southeast of Moose Lake, Cariboo district.
- SCHIST (MICA): High bluff, 5 miles north of Prince Rupert, at Prince Rupert Harbor.
- SKARN: Marble Bay mine, Texada Island.
- SKARN: On Needlepoint Mountain, McDame area, 2 miles

northeast of junction of Bass Creek and Cottonwood River.

- SLATE: Near summit of Rose Pass, 5 miles northeast of Crawford Bay on Kooteney Lake.
- SYENITE: Rock Candy mine, 15 miles north of Grand Forks.
- TRACHYTE: Rexpar property, 3 miles south of Birch Island station, Canadian National Railroad, 80 miles north of Kamloops.
- TRAVERTINE: Near Hudson Hope, in Peace River mining district.

Manitoba

- BASALT (AMYGDALOIDAL): North end of Lake Manitoba and on Sugar Island in Lake St. Martin.
- DIORITE: Quarry east of East Braintree.
- GABBRO: South of Hub Bay, on Wekusko Lake.
- GNEISS: At Sherridon.
- GRANITE: Pigeon Lake, 9 1/2 miles southwest of Bathurst, Gloucester County.
- GRANODIORITE: 6 miles north of Barren Lake, Falcon Lake area.
- GYPSUM: East of Highway 75, 30 miles south of Winnipeg, at Silver Plains gypsum mine.
- GYPSUM (IN BLACK SHALE): Morden–Miami area.
- GYPSUM (WITH ANHYDRITE): Gypsumville district, north of Lake St. Martin.
- GYPSUM (WITH QUARTZ CONCRETIONS): Mine at Amarath.
- PEGMATITE: Montgary property at west end of Bernic Lake, and at east end of lake.
- PEGMATITE: Chemally mine, Bernic Lake.
- PEGMATITE: North of Falcon Lake.
- PEGMATITE: West of Cross Lake, Cross Lake area.
- PEGMATITE: 3 miles southeast of Lamprey Falls of Winnipeg River.
- PEGMATITE: In Shatford–Ryerson Lake area, near east end of Shatford Lake.
- PEGMATITE: Near Bird River, southeast of Lake Winnipeg.
- PEGMATITE: 1/2 mile inland from point on southeast shore of Winnipeg River, 9 miles above Pointe du Bois.

- PEGMATITE: At mines near Cat Lake.
- PEGMATITE (IN GRANITE): Birse Lake, east-northeast of Winnipeg.
- PERIDOTITE (AND GABBRO): Bird River area.
- RHYOLITE (AND GABBRO): West of Alberts Lake.
- SCHIST: Northwest of Shoal Lake, near Ontario border, Falcon Lake area.
- SCHIST: Outcrops along shores of Snow, Anderson, File, and Corley lakes, at Herb Lake, and in Niblock Lake area—all north of Narrows of Crowduck Bay.
- SCHIST (AND ANDESITE): On east side of Thompson Lake.
- SCHIST (AND GNEISS): 1 mile west of Star Lake and 10 miles east of Rennic Station.
- STEATITE: Old quarry near Manigotagan.

Newfoundland

- ANORTHOSITE: Grenfell quarry on south side of Tabor Island, south of Nain, Labrador.
- APLITE: South shore of Northern Adlavik Island, 1 mile east of Maconit Bay, Labrador.
- BASALT (AMYGDALOIDAL): Ridge 1 mile west of Paradise River bridge and 1/4 mile south of Terenceville Road.
- DUNITE (AND PERIDOTITE): At Stowbridge and at south end of North Arm Mountain.
- GNEISS: Hickey's Pond, 5 miles west of the head of Placentia Bay.
- GNEISS (GRAPHITIC): North coast of Labrador between Grenville Sound and Port Manvers.
- GRANITE: St. Lawrence on Buril Peninsula.
- GRANITE: Along the highway, 1 mile north of the bridge at east end of Gander Lake.
- GRAYWACKE: Near north end of Snows Pond, 6 miles southwest of Clarke's Beach.
- GYPSUM: Southeast of St. George's Bay, between St. George's and Searston.
- HORNFELS (AND PHYLLITE): On North Arm Mountain at Bay of Islands.
- SCHIST: South of Long Pond, near Manuels, in Torbay area.
- SYENITE: Seal Lake, Labrador.

New Brunswick

- CONGLOMERATE: Goose Creek near Martin Head.
- GABBRO: Point Wolfe River, St. John County.
- GRANITE: Northwest of Pabineau Lake, 10 miles southwest of Bathurst.
- GRAPHITE (AND SCHIST): On Golden Grove Mountain, St. John County, and between it and Grassy Lake.
- GYPSUM (AND ANHYDRITE): South side of Wilson Brook, Hillsborough, Albert County, and at Whitehead quarry.
- MARBLE (SERPENTINE): Along Burpee Avenue in St. John.
- RHYOLITE: Lords Cove, Charlotte County.
- RHYOLITE: Mount Pleasant, Charlotte County.
- RHYOLITE: Burchil Camp, Northumberland County.
- SCHIST (MICA): Moores Mills, Moose Lake, Charlotte County.
- SHALE: Gouldville, Westmoreland County.
- SLATE: Lower Birch Island, York County.
- SLATE (WITH HEMATITE): Coal Creek, Queen's County.

Northwest Territories

- DOLOMITE: Camsell River Silver Mines on Camsell River, 20 miles south of Great Bear Lake.
- GYPSUM: Gypsum Point on north shore of Great Slave Lake, and on southwest shore of north arm of Great Bear Lake.
- PEGMATITE: Ross Lake area, Mackenzie district.
- PEGMATITE: Just north of Hearne Channel, Great Slave Lake.
- PEGMATITE: 5 miles southwest of the north end of Buckham Lake.
- SCHIST: At west end of Baker Lake.
- SCHIST (GREENSTONE): Near McLeod Bay, Great Slave Lake.

Nova Scotia

- ANHYDRITE: Cliffs near Port Hastings, on east side of road to Hawkesbury.

- BASALT: Generally along the south shore of the Bay of Fundy from Digby Neck to Cape Blomidon, and on the north shore of Minas Channel and basin; especially at Canada Creek Village, 3 miles northeast of Harbourville, and at Hall's Harbor.
- BRECCIA (LIMESTONE): At mine 13 miles east of Brookfield Station.
- CONGLOMERATE: Atkinson, Cumberland County.
- CONGLOMERATE: Gays River, southwest Colchester County.
- DIABASE: Cape Blomidon and Partridge Island, Bay of Fundy.
- GRANITE: Between New Ross and Lake Ramsay, Lunenburg County.
- GRANITE: Near Six-Mile Lake, on St. Margaret's Bay Road, Halifax County.
- GYPSUM: Clifton quarry near Windsor, Hants County, and quarries in Walton and Cheverie, Hants County, and at Little Narrows, Cape Breton Island.
- GYPSUM (WITH ANHYDRITE): On west bank of the Shubenacadie River between South Maitland and Urbania.
- LIMESTONE: 6 miles northeast of Truro, Colchester County.
- LIMESTONE (WITH CONCRETIONS): Quarry on Dewar's Hill, 3 miles southwest of Pugwash.
- LIMESTONE (COQUINA): 3 miles west of Hilden.
- MARBLE: Headwaters of French Creek, 2 miles southwest of Meat Cove, north end of Cape Breton Island.
- MARBLE: Near Eskasoni, on the west side of East Bay, and in quarry near shore of West Bay—both on Bras d'Or Lake.
- MARBLE: Quarry at Scotch Lake, west of Scotch Lake Village.
- PEGMATITE: Reeves farm, 3 miles west of New Ross, Lunenburg County.
- PEGMATITE: Along coastline from Sandy Cove to Western Head, Queens County.
- SALT: Quarries near Newport Landing, north of Windsor, Hants County.
- SANDSTONE: Clarke's Head and Crane Point, Cumberland County.

- SCHIST (MICA): Along Broad River, 1 1/2 miles from its mouth.
- SCHIST (MICA): Near Guysborough.
- SLATE: Rawdon and West Gore, Hants County.
- SLATE: Along the Bass and East rivers, Colchester County.
- SLATE: Scotia mine, Springhill, Cumberland County.
- SLATE: Glencoe Brook, Pictou County.
- SLATE (AND GRANITE): Near Halifax.

Ontario

- AMPHIBOLITE: North shore of Fishtail Lake, Harcourt Township.
- BASALT: McGill gold mines, Hincks Township, Kirkland Lake area.
- BASALT: Near Bruce Mines on island opposite Desbarats.
- BASALT: Michipicoten Island in Lake Superior.
- BASALT: Near Madoc, Hastings County.
- CALCITE (WITH MICA): Silver Crater mine, Faraday, Hastings County.
- CONGLOMERATE: North of Bruce Mines; along a ridge 1/2 mile from the north end of Goulais Bay, Lake Superior; along St. Mary's River, 4 miles west of Campement d'Ours Island; on the east shore of Lake George.
- CONGLOMERATE: Near Massey; on St. Joseph's and Drummond islands.
- DIABASE: Gowganda mines, Timiskaming district.
- DIABASE: In railroad cuts between Orient Bay and Fairclough in Lake Nipigon area.
- DIABASE: Between Longlac and Jellicoe.
- DIABASE: Belmont Township, Peterborough County.
- DIABASE: Emo area, Sudbury district.
- DOLOMITE: Credit Forks, Caledon Township, Peel County.
- DOLOMITE: South side of Highway 17, 1/3 mile east of the bridge over Pimisi Bay near Rutherglen, Colvin Township.
- DOLOMITE: Haley Station, Ross Township, Renfrew County.
- DOLOMITE: Quarries at Port Colborne; Walker quarry near Thorold.

- GABBRO: North end of Dog Lake, 1 1/2 miles southeast of Lochalsh.
- GNEISS: Just north of Stormy Lake, Glamorgan Township.
- GNEISS: Outcrop 12 miles east of Sudbury.
- GNEISS: North of Christie Lake and on east side of rock cut along Canadian Pacific Railroad, South Sherbrooke Township, Lanark County.
- GNEISS (AND DOLOMITE): Richardson mine near Eldorado, Madoc Township.
- GNEISS (WITH CALCITE): Markill quarry, 2 miles west of Robertsville, Palmerston Township, Frontenac County.
- GNEISS (WITH NEPHELINE): Near Egan Chute on York River.
- GRANITE: Thunder Bay mine, 35 miles northeast of Thunder Bay.
- GRANITE (AND SYENITE): 7 miles east of Schreiber, Duck Lake area.
- GYPSUM: Caledonia, Haldiman County.
- GYPSUM: Faraday mine, Hastings County.
- GYPSUM: South and west of Hamilton, east of Hagersville, and at Princeton.
- GYPSUM: Along banks of Moose River near village of Moose River, and along the Cheepash 20 miles above its junction with Moose River.
- JASPILITE: South edge of Heenan Township, Sudbury district.
- LIMESTONE: Steep Rock mines at Steep Rock Lake.
- LIMESTONE: At quarry at Amherstburg, Essex County.
- LIMESTONE: Near Newboro, South Crosby Township.
- LIMESTONE: Quarries at Woodstock and St. Marys.
- LIMESTONE: Beachville, Oxford County.
- LIMESTONE: In railroad cut near Chaffeys Locks.
- LIMESTONE: Near Mississagua Lake, Cavendish Township, Peterborough County.
- LIMESTONE (RED): In South Burgess Township, Leeds County.
- MARBLE (BLACK): Southeast end of Madoc Village in Madoc Township, Hastings County.
- NEPHELINE SYENITE: Quarries at Blue Mountain, Methuen Township, Peterborough County.

- NEPHELINE SYENITE: Princess quarry, 2 1/2 miles east of Bancroft, Hastings County.
- NEPHELINE SYENITE: Craig mine, Raglan Township, Renfrew County.
- NEPHELINE SYENITE: In belt 5 miles long, striking north from point on French River 4 miles below French River station on Canadian Pacific Railroad, Bigwood Township.
- PEGMATITE: Richardson mine, Verona, Frontenac County.
- PEGMATITE: Purdy mine at Eau Claire, near Mattawa.
- PEGMATITE: Lacey mine, Sydenham, Frontenac County.
- PEGMATITE: Just north of Lily Lakes in Fort Hope area.
- PEGMATITE: Yeo's Island, near upper end of Tar Island, north side of English Channel, Thousand Islands.
- PEGMATITE: McDonald mine, Monteagle Township, Hastings County.
- PEGMATITE: 1 1/2 miles north of Quadeville, Lyndoch Township.
- PEGMATITE: Echo Township, Kenora district.
- PEGMATITE: Quarries 3 miles west of Balderson.
- PEGMATITE: 1 1/2 miles west of west end of Cosgrave Lake, Port Arthur district.
- PEGMATITE: Dokis Island, Key Harbour area, Parry Sound district.
- PEGMATITE: Gale property, Murchison Township, Nipissing district.
- PEGMATITE: Along Stoney Lake near Eel Creek, Burleigh Township, Peterborough County.
- PEGMATITE: East of Wilberforce in north half of Cardiff Township, Haliburton County.
- PEGMATITE: Near Fry Lake just south of Seguin Falls, Monteith Township, Parry Sound district.
- PEGMATITE: Between Strain and Burns lakes, Griffith Township, Renfrew County.
- PORPHYRY: 19 miles west of Matchewan at Rahi Lake, Bannockburn Township.
- PORPHYRY: Lake Shore mine, Kirkland Lake.
- QUARTZITE: Whitefish Falls, Manitoulen district.
- QUARTZITE: North shore of St. Joseph Island and Campement d'Ours Island, Lake Huron.

- RHYOLITE: Mine on Temagami Island.
- SANDSTONE: Sault Ste. Marie.
- SCHIST: Iron mine at Skibi Lake, 30 miles northwest of Nakina.
- SCHIST (CHLORITIC): Horseshoe mine on Whitefish Bay, Lake of the Woods area.
- SCHIST (CHLORITIC): Denison mine near Worthington station, Sudbury district.
- SCHIST (CHLORITIC): Jardun mine, 18 miles northeast of Sault Ste. Marie.
- SCHIST (HORNBLENDE): Extreme southeast of Marmora Township, Hastings County.
- SCHIST (MICA): In a band running northeast across Clarendon Township, 50 miles northwest of Kingston.
- SCHIST (MUSCOVITE): Clarendon–Dalhousie area, Barrie Township, Frontenac County.
- SCHIST (AND GRANITE): St. Anthony mine, Sturgeon Bay.
- SERPENTINE: In marble at Marble Bluff, Lanark County.
- SERPENTINE: Crow Lake, Marmora Township.
- SERPENTINE: Along border of Beatty and Munro townships.
- SERPENTINE: On north shore of Bear Lake in Schreiber–Duck Lake area.
- SERPENTINE (IN LIMESTONE): 1/2 mile east of Foresters Falls, Ross Township.
- SHALE: Pigeon River, Thunder Bay district.
- SKARN: Williams Bay deposit, 2 miles northwest of Calabogie, Bagot Township.
- STEATITE (SOAPSTONE): Eldorado talc mine, Madoc Township.
- STEATITE (SOAPSTONE): Trap Lake, south of Wabigoon Lake.
- SYENITE: On mainland, Thunder Bay district, opposite Pic Island, Lake Superior.
- SYENITE: East bank of York River, Monteagle Township, 10 miles northeast of Bancroft.
- SYENITE (RED): West shore of Browning Lake in north part of Cairo Township, Matachewan area.
- TALC: Henderson mine, Huntingdon Township, Hastings County.
- TUFF (BRECCIA): Madsen gold mine, Red Lake area.

Quebec

- ANORTHOSITE: St. Charles River, Bourget Township, Chicoutimi County.
- ANORTHOSITE: Below falls of Ste. Marguerite River at Clark City.
- ANORTHOSITE: At Sheldrake along the St. Lawrence River.
- ANORTHOSITE: Northeast of Lake St. John, Roberval and Chicoutimi counties.
- ARAGONITE: At Montreal Chrome Pit, 3/4 mile east of the south end of Little Lake St. Francis, Coleraine Township, Megantic County.
- BRECCIA (ANORTHOSITE): Kayrand mine, Obalski Township, Abitibi East.
- CONGLOMERATE (AGATE PEBBLES): Chaleur Bay, Gaspé County.
- DIABASE (AND SERPENTINE): Old mine in South Ham Township, Wolfe County.
- DOLOMITE: 10 miles north of Grenville, Harrington Township.
- GABBRO: Along Romaine-Est river, upstream 2 1/2 miles, from 1/2 mile north of mouth of Metivier River.
- GABBRO: East of Barbie Lake in Bachelor Lake area, Abitibi district.
- GNEISS (WITH MIGMATITE): Near Montauban les Mines, Chavigny Township, Portneuf County.
- GRANITE: Batholith in Meach Lake–Camp Fortune area, Hull Township.
- GRANITE: Lac a Baude, Normand Township, Laviolette County.
- GRANITE: Wentworth Township, Argenteuil County.
- KIMBERLITE: Near Bachelor Lake, Lesueur Township, Abitibi district.
- LIMESTONE: Laurel, Argenteuil County.
- LIMESTONE: Sault de la Puce, Montmorency County.
- LIMESTONE: Along roadcut from Calumet Island to Campbell Bay.
- LIMESTONE: Near Clement Station, Campbell County, Labelle County.

- MARBLE: Quarry 1 1/4 miles north of South Stukely, Stukely Township, Shefford County.
- MARBLE: Quarry 3/4 mile north of Philipsburg on Missisquoi Bay of Lake Champlain, Missisquoi County.
- MARBLE: Quarry on east side of Bowker Lake, Orford Township, Sherbrooke County.
- NEPHELINE SYENITE: Along the Metawishish River, north of Lake Grenier and 12 miles east of Lac Albanal.
- NEPHELINE SYENITE: On northwest flank of Mount Royal at Corporation quarry, Outremont, Montreal.
- PEGMATITE: South of Lake Lortie, Lacorne Township, Abitibi district.
- PEGMATITE: Maisonneuve mine, Berthier County.
- PEGMATITE: Windpass mine, 7 miles northeast of Chu Chua, North Thompson River district.
- PEGMATITE: Mine near Barraute, Lacorne, and Fiedmont Townships, Abitibi County.
- PEGMATITE: Mine 6 miles south from a point 17 miles east of Amos on Highway 45, Lacorne Township, Abitibi County.
- PEGMATITE: Lac Pied des Monts, 17 miles northwest of La Malbaie, Charlevoix County.
- PEGMATITE: In northeast corner of Lac Expanse, Delbreuil Township, Temiskaming County.
- PEGMATITE (SKARN): 10 miles north of Lachute, Wentworth Township, Argenteuil County.
- PERIDOTITE (DUNITE): In asbestos mines, Thetford mines area.
- QUARTZITE: 7 miles south of Irene Lake, in Nipissis River area, Saguenay County.
- SANDSTONE: Island of Orleans.
- SCHIST: Southwest bank of Gatineau River, near Hinks bridge, Alwyn Township.
- SCHIST (BIOTITE): Roadcut in Highway 19, 3 1/2 miles west of bridge on Mekinac River, Mekinac Township, Laviolette County.
- SCHIST (CHLORITIC): Huntingdon mine, near Eastman, Brome County.
- SERPENTINE: Canada Marble & Line Company quarry, west of L'Annonciation.

- SERPENTINE: Lower pit, Megantic-Lambly mine, Ireland Township, Megantic County.
- SERPENTINE: West bank of Port Daniel River, 6 miles from its mouth, Port Daniel Township, Gaspé Peninsula.
- SERPENTINE: Montreal Chrome pit, Coleraine Township, Megantic County.
- SHALE: Mines at Acton, Bagot County.
- SLATE: Lake St. Francis, Frontenac County.
- SLATE (AND LIMESTONE): On St. Helen Island.
- SYENITE: Duvex property, Mitchell Township.
- TALC: Bolton Township, Brome County.
- TUFF (AND PERIDOTITE): 1/4 mile north of Rivière des Plantes, Beauceville.

Saskatchewan

- BRECCIA: 24 miles northeast of Goldfields.
- GRANITE: Frontier Trust property on lake northwest of Frontier Lake.
- PEGMATITE: West side of Viking Lake in Goldfields area.
- PEGMATITE: Eldorado dike on Middle Foster Lake.
- SCHIST: Amisk Lake.

Yukon

- BRECCIA: At overlook at Watson Valley, 4 miles north of Mount Skukum.
- GRANITE (AND LIMESTONE): Along the valley of the Yukon River in the Whitehorse area.
- GRANODIORITE: Porter property, Carbon Hill, Wheaton district.
- PERIDOTITE: Near top of Miles Ridge, 2 miles west of Alaska Highway bridge over White River.
- PHYLLITE: 35 miles north of Watson Lake.
- PHYLLITE (AND GRANODIORITE): Canol mine at head of Upper Sheep Creek, 36 miles south-southeast of Ross River.
- PORPHYRY (SYENITE): Mine at Freegold Mountain, between Seymour and Stoddard creeks.
- SKARN: On south shore of Dragon Lake.

Mexico

- ANDESITE: Mine 3 miles east of El Rosario, Baja California.
- BASALT: Guadalupe Island, Baja California.
- BASALT: Pinacate volcanic field, Sonora.
- GRAPHITE: La Colorada, Sonora.
- OBSIDIAN: Along Highway 15, northwest of Guadalajara, near Tequila, Jalisco.
- PEGMATITE: El Alamo, 38 miles southeast of Ensenada, Baja California.
- PEGMATITE: 4 miles southeast of La Huerta, east of Ojos Negro, Baja California.
- PEGMATITE: La Jolleta Hills, 27 miles east of Tecate, Baja California.
- RHYOLITE: Tepetate, San Luis Potosi.
- RHYOLITE: Magdalena, Jalisco.
- RHYOLITE: Cerro Mercado mine, Ciudad Durango, Durango.

Nearly every state has a geological survey that publishes specialized reports on its mineral resources. Lists of such reports and maps can be obtained by writing to the bureaus listed in the section on Sources of Information. The various state tourist agencies occasionally have something specific enough to be useful.

The U.S. Bureau of Mines and the U.S. Geological Survey have issued a large number of professional papers, reports, and guides. These are indexed in a volume issued occasionally and available in large libraries, where many of the major publications themselves may be available.

The Bureau of Mines will supply preprints of state reports that appear in its *Minerals Yearbook.* It has recently published six *Visitor's Guides* that locate and list as well as describe mining areas open to the public. These cover, respectively, the New England and Middle Atlantic States, the South Atlantic States, the North Central States, the South Central States, the Rocky Mountain States, and the Pacific States. They are obtainable from the Superintendent of Documents, U.S. Government Printing Office, Washington, D.C. 20402. The price is $3.45 each. The information is rather general but interesting.

The McGraw-Hill Book Company, 1221 Avenue of the Americas, New York, New York 10020, publishes the *International Directory of Mining and Mineral Processing Operations,* costing $30. It is comprehensive as a guide to mines and quarries in the United States and elsewhere, and may be available in large libraries.

Since no listing of rock exposures as such exists, those appearing in this chapter have necessarily been compiled from incidental references in sources of information about minerals, physical geology, and gems. The author would welcome comments, corrections, and amplifications of the listings.

glossary

Aa: rough, clinkery, hardened lava. See *Pahoehoe*.
Amphibole: a member of a family of rock-forming silicates, such as hornblende.
Andesite: the fine-grained analog of diorite.
Anorthosite: a rock related to gabbro, composed mostly of plagioclase feldspar.
Anthracite: coal formed by metamorphism that is almost pure carbon.
Anticline: a fold or rise of rock that dips outward from its apex.
Arkose: a sandstone containing much feldspar and other mineral grains.
Basalt: a fine-textured, dark, heavy extrusive rock, the most abundant volcanic rock.
Basin: area formed by rock formations sloping to a center.
Batholith: a major intrusion of igneous rock, frequently the core of a mountain range, such as the Sierra Nevada.
Breccia: a conglomerate rock formed of cemented broken rock fragments.
Caldera: basinlike depression in the peak of a volcano, usually from subsidence of the crater.
Chalk: a sedimentary rock formed of the skeletons of tiny plants and animals, related to limestone.
Cirque: steep basin cut into the side of a mountain by a glacier.
Clay: A compacted deposit of decomposed rock particles.
Cleavage: capacity of a mineral to part along a smooth plane, a quality derived from the mineral's crystal structure.

Coastal plain: the low, broad area bordering a seacoast.

Concretion: a concentration of a rock's constituent materials, usually formed by action of cementing agents in sedimentary rocks.

Conglomerate: a rock formed of pebbles cemented together.

Continental drift: a theory that the continents were once parts of a single mass and have drifted into their present positions.

Continental shelf: a sloping plain lying beneath the sea along the border of a continent.

Contour line: line on a topographic map connecting all points on a land surface that are at the same level.

Coquina: a limestone formed principally of visible shell fragments.

Country rock: the predominant rock in an area, often altered by igneous intrusions.

Crossbedding: planes of sediments, usually in sandstone, that cut across and are inclined to the bedding of the rock mass.

Crust: the rocky outer shell of the earth.

Crystal: natural solid that expresses externally the regularity of its inner atomic structure.

Desert: an area of the earth's surface that gets less than 10 inches of rain annually.

Diabase: a gabbrolike rock, dark and heavy but finer-grained.

Dike: a narrow igneous intrusion that cuts at a more or less vertical angle through country rock.

Diorite: a coarse-textured igneous rock, dark and containing little quartz.

Dolomite: a sedimentary rock closely related to limestone but containing magnesium as well as calcium.

Drift: earth, clay, and rock deposited by a continental glacier.

Drumlin: an elongated hill formed of glacially transported material and parallel to the direction of the glacier's movement.

Dune: a mound of drifted sand, usually windblown.

Dunite: a rock related to peridotite but formed almost entirely of olivine.

Element: a basic building block of the chemical system, indivisible by ordinary chemical methods.

Erosion: destruction of rocks by wind, water, ice, and changing temperatures.

Escarpment: a steep cliff formed by faulting or erosion.

Esker: a narrow ridge formed by material deposited by a stream flowing within a glacier.

Extrusive: a term applied to igneous rocks that have hardened above the surface of the earth, such as lava.

Fault: a fracture in the crust caused by an earth movement. Faults are of several types, such as normal, reverse, and strike-slip faults.

Ferromagnesian: term applied to common rock-forming silicates containing iron and magnesium. Such rocks are usually dark.

Flow structure: lines and structures in igneous rocks indicative of the movement of the magma before it hardened.

Foliation: visible layering in a metamorphic rock caused by parallel alignment of such minerals as mica.

Formation: a distinctive rock or group of rock units large enough to be marked on a geologic map.

Fracture: appearance of the surface of a rock that has been broken apart. Unlike the appearance in a cleavage, the surface is usually rough and hackly.

Gabbro: a coarse-textured igneous rock, dark from pyroxenes and plagioclase feldspar, the intrusive equivalent of extrusive basalt.

Geode: a hollow, usually spherical body formed in a rock cavity by deposition of a shell of quartz or calcite in a sedimentary rock such as limestone.

Geology: the science that treats of things and processes of the earth.

Geologic map: a topographic map with additions that show the nature and location of rock formations present in the mapped area.

Gneiss: a coarse-grained metamorphic rock much like granite but distinguished by the segregation of its light and dark minerals into separate layers.

Graben: a depression caused by the faulting of a block of the earth's surface. See *Horst.*

Granite: a coarsely crystalline, light-colored rock, the basic rock of the continents.

Granodiorite: an igneous rock midway in color and mineral substance between granite and diorite.

Graywacke: impure sandstone containing rock fragments and clay particles.

Gypsum: a sedimentary rock composed of calcium sulfate, often found with salt deposits.

Hornfels: a slatelike metamorphic rock, harder than slate and not readily cleaved.
Horst: block of the earth's crust elevated by faulting. See *Graben.*
Igneous: a term applied to rocks formed of molten magma.
Intrusive: a term applied to igneous rocks that have hardened below the earth's surface.
Jade: common name for two different silicate rocks, jadeite and nephrite, both hard and often green in color.
Kame: a conical hill of drift left by meltwater from a glacier.
Kimberlite: an altered peridotite breccia; the host rock of diamonds.
Laccolith: an intrusion of igneous rock that raises rock layers into a dome.
Latite: fine-grained igneous rock; the counterpart of monzonite.
Lava: molten magma that reaches the surface through a volcano or other vent.
Limestone: a sedimentary rock formed of shell fragments and chemically deposited calcium carbonate. See *Dolomite.*
Loess: a deposit of fine, windblown rock fragments.
Luster: the appearance of a rock surface by reflected light, described by such a term as "glassy."
Magma: molten material beneath the earth's surface; the source of igneous rock.
Mantle: the part of the earth that lies immediately below the crust. It is the source of magma.
Marble: a metamorphic rock composed mainly of interlocked crystals of calcite. It is normally light-colored and often figured or mottled.
Mass wasting: the downslope movement of rock by the force of gravity.
Mesa: an isolated elevated area with steep sides and a flat top.
Metamorphic: a term applied to rocks formed by alteration of other rocks by heat, pressure, and other natural forces.
Mineral: a crystalline inorganic substance with a definite chemical composition and physical properties.
Mohs hardness scale: in increasing order of hardness:

1. Talc	6. Orthoclase feldspar
2. Gypsum	7. Quartz
3. Calcite	8. Topaz
4. Fluorite	9. Corundum
5. Apatite	10. Diamond

Monzonite: a coarse-grained intrusive rock intermediate between diorite and syenite.
Moraine: a ridge or other mass of earth and stones deposited during the retreat of a glacier.
Nodule: a foreign body, usually rounded, different in composition from the rock in which it exists.
Obsidian: an extrusive rock that looks like glass; usually black or red.
Olivine: a magnesium silicate; an important rock-forming mineral; the principal mineral of dunite.
Outcrop: bedrock exposed to view, as in a cliff.
Pahoehoe: lava that has cooled with a smooth or pillowlike surface. Pronounced with five syllables. See *Aa.*
Pegmatite: igneous rock characterized by the large size of its crystals, but like granite in composition.
Peridotite: a dark-colored igneous rock composed mostly of pyroxene and olivine.
Period: a division of geological time, part of an era, as the Cambrian period of the Paleozoic era.
Phenocryst: the large, conspicuous crystals in a porphyry.
Phyllite: a gray metamorphic rock distinguished by its pearly surface and easy cleavage.
Pitchstone: a variety of obsidian.
Plate tectonics: a comprehensive theory of global dynamics involving the interrelationships of drifting continental plates.
Plateau: an elevated and largely flat surface of considerable extent.
Porphyry: a fine-grained igneous rock containing large crystals that formed before the mass cooled.
Pumice: a frothy form of the glassy extrusive rock obsidian.
Pyroxenes: a family of mineral silicates that are common rock-formers.
Quartzite: a product of the metamorphism of sandstone, hard, light-colored, and grainy.
Rhyolite: an extrusive rock that is chemically the equivalent of granite but is fine-grained because of rapid cooling.
Rock: a solid, naturally occurring substance; usually a mixture of crystals of several minerals.
Sandstone: a sedimentary rock formed by hardening of sand-sized particles; usually predominantly quartz.
Schist: a coarse metamorphic rock characterized by a wavy surface and often by an abundance of mica.
Sedimentary: a term applied to rocks formed on the earth's

surface, usually from products of erosion of other rocks.

Serpentine: a metamorphic rock with a waxy appearance and texture; usually some shade of green or yellow.

Shale: clay and silt cemented into rock that has a platy, easily cleaved texture.

Shield: the rocky central nucleus about which a continent has been built.

Silica: silicon dioxide, the mineral of quartz.

Sill: an igneous intrusion as a tabular, usually horizontal body, between layers of the preexisting rock.

Silt: rock dust smaller than .05 millimeter.

Skarn: a rock often rich in mineral crystals that has been created by the intense heat of contact metamorphism acting on limestone.

Slate: a dark metamorphic rock characterized by easy cleavage.

Specific gravity: the ratio of the weight of a material to an equal volume of water. Specific gravity (symbol sg) is expressed as a number, such as quartz 2.65.

Stalactite: a pillarlike cave formation growing from the ceiling. A like formation growing from the floor is a stalagmite.

Stock: a steep-sided rock intrusion.

Stratum: a distinct layer in a rock mass; usually sedimentary rock. The plural is strata.

Streak: color of the powder rubbed from a specimen when it is drawn across an unglazed tile.

Styolite: a columnlike formation in limestone inclined to the bedding plane.

Syenite: an extrusive, coarse-grained igneous rock like granite but containing less quartz.

Syncline: a downfolded trough of rock; the opposite of an anticline.

Talus: rock debris at the foot of a cliff or mountain slope.

Texture: the grain size and interrelationship of mineral constituents in a rock.

Till: a deposit of loose glacial debris, especially sand, gravel, and clay.

Tonalite: a form of diorite, but containing more quartz.

Topographic map: a map that shows the shape and position of physical features of an area of the earth's surface.

Trachyte: an extrusive rock, the fine-grained equivalent of syenite.

Trap rock: dark, dense igneous rocks, such as basalt, gabbro, and diabase, that are quarried for road material.

Travertine: a porous limestone formed in springs and caves; often used for tabletops and ornamental purposes.
Tufa: a coarse travertine.
Tuff: a rock formed by cementation of small volcanic particles.
Volcano: Elevated vent in the earth's surface from which molten rock material is emitted.
Weathering: the disintegrating action of natural agents such as wind, weather, and ice.
Xenolith: a foreign rock fragment included in an igneous rock mass; picked up from the country rock while the invading rock was molten.

Official State Stones

Alabama	Marble
Alaska	Jade
Arkansas	Bauxite
California	Serpentine
Indiana	Limestone
Iowa	Geode
Maine	Red Garnet
Michigan	Petosky Stone
Mississippi	Petrified Wood
Missouri	Mozarkite
Montana	Montana Agate
Nebraska	Prairie Agate
North Dakota	Petrified Teredo Wood
Oklahoma	Barite Rose
Oregon	Thunderegg
Rhode Island	Cumberlandite
South Carolina	Blue Granite
Texas	Petrified Palm Wood
Washington	Petrified Wood
Wisconsin	Red Granite

metric equivalents for rockhounds

With the metric system now nearly universal in most scientific writing, it is helpful to be able to translate it into more familiar units. Equivalents useful for collectors are given below:

LENGTH

1 inch	= 2.54 centimeters (cm)
1 foot	= 30 centimeters or 0.3 meter
1 yard	= 0.91 meter
1 mile	= 1.61 kilometers (km)

WEIGHT

1 ounce	= 141 carats or 28.2 grams (31.1 Troy grams)
1 gram	= 5 carats
1 carat	= 200 milligrams (mg)
1 pound	= 0.45 kilogram (kilo)
1 ton	= 0.91 metric ton

CAPACITY

1 quart	= 0.95 liter

TEMPERATURE

To convert Celsius (often called Centigrade) to Fahrenheit, multiply the Celsius reading by 9, divide the result by 5, and add 32. To convert Fahrenheit to Celsius, subtract 32 from the Fahrenheit reading, multiply the result by 5, and divide by 9.

sources of information

Information and example are essential to enjoyment of any hobby, and this is especially true of rock collecting, where the whole continent is the field of interest. Museums and university collections of minerals and rocks, as well as federal, state, and regional centers of information, are listed below.

It is advisable to make an appointment to see a university collection. Many academic institutions have dispersed their collections or withdrawn them from public view as financial pressures and changing emphases in geological teaching have been felt. Since federal money has poured into state agencies, they have regrouped so rapidly that some addresses listed below may have changed since publication of this book.

In the listing by states and cities that follows, the symbol (1) identifies the state agency concerned with geological matters—the place to go or write for publications and information—and the symbol (2) introduces the listing of major museums and academic collections and displays as well as local sources of information.

United States

Alabama: (1) Geological Survey, Tuscaloosa 35401. (2) Regar Memorial Museum of Natural History, Anniston; Alabama Polytechnic University, Auburn; Alabama Museum of Natural History, Tuscaloosa.

Alaska: (1) Natural Resources Department, Division of Geology and Geophysical Surveys, 3001 Porcupine Drive, Anchorage 99501. (2) State Museum, State Capitol, Juneau; University of Alaska Museum, Fairbanks.

Arizona: (1) Mineral Resources Department, 1826 West McDowell, Phoenix 85007. (2) Museum of Northern Arizona, Flagstaff; Petrified Forest National Monument, Holbrook; Mineral Museum, Fairgrounds, Phoenix; Center for Meteorite Studies, Tempe; Public Museum, Tombstone; Arizona State Museum at University of Arizona, and Arizona–Sonora Desert Museum, both in Tucson.

Arkansas: (1) Commerce Department, Geological Commission, Vardell Parkham Geology Center, 3815 West Roosevelt Road, Little Rock 72204. (2) State Museum at University of Arkansas, Fayetteville; Hendrix College, Conway.

California: (1) Conservation Department, Division of Mining and Geology, 1416 Ninth Street, Sacramento 95814. (2) University of California Museum, Berkeley; Western Trails Museum, Knott's Berry Farm, Buena Park; Museum of Natural History, Fresno; County Museum of Natural History, Museum of Science and Industry, and museums at the University of California and the University of Southern California, all in Los Angeles; Public Museum, Oakland; Museum of Natural History, Pacific Grove; Natural History Museum and San Diego Gem and Mineral Society exhibit, both in Balboa Park, San Diego; Riverside County Museum, Riverside; Mines Museum in Ferry Building, Academy of Sciences Museum in Golden Gate Park, Museum of Wells Fargo Bank, all in San Francisco; New Almaden Museum, San Jose; Museum of Natural History, Santa Barbara; University of California Museum, Santa Clara; City-County Museum, Sacramento.

Colorado: (1) Natural Resources Department, Geological Survey, 1313 Sherman Centennial Building, Room 715, Denver 80203. (2) University of Colorado Museum, Boulder; Western Museum of Mining and Industry, Colorado College, both in Colorado Springs; Cripple Creek District Museum, Cripple Creek; Denver Museum of Natural History in City Park, State Museum, and Mines Museum in State Capitol, all in Denver; Colorado School of Mines, Golden.

Connecticut: (1) Environmental Protection Department, Bureau of Geology, State Office Building, Hartford 06115. (2) Bruce Museum, Greenwich; Trinity College and Wadsworth Athenaeum, both in Hartford; Wesleyan University, Middletown; Peabody Museum and Geology Laboratory of Yale University, New Haven; Choate School, Wallingford.

Delaware: (1) Geological Survey, 16 Robinson Hall, University of Delaware, Newark 19711. (2) State Museum, Dover; Delaware Museum of Natural History, Greenville; Irene Du-Pont Collection, Penny Hall, University of Delaware, Newark; Hagley Museum, Museum of Natural History, Wilmington.

District of Columbia: (1) Geological Survey, 12201 Sunrise Valley Drive, Reston, Virginia 22092; Bureau of Mines, Department of the Interior, 2401 E Street, N.W., Washington 20241. (2) National Museum of the Smithsonian Institution.

Florida: (1) Department of Natural Resources, Division of Resource Management, Bureau of Geology, Pennington Building, Tallahassee 32304. (2) John B. Stetson Museum, DeLand; Florida State Museum, Gainesville; Geological Survey Museum and Geology Department of Florida State Museum, Tallahassee; Museum of Natural History, Tampa.

Georgia: (1) Natural Resources Department, Earth and Water Division, Geological Survey, 19 Hunter Street S.W., Atlanta 30334. (2) Hurt Museum, Atlanta; Museum of University of Georgia, Athens.

Hawaii: (1) Land and Natural Resources Department, 1151 Punchbowl, Honolulu 96813. (2) Bernice P. Bishop Museum, Honolulu; Kauai Museum, Lihue.

Idaho: (1) Earth Resources Division, Room 121, Statehouse, Boise 83720. (2) State Museum, Boise; University of Idaho Museum, Moscow; Idaho State University Museum, Pocatello.

Illinois: (1) Geological Survey, Natural Resources Building, University of Illinois, Urbana 61801. (2) Southern Illinois University, Carbondale; Academy of Sciences, Field Museum of Natural History, both in Chicago; Lizzadro Museum of Lapidary Arts, Elmhurst; Illinois State University Museum, Normal; Fryxell Museum of Augustana College, Rock Island; Funk Museum, Shirley; Illinois State Museum, Springfield; University Museum of Natural History, Urbana.

Indiana: (1) Natural Resources Department, Geological Survey, Indiana University, Bloomington 47401. (2) University Museum, Bloomington; State Museum in the State Capitol, and Children's Museum, Indianapolis; Purdue University School of Engineering, Lafayette; Earlham College, Richmond; Indiana State University, Terre Haute.

Iowa: (1) Geological Survey, 123 North Capital Street, Iowa City 52240. (2) University of Northern Iowa, Earth Science Department, and University Museum, Cedar Falls; Public Museum, Davenport; Porter House Museum, Decorah; Straight Memorial Museum, Drake University, State Historical Museum, both in Des Moines; Geological Survey in Trowbridge Hall, University of Iowa, Iowa City; Cornell College Geology Department, Mt. Vernon; Grout Museum, Waterloo.

Kansas: (1) Park and Resources Authority, Natural Resources Department, 503 Kansas Street, 5th Floor, Topeka 66603. (2) St. Benedict's College, Atchison; Natural History Museum and Geology Department Museums at University of Kansas, Lawrence; Smoky Hills Historical Museum, Salina; State Historical Society Museum in Memorial Building, Topeka; Historical Museum, Wichita.

Kentucky: (1) Geological Survey, 307 Mineral Industries Building, 120 Graham Avenue, Lexington 40506. (2) Museum at Western Kentucky University, Bowling Green; Baker Hunt Foundation, Covington; Geology Department Museum, University of Kentucky, Lexington; Public Library Museum, Louisville.

Louisiana: (1) Geological Survey, Louisiana State University, Geology Building, Baton Rouge 70804. (2) University Museum, Baton Rouge; Lafayette Natural History Museum, Lafayette; State Museum and Museum of Tulane University, both New Orleans.

Maine: (1) Department of Conservation, Bureau of Geology, Ray Building, Hospital Street, Augusta 04333. (2) State Museum, Augusta; Bates College, Lewiston Museum of University of Maine, Orono; Hamlin Memorial Hall, Paris; Natural History Society Museum and Beach Museum, both in Portland; Colby College, Waterville.

Maryland: (1) Natural Resources Department, Geological Survey, Johns Hopkins University, Baltimore 21218. (2) Johns Hopkins University Geology Department, Natural History Society Museum, and Academy of Sciences, all in Baltimore.

Massachusetts: (1) Environmental Management Department, 100 Cambridge Avenue, Boston 02100. (2) Pratt Museum of Amherst College, Amherst; Society of Natural History Museum, Museum of Science, Children's Museum, all in Boston; Mineralogical Museum of Harvard University, Cambridge; Smith College, Northampton; Peabody Museum, Salem; Mount Holyoke College, South Hadley; Museum of Natural History, Springfield; Williams College, Williamstown; Natural History Museum, Science Center, Clark University Museum, Worcester.

Michigan: (1) Natural Resources Department, Geological Survey Division, Mason Building, Lansing 48913. (2) Mineralogical Museum of the University of Michigan, Ann Arbor; Kingman Museum, Battle Creek; Cranbrook Institute of Science, Bloomfield Hills; Ft. Wilkins State Park Museum, Copper Harbor; Science Museum and Wayne State University Museum, both in Detroit; Public Museum, Grand Rapids; Seaman Museum of Michigan Technological University, Houghton; Michigan State University Museum and State Historical Museum, both in East Lansing; Public Museum, Western Michigan University, Kalamazoo; Port Huron Public Library Museum, Port Huron; Saginaw Museum, Saginaw.

Minnesota: (1) Natural Resources Department, Geology Division, Centennial Building, St. Paul 55155. (2) James Ford Bell Museum of Natural History, Science Museum at Public Library, both in Minneapolis; Carleton College, Northfield; Science Museum, St. Paul.

Mississippi: (1) Geological Survey, 2525 North West Street, Jackson 39205. (2) Mississippi State College, State College; University of Mississippi, University.

Missouri: (1) Division of Geological Survey, Buehler Park, P.O. Box 205, Rolla 65401. (2) Museum of University of Missouri, Columbia; Missouri Resources Museum, Jefferson City; Kansas City Museum of History and Science, Geological Museum at the University of Missouri, both in Kansas City; School of Mines Museum, Rolla; Public Schools Educational Museum, Museum of Washington University, Museum of Science and Natural History, all in St. Louis; Palmer Little Museum, Webb City.

Montana: (1) Natural Resources and Conservation Department, 32 Ewing Street, Helena 59601. (2) School of Mines, Butte; Museum of the Historical Society, Helena; State University Museum, Missoula.

Nebraska: (1) Natural Resources Commission, 301 Centennial Mall South, 4th Floor, Lincoln 68509. (2) University of Nebraska, State Museum, Lincoln.

Nevada: (1) Conservation and Natural Resources Department, 201 South Fall Street, Carson City 89701. (2) Lake Mead Natural History Association, Boulder City; State Museum, Carson City; Northeastern Nevada Museum, Elko; Mackay School of Mines Museum, Reno.

New Hampshire: (1) Resources and Development Department, Natural Resources Development Division, State House Annex, Concord 03301. (2) Woodman Institute, Dover; Geology Department of the University of New Hampshire, Durham; Wilson Museum of Dartmouth College, Hanover; Institute of Arts and Sciences, Manchester.

New Jersey: (1) Bureau of Geology and Topography, Department of Environmental Protection, P.O. Box 2809, Trenton 08625. (2) Museum of the Newark Mineralogical Society, Newark; Rutgers University Geology Museum, New Brunswick; New Jersey Mineralogical Society, Paterson; Princeton University Geology Museum, Princeton; State Museum in State House Annex, Trenton.

New Mexico: (1) Natural Resources Conservation Commission, 321 West San Francisco Street, Santa Fe 87501. (2) University of New Mexico Museum, Albuquerque; Carlsbad Caverns National Park Museum, Carlsbad; Public Museum, Roswell; State Museum in Palace of the Governers, Santa Fe; Institute of Mining and Technology, Socorro.

New York: (1) Education Department, Geological Survey, Education Building, Albany 12224. (2) State Museum, Albany; Museum of Science, Buffalo; Knox Museum of Hamilton College, Clinton; Museum of Natural History of Colgate

University, Hamilton; Cornell University, Ithaca; American Museum of Natural History, Columbia University Geology and Mineralogy Museum, Metropolitan Museum of Art, all in New York; Vassar College, Poughkeepsie; University of Rochester Museum of Geology, Ward's Natural Establishment, Museum and Science Center, all in Rochester; Union College, Schenectady; Rensselaer Polytechnic Institute, Troy.

North Carolina: (1) Natural and Economic Resources Department, Old YMCA Building, Raleigh 27611. (2) Colburn Mineral Museum, Asheville; University of North Carolina, Chapel Hill; Nature Museum, Charlotte; Duke University, Durham; Museum of North Carolina Minerals of National Park Service, Gillespie Gap, near Spruce Pine; North Carolina State University, and State Museum, Raleigh; Nature Science Museum, Winston-Salem; Franklin Gem and Mineral Museum, Franklin; Schiele Museum of Natural History, Gastonia; Natural Science Museum, Greensboro; Arts and Sciences Museum, Stateville.

North Dakota: (1) Geological Survey, 209 East Broadway, Bismarck 58501. (2) University of North Dakota, Grand Forks.

Ohio: (1) Department of Natural Resources, Division of Geological Survey, Fountain Square, Columbus 43224. (2) Ohio University Museum of Natural History, Athens; Bowling Green State University, Bowling Green; Museum of Natural History, Cincinnati; Case Institute, Museum of Natural History, Western Reserve University, all in Cleveland; Science Center, Orton and Lord Halls of Ohio State University, both in Columbus; Johnson-Humrickhaus Memorial Museum, Coshocton; Museum of Natural History, Dayton; Oberlin College, Oberlin; Clark County Historical Society, Springfield; Heidelberg College Science Hall, Tiffin.

Oklahoma: (1) Geological Survey, 830 Van Vlett Oval, Room 163, Norman 73069. (2) Woolaroc Museum, Bartlesville; Gould Hall and Stovall Museum of Science and History of the University of Oklahoma, both in Norman; University of Tulsa and the County Museum, both in Tulsa.

Oregon: (1) Department of Geology and Mineral Industries, 1400 Southwest Fifth Street, Portland 97201. (2) Oregon State College, Corvallis; Museum of Natural History of the

University of Oregon, Eugene; Museum of Science and Industry, Lewis and Clark College, Portland; Prehistoric Life Museum, U.S. 101, Yachats.

Pennsylvania: (1) Environmental Resources Bureau of Topographic and Geologic Survey, Towne House Apartments Building, Second and Chestnut Streets, Harrisburg 17101. (2) Lehigh University, Bethlehem; Bryn Mawr College, Bryn Mawr; Dickinson College, Carlisle; Lafayette College, Easton; North Museum, Franklin and Marshall College, Lancaster; Allegheny College, Meadville; Delaware County Institute of Science, Media; Academy of Natural Sciences, Museum of the University of Pennsylvania, Franklin Institute Science Museum, Wagner Free Institute of Science, all in Philadelphia; Carnegie Museum of Natural History, Pittsburgh; Mineral Industries Building of Pennsylvania State University, University Park.

Rhode Island: (1) Natural Resources Department, 83 Park Street, Providence 02903. (2) University of Rhode Island, Kingston; Roger Williams Park Museum, Rhode Island Hall of Brown University, both in Providence; Public Library, Westerly.

South Carolina: (1) Development Board, Geology Division, Harbison Forest Road, Columbia 03903. (2) Museum of Art and Science, Howard Collection at University of South Carolina, both in Columbia.

South Dakota: (1) Geological Survey, Science Center, Vermillion 57069. (2) School of Mines and Technology, Rapid City; W. H. Over Dakota Museum at the University of South Dakota, Vermillion.

Tennessee: (1) Department of Conservation, Division of Geology, G-5 State Office Building, Nashville 37219. (2) Students Museum and the University of Tennessee, Knoxville; Vanderbilt University Geology Department, State Museum in War Memorial Building, both in Nashville.

Texas: (1) Bureau of Economic Geology, University of Texas, Austin 78701. (2) Texas Memorial Museum, Austin; Centennial Museum, El Paso; Museum of Science and History, Fort Worth; Museum of Natural Science, Houston; Witte Memorial Museum, San Antonio; Baylor University, Waco.

Utah: (1) Geological and Mineral Survey, Geological Survey

Building, University of Utah, Salt Lake City 84112. (2) John Hutchings Museum, Lehi; Geology Museum of the University of Utah, Westminster College, both in Salt Lake City; Fieldhouse of Natural History, Vernal State Park, Vernal.

Vermont: (1) Environmental Conservation Agency, 5 Court Street, Montpelier 05602. (2) Fleming Museum of the University of Vermont, Burlington; Vermont Museum, Montpelier; Fairbanks Museum, St. Johnsbury.

Virginia: (1) Conservation and Economic Development Department, Geology Division, Charlottesville 22902. (2) Holden Hall of Virginia Polytechnic Institute, Blacksburg; Brooks Museum of the University of Virginia, Charlottesville; Washington and Lee University, Lexington; Science Museum of Virginia, Richmond.

Washington: (1) Natural Resources Department, Division of Geology, Public Lands Building, Olympia 98504. (2) State Capitol Museum, Olympia; Burke Memorial Museum at the University of Washington, Seattle; Grace Campbell Memorial Public Museum, Spokane; Washington State Historical Society, Tacoma; Ginkgo Petrified Forest Museum, Vantage; Whitman College, Walla Walla; North Central Washington Museum, Wenatchee.

West Virginia: (1) Mines Department, Division of Geology, MB3-A State Capitol, Charleston 25305. (2) Archives and History Museum, Charleston; Geology Museum of Marshall College, Huntington; West Virginia University, Morgantown.

Wisconsin: (1) Geological and Natural History Survey, 1815 University Avenue, Madison 53706. (2) Lawrence College, Appleton; Beloit College, Beloit; University of Wisconsin, Madison; Public Museum, Museum of University of Wisconsin both in Milwaukee.

Wyoming: (1) Geological Survey, University Station, Box 3008, Laramie 82071. (2) State Museum, Cheyenne; Geology Building of University of Wyoming, Laramie; Norris Museum, Yellowstone Park.

Canada

(1) Geological Survey of Canada, 601 Booth Street, Ottawa, Ontario. (2) University of Alberta and Provincial Museum, Edmonton, and Glenbow-Albert Museum, Calgary, Alberta. University of British Columbia, City Museum, and British Columbia and Yukon Chamber of Mines, all in Vancouver, and Provincial Museum, Victoria, British Columbia. Museum of Man and Nature, Winnipeg, Manitoba. New Brunswick Museum, St. John, University of New Brunswick, Fredericton, and Mount Allison University, Sackville, New Brunswick. Memorial Museum, St. John's, Newfoundland. Museum of Science and Dalhousie University Museum, Halifax, Nova Scotia. National Museum of Natural Sciences and Victoria Museum, Ottawa, Miller Hall of Queen's University, Kingston, and Royal Ontario Museum, Toronto, Ontario. Confederation Centre Museum, Charlottetown, Prince Edward Island. Redpath Museum of McGill University, College de Montreal, Montreal, Musee du Quebec and Musee de Mineralogie of Laval University, Quebec, Quebec.

for further reading

General Geology

Anatomy of the Earth, Andre Cailleux. McGraw-Hill Book Company, New York, 1968, 255 pages.

Continents in Motion, Walter Sullivan. McGraw-Hill Book Company, New York, 1974, 399 pages.

Down to Earth, Carey Croneis and William C. Krumbein. University of Chicago Press, Chicago, 1936, 499 pages.

The Earth Beneath Us, Kirtley F. Mather. Random House, New York, 1964, 320 pages.

The Evolution of North America, Philip B. King. Princeton University Press, Princeton, 1959, 189 pages.

Field Guide to Landforms in the United States, John A. Shimer. The Macmillan Company, New York, 1972, 272 pages.

The Forging of Our Continent, Charlton Ogburn, Jr. D. Van Nostrand Company, Smithsonian Library, Princeton, N.J., 1968, 160 pages.

Geological Evolution of North America (2d edition), Thomas H. Clark and Colin W. Stearn. Roland Press, New York, 1968, 570 pages.

Geology in the Service of Man, W. G. Fearnsides and O. M. Bulman. Pelican paperback, London, 1961, 217 pages.

Invitation to Geology, William H. Matthews III. Natural History Press, Garden City, N.Y., 1971, 148 pages.

Physics of the Earth and Planets, A. H. Cook. John Wiley & Sons, New York, 1973, 316 pages.

Regional Geomorphology of the United States, William D. Thornbury. John Wiley & Sons, New York, 1965, 609 pages.

The Restless Earth, Nigel Calder. Viking Press, New York, 1972, 152 pages.

Rock, Time, and Landforms, Jerome Wykoff. Harper & Row, New York, 1966, 372 pages.

This Sculptured Earth, John A. Shimer. Columbia University Press, New York, 1959, 255 pages.

The Way the Earth Works, Peter J. Wyllie. John Wiley & Sons, New York, 1976, 296 pages.

Lore About Rocks

Dictionary of Geological Terms (revised edition), prepared under the direction of the American Geological Institute. Anchor Books, Garden City, N.Y., 1976, 472 pages.

Discovering Rocks and Minerals, Roy A. Gallant and Christopher J. Schuberth. The Natural History Press, Garden City, N.Y., 1967, 126 pages.

Field Guide to Rocks and Minerals (4th edition), Frederick H. Pough. Houghton Mifflin Company, Boston, Mass. 1976, 317 pages.

Geology of the Industrial Rocks and Minerals, Robert L. Bates. Harper and Company, New York, 1960.

The Gem Hunter's Guide (5th revised edition), Russell P. MacFall. Thomas Y. Crowell Company, New York, 1975, 323 pages.

A Guide to Minerals, Rocks and Fossils, W. R. Hamilton, A. R. Woolley, and A. C. Bishop. Crescent Books, New York, 1974, 320 pages.

Guide to the Natural Wonders of America, edited by Beverley da Costa. American Heritage Publishing Company, New York, 1972, 320 pages.

How to Know the Minerals and Rocks, Richard M. Pearl. McGraw-Hill Book Company, New York, 1955, 192 pages.

Introduction to Petrology, Brian Bayly. Prentice-Hall, Inc., Englewood Cliffs, N.J., 1968, 371 pages.

Meteorites, Fritz Heide. University of Chicago Press, Chicago, 1964, 144 pages.

Minerals and Gems, edited by Russell P. MacFall. Thomas Y. Crowell Company, New York, 1975, 242 pages.

Nature of Earth Materials, Anthony C. Tennissen. Prentice-Hall, Inc., Englewood Cliffs, N.J., 1974, 317 pages.

The Rock Book, Carroll Lane Felton and Mildred Adams Felton. Doubleday, Doran, Garden City, N.Y., 1940, 357 pages.

The Rockhound's Manual, Gordon S. Fay. Barnes & Noble, New York, 1972, 290 pages.

Rocks and Minerals, Joel Arem. Bantam Books, New York, 1973, 145 pages.

Western National Parks, Michael Frome, photos by David Muench. Rand McNally & Company, Chicago, 1977, 72 pages.

Crafts with Stones

Contemporary Stone Sculpture, Dona Z. Meilach. Crown Publishers, Inc., New York, 1970, 211 pages.

The Fundamentals of Gemstone Carving, Gordon S. Kennedy, edited by Pansy D. Kraus. Lapidary Journal, San Diego, 1967, 128 pages.

Gemcraft (2d edition), Lelande Quick and Hugh Leiper, revised by Pansy D. Kraus. Chilton Book Company, Radnor, Pa., 1977, 195 pages.

Gem Cutter's Guide, Ronald J. Balej. Minnesota Lapidary Supply Company, Minneapolis, Minn., 1963, 43 pages.

Gem Cutting (2d edition), John Sinkankas. Van Nostrand Reinhold Publishing Company, New York, 1962, 297 pages.

Gem Cutting Is Easy, Martin Walter. Crown Publishers, Inc., New York, 1972, 96 pages.

Gem Cutting Shop Helps, Hugh Leiper and Pansy S. Kraus. Lapidary Journal, San Diego, 1964, 230 pages.

Gem Tumbling, Arthur and Lila Mae Victor. Victor Agate Shop, Spokane, Wash., 1962, 58 pages.

How to Plan, Establish and Maintain Rock Gardens, George Schenk. Lane Book Company, Menlo Park, Calif., 1964, 112 pages.

Mosaics with Natural Stones, Walter Lauppi. Sterling Publishing Company, New York, 1974, 96 pages.

New Improved Methods of Tumbling Gem Stones, Erwin C.

Gilman. Published by the author, Hellerstown, Pa., 1971, 57 pages.

Pebble Collecting and Polishing, Edward Fletcher. Sterling Publishing Company, New York, 1973, 96 pages.

Practical Gemstone Craft, Helen Hutton. Viking Press, New York, 1972, 103 pages.

Rock Gardens and Water Plants, Francis B. Stark and Conrad B. Link. Doubleday & Company, Garden City, N.Y., 1969, 64 pages.

Rock and Stone Craft, Elyse Sommer. Crown Publishers, Inc., New York, 1973, 96 pages.

Stone Grinding and Polishing, David F. Olson. Sterling Publishing Company, New York, 1973, 48 pages.

Location References

United States

Mineralogy of Arizona, John W. Anthony, Sidney A. Williams, and Richard A. Bideaux. University of Arizona Press, Tucson, Ariz., 1977, 255 pages.

Arkansas Rock and Mineral Collecting Localities, published by the Arkansas Geological Commission, Little Rock, Ark., 19 pages. With "Geology of Magnet Cove," 6 pages, plus map.

Rockhounding in Arkansas, David and Sarah Dodson. Published by the authors, Little Rock, Ark., 1974, 47 pages.

California's Changing Landscapes, Gordon B. Oakeshott. McGraw-Hill Book Company, New York, 1971, 416 pages.

Rocks and Minerals of California (2d revised edition), Vinson Brown and David Allan. Naturegraph Publishers, Healdsburg, Calif., 1964, 121 pages.

Geologic History of the Yosemite Valley, Francois E. Matthes. U.S. Geological Survey Professional Paper 160, 1930, 137 pages.

Minerals of Colorado, a 100-Year Record, Edwin B. Eckel. U.S. Geological Survey Bulletin 1114, 1961, 399 pages.

The Geology of Eastern Connecticut, Wilbur G. Foye.

Published by the state, Geological Survey Bulletin 74, Hartford, Conn., 1949, 100 pages.

The Geology of Jefferson County, Fla., J. William Yon, Jr. Florida Geological Survey Bulletin 48, Tallahassee, Fla., 1966, 119 pages.

Rocks and Minerals of Florida, Ernest W. Bishop and Lawrence L. Dee, Jr. Florida Geological Survey Special Publication 8, Tallahassee, Fla., 1961, 41 pages.

Summary of the Geology of Florida and a Guidebook to the Classic Exposures, Harbans S. Puri and Robert O. Vernon. Florida Geological Survey Special Publication 5, Revised, Tallahassee, Fla., 1964, 312 pages.

The Common Rocks and Minerals of Georgia, A. S. Furcron. Department of Mines, Mining and Geology Information Circular 5, Atlanta, Ga., 1964, 6 pages.

The Flagstone Industry of Georgia, A. S. Furcron. Department of Mines, Mining and Geology Information Circular 12, Atlanta, Ga., 1964, 7 pages.

Geology of the Crystalline Rocks of Georgia, Geoffrey W. Crickmay. Department of Mines, Mining and Geology Bulletin 58, Atlanta, Ga., 1952, 56 pages.

The Georgia Marble District, a Field Excursion, W. Robert Power and Ernest H. Wade. Department of Mines, Mining and Geology Guidebook 1, Atlanta, Ga., 1962, 21 pages.

Minerals of Georgia, Robert B. Cook, Department of Natural Resources, Atlanta, Ga., 1978, 189 pages.

Geology of the Hawaiian Islands, H. T. Stearns. Bulletin 8, Honolulu, Hawaii, 1946, 226 pages.

The Minerals of Idaho, Earl V. Shannon. National Museum Bulletin 131, Washington, D.C., 1926, 483 pages.

The Minerals of Iowa, Paul J. Horick. Published by the state, Iowa Geological Survey Educational Series, Iowa City, Iowa, 1974, 88 pages.

Kentucky's Rocks and Minerals, Walter L. Helton. Geological Survey, Special Publication 9, Lexington, Ky., 1964, 55 pages.

The Petrography of Certain Igneous Dikes of Kentucky, James B. Koenig. Kentucky Geological Survey Series 9, Bulletin 21, Lexington, Ky., 1956, 57 pages.

Guidebook to Mineral Collecting in the Maine Pegmatite Belt, published by the Federation of Maine Mineral and Gem Clubs, 1973, 22 pages.

Maine Granite Quarries and Prospects. Maine Geological Survey Mineral Resources Index No. 2, Augusta, Maine, 1958, 50 pages, plus map.

Maine Pegmatite Mines and Prospects and Associated Minerals, John R. Rand. Maine Geological Survey Mineral Resources Index No. 1, Augusta, Maine, 1957, 43 pages.

Bedrock Geology of the Salem Quadrangle and Vicinity, Massachusetts, Priestley Toulmin, III. U.S. Geological Survey Bulletin 1163-A, 1964, 79 pages.

Geology of Massachusetts and Rhode Island, B. K. Emerson. U.S. Geological Survey Bulletin 597, 1917, 289 pages.

Massachusetts Mines and Minerals, John Hiller, Jr. Privately published, Stratford, Conn., 1974, 51 pages.

Geology of Michigan, John A. Dorr, Jr., and Donald F. Eschman. University of Michigan Press, Ann Arbor, Mich., 1970, 476 pages.

The Mineralogy of Michigan, E. Wm. Heinrich. Bulletin 6, Department of Natural Resources Geological Survey Division, Lansing, Mich., 1976, 225 pages.

Rocks and Minerals of Michigan, O. F. Poindexter, H. M. Matin, and S. G. Bergquist. Michigan Department of Natural Resources, Hillsdale Educational Publishers, Hillsdale, Mich., 1971, 45 pages.

Minerals and Gemstones of Nebraska, Roger K. Pabian. University of Nebraska Educational Circular 2, Lincoln, Nebr., 1971, 80 pages.

The Rare Alkalis in New England, Frank L. Hess, Roscoe J. Whitney, Joseph Trefethen, and Morris Slavin. U.S. Department of the Interior, Bureau of Mines, Information Circular 7232, 1943, 51 pages.

The Geology of the Monadnock Quadrangle, New Hampshire, Katharine Fowler-Billings. New Hampshire Planning and Development Commission, Concord, N.H., 1949, 43 pages.

The Geology of the Seacoast Region of New Hampshire, Robert F. Novotny. New Hampshire Department of

Resources and Economic Development, Concord, N.H., 1969, 46 pages.

The Geology and Geography of New Jersey, Kemble Widmer. D. Van Nostrand Company, New York, 1964, 189 pages.

Geology of the Catskill and Kaaterskill Quadrangles, John H. Cook and David H. Newland. University of the State of New York, State Museum Bulletin 331, Albany, N.Y., 1942, 251 pages.

The Geology of New York City and Environs, Christopher J. Schuberth. Natural History Press, New York, 1968, 304 pages.

Minerals of New York State, David E. Jensen. Ward's Natural Science Establishment, Rochester, N.Y., 1978, 220 pages.

Geology of the Spruce Pine District, Avery, Mitchell and Yancey Counties, North Carolina, Donald A. Brobst. U.S. Geological Survey Bulletin 1122-A, 1962, 26 pages.

Mineral Collecting Sites in North Carolina, W. F. Wilson and B. J. McKenzie. Geological Survey Section, Department of Natural Resources and Community Development, Information Circular 24, Raleigh, N.C., 1978, 122 pages.

About Ohio Rocks and Minerals, Carolyn Farnsworth. Ohio Division of Geological Survey, Educational Leaflet Series 5, Columbus, Ohio, 1961, 30 pages.

The Occurrence of Flint in Ohio, Wilber Stout and R. A. Schoenlaub. Ohio Geological Survey Bulletin 46, Fourth Series, Columbus, Ohio, 1945, 110 pages.

Central Oregon Rockhound Guide, map and brochure published by the U.S. Bureau of Land Management and Prineville-Crook County Chamber of Commerce, 1968.

The Mineralogy of Pennsylvania, Samuel G. Gordon. Academy of Natural Sciences Special Publication 1, Philadelphia, Pa., 1922, 255 pages.

The Mineralogy of Pennsylvania, 1966–1975, Robert C. Smith II. Friends of Mineralogy, Pennsylvania chapter, 1978, 304 pages.

Minerals of Rhode Island, Clarence E. Miller. University of Rhode Island, Department of Geology, Kingston, R. I., 1972, 83 pages.

Badlands National Monument, Carl R. Swartzlow and Robert F. Upton. National Park Service Natural History Handbook Series 2, 1954, 48 pages.

Minerals of the Black Hills, Willard L. Roberts and George Rapp, Jr. School of Mines and Technology Bulletin 18, Rapid City, S. Dak., 1965, 268 pages.

Preliminary Report on the Pegmatites of the Custer District, D. Jerome Fisher. University of South Dakota Report of Investigations 44, Vermillion, S.Dak., 1949, reprint, 35 pages.

Geology of the Eastern Great Smoky Mountains, North Carolina and Tennessee, Jarvis B. Hadley and Richard Goldsmith. U.S. Geological Survey Professional Paper 349-B, 1963, 118 pages.

Geology of the Central Great Smoky Mountains, Tennessee, Philip B. King. U.S. Geological Survey Professional Paper 349-C, 1964, 148 pages.

Texas Rocks and Minerals, Roselle M. Girard. Bureau of Economic Geology Guidebook 6, Austin, Tex., 1964, 109 pages.

Geology and Geography of the Henry Mountains Region, Utah, Charles B. Hunt, Paul Averitt, and Ralph L. Miller. U.S. Geological Survey Professional Paper 228, 1953, 234 pages.

Minerals of Virginia, R. V. Dietrich. Virginia Polytechnic Institute Research Division Bulletin 47, Blacksburg, Va., 1970, 325 pages.

Minerals of Washington, Bart Cannon. Cordilleron, Mercer Island, Wash., 1964, 184 pages.

The Rockhound's Guide to Washington, Bob and Kay Jackson. Jax Products, Seattle, Wash., 1974, 48 pages.

Surficial Geology of Mount Rainier National Park, Washington, Dwight R. Crandell. U.S. Geological Survey Bulletin 1288, 1969, 41 pages.

Wisconsin Through 5 Billion Years of Change, Byron Crowns. Wisconsin Earth Science Center, Wisconsin Rapids, Wis., 1967, 318 pages.

Geology of Sedimentary Rocks in Southern Yellowstone National Park, Wyoming, J. D. Love and W. R. Keefer. U.S. Geological Survey Professional Paper 729-D, 1975, 60 pages.

Wyoming's Mineral Resources, F. W. Osterwald and Doris B. Osterwald. University of Wyoming, Bulletin 45, Geological Survey, Laramie, Wyo. 1952, 76 pages.

Canada

A Catalog of Canadian Minerals, R. J. Traill. Geological Survey of Canada Paper 69–45, Ottawa, 1970, 649 pages.

Supplement 1974, Paper 73–22, 260 pages.

Rockhounding and Beachcombing on Vancouver Island (2d edition), Bill and Julie Hutchinson. The Rockhound Shop, Victoria, 1975, 77 pages.

Rocks and Minerals of Ontario, D. F. Hewitt. Ontario Department of Mines, Geological Circular 13, Toronto, 1964, 108 pages.

Magazines

United States

Earth Science. Box 1815, Colorado Springs, Colo. 80901.

Gems and Gemology. Gemological Institute of America, 1660 Stewart Street, Santa Monica, Calif. 90406.

Gems and Minerals. P.O. Box 687, Mentone, Calif. 92359.

Geotimes. American Geological Institute, 5205 Leesburg Pike, Falls Church, Va. 22041.

Lapidary Journal. P.O. Box 80937, San Diego, Calif. 92138.

Mineralogical Record. P.O. Box 783, Bowie, Md. 20715.

Rockhound Magazine. P.O. Box 328, Conroe, Tex. 77301.

Rocks and Minerals. Room 500, 4000 Albemarle Street N.W., Washington, D.C. 20016.

Canada

Canadian Rockhound. 941 Wavertree Road, North Vancouver, British Columbia.

Rocks and Minerals in Canada. Unit 310, 12 Crescent Town Road, Toronto, Ontario M4C 5L3.